Transport, the Environment and Sustainable Development

Other Titles from E & FN Spon

Rebuilding the City
Property-led urban regeneration
P. Healey, D. Usher, S. Davoudi, S. Tavsanoglu and M. O'Toole

Urban Regeneration, Property Investment and Development
J. Berry, S. McGreal and B. Deddis

From Garden Cities to New Towns
Campaigning for Town and Country Planning 1899–1946
D. Hardy

From New Towns to Green Politics
Campaigning for Town and Country Planning 1946–1900
D. Hardy

The Garden City
Past, present and future
S. Ward

The World Environment 1972–1992
Two decades of challenge
M.K. Tolba, O.A. El-Kholy

Saving our Planet
Challenges and hopes
M.K. Tolba

Environmental Dilemmas
Ethics and decisions
R.J. Berry

City Centre Planning and Public Transport
B.J. Simpson

Development and Planning Economy
Environmental and resource issues
P.A. Stone

Passenger Transport after the year 2000
G.B.R. Freiden, A.H. Wickens and I.R. Yates

Project Management Demystified
Today's tools and techniques
G. Reiss

Transport Planning: in the UK, USA and Europe
D. Banister

Urban Public Transport Today
B. Simpson

Effective Writing
Improving scientific, technical and business communication
2nd Edition
C. Turk and J. Kirkman

Effective Speaking
Communicating in speech
C. Turk

Good Style
Writing for science and technology
J. Kirkman

Writing Successfully in Science
M. O'Connor

For more information on these and other titles published by us, please contact:
The Promotion Department, E & FN Spon, 2–6 Boundary Row, London, SE1 8HN

Transport, the Environment and Sustainable Development

Edited by David Banister and Kenneth Button

E & FN SPON

An Imprint of Chapman & Hall

London · Glasgow · Weinheim · New York · Tokyo · Melbourne · Madras

**Published by E & FN Spon, an imprint of Chapman & Hall,
2-6 Boundary Row, London SE1 8HN, UK**

Chapman & Hall, 2-6 Boundary Row, London SE1 8HN, UK

Blackie Academic & Professional, Wester Cleddens Road, Bishopbriggs, Glasgow G64 2NZ, UK

Chapman & Hall GmbH, Pappelallee 3, 69469 Weinheim, Germany

Chapman & Hall USA., 115 Fifth Avenue, New York, NY 10003, USA

Chapman & Hall Japan, ITP-Japan, Kyowa Building, 3F, 2-2-1 Hirakawacho, Chiyoda-ku, Tokyo 102, Japan

Chapman & Hall Australia, 102 Dodds Street, South Melbourne, Victoria 3205, Australia

Chapman & Hall India, R. Seshadri, 32 Second Main Road, CIT East, Madras 600 035, India

First edition 1993
Reprinted 1995, 1996

© 1993 David Banister and Kenneth Button

Typeset in 10/12½ Times by Intype, London
Printed in Great Britain by The Ipswich Book Company, Ipswich

ISBN 0 419 17870 8

A Catalogue record for this book is available from the British Library

Library of Congress Cataloging-in-Publication Data available

Disclaimer

The views expressed in the chapters of this book are those of the authors and do not necessarily represent those of the companies, organizations or institutions for which they work.

John Roberts died in July 1992. All the contributors to this book would like to acknowledge John's dedication to his principles of fairness and equity in transport policy and the important role that TEST has played in promoting environmental and non-car-based solutions to transport problems.

Contents

PART III. Analysis: Problems and Prognoses

Contributors

DAVID BANISTER is Reader in Transport Planning at University College London and Director of the Planning and Development Research Centre at UCL.

TERENCE BENDIXSON is a Transport Consultant and Freelance Writer.

KENNETH BUTTON is Professor of Applied Economics and Transport and Director of the Applied Micro-Economics Research Group, Loughborough University.

DAVID COPE is Director of the UK Centre for Economic and Environmental Development

ELIZABETH DEAKIN is Associate Professor in the Faculties of City and Regional Planning and Transportation Engineering, University of California, Berkeley.

PHILIP GOODWIN is Reader in Transport Studies and Director of the Transport Studies Unit, Oxford University.

NATHANIEL LICHFIELD is Director of Nathaniel Lichfield and Partners and Emeritus Professor of Environmental Planning at University College London.

DAVID MARTIN is in the Energy Efficiency Technical Department, Energy Technology Support Unit, Harwell.

TONY MAY is Professor of Transport Engineering and Director of the Institute of Transport Studies at Leeds University.

BERT MORRIS is Manager, Highways and Traffic in the Public Policy Division at the Automobile Association.

DAVID PEARCE is Professor of Economics at University College London and Director of the London Environmental Economics Centre.

EMILE QUINET is Director of the Department of Economics, École Nationale des Ponts-et-Chaussées, Paris.

PIET RIETVELD is Professor of Environmental Economics, Free University of Amsterdam.

JOHN ROBERTS was Director and Founder of TEST (Transport and Environmental Studies).

WERNER ROTHENGATTER is Professor of Transport at the University of Karlsruhe.

NEIL SCHOFIELD is in the Transport Policy Unit, Department of Transport.

HUGH SOMERVILLE is Head of Environment at British Airways.

JACK SHORT is Principal Administrator, European Conference of Ministers of Transport, Paris.

JOHN WHITELEGG is Head of Department of Geography at Lancaster University.

DEREK WOOD QC is Chairman of the Standing Advisory Committee on Trunk Road Appraisal.

Foreword

DAVID PEARCE

The topic of transport and the environment is once again to the fore. Where previously the concerns were noise nuisance, congestion costs, community severance and landscape loss, they have now expanded to include the impact of the 'traditional' air pollutants such as nitrogen oxides and the 'new' pollutant carbon dioxide. Few other economic activities offer such conspicuous social benefits in the form of comfort, convenience, and time saving at the cost of such a wide ranging 'bundle of bads' as road transport.

The background to the transport-environment debate goes beyond the everyday observation that there is underinvestment in public transport systems, and particularly in the more imaginative urban mass-transit systems, and excess demand for the available road space. The context is one of a projected approximate *doubling* of traffic in the UK by the year 2025. Understandably, not just environmentalists find the implications of such projections breathtaking. Self-evidently, the solution to meeting such growth in demand at minimum social cost must be a combination of supply-side policies and demand constraint. Road-building lobbies and car lobbies tend to favour the former, environmentalists the latter. The arguments are generic to any polluting activity: arguably, reducing pollution affects the poorest most, inhibits economic growth, denies freedom of choice, and accelerates inflation as cost increases are shifted forwards. Many argue that such arguments tend to miss the point which is that the transport system has grown in response to a highly distorted set of price signals. It would be surprising therefore if correcting those distortions were painless. Others suggest that the prevailing prices, particularly of fuels, already encapsulate the economist's concept of 'externality' – i.e. tax rates already reflect the social damage done (even though this corrective feature was not an original part of the tax regime). Clearly, this is just one of the issues that needs to be investigated. There are many others, not least the response of the policy-makers that it simply is not possible to price people off the road unless public transport investments beyond the feasible are made.

We all need a much clearer picture of just exactly what price we are paying for a transport system that creaks and groans under the weight of generally unfettered demand. The papers in this volume are a start, and a good one too.

Acknowledgements

The editors would like to thank the UK Economic and Social Research Council and the UK Science and Engineering Research Council for supporting the production of this book.

They also thank Tim Aspden for preparing the illustrations.

1

Environmental Policy and Transport: An Overview

DAVID BANISTER and KENNETH BUTTON

Transport conveys many benefits. It allows personal mobility for both work and leisure activities. People in most industrialized countries now have a much wider choice of where they can live in relation to their employment than they enjoyed in the past. They also have access to a much wider and more diverse range of leisure pursuits – a fact of no small consequence as more time is given over to non-work activities. Transport, perhaps in some ways more importantly, also provides a vital lubricant to trade and has permitted the advantages of geographical specialization in production to be more fully exploited. It is no accident that, as the post-socialist countries of Eastern Europe seek to develop their out-of-date industrial bases and to expand their trade with the West, one of their priorities is the modernization of their transport systems. Here the problem is not so much one of the quantity of the existing transport systems – many of these countries have extensive rail and road networks – but rather the quality of the infrastructure (Button, 1991).

Despite the unquestionable benefits that appropriate transport provision can bring, there is an inevitable opportunity cost involved. Some elements of this cost are taken into account in the charges borne by those supplying transport services and by the users of these services. This is really what the notion of markets is all about. Other costs, though – and here we will focus particularly on the environmental aspects – are outside of traditional markets and tend not to be brought within the domain of decisions regarding transport provision and use. One must add, of course, that not even all of the conventional costs of transport provision and use are perfectly reflected in market prices. Monopoly power, government subsidies, inefficient management, and a range of other factors mean that markets may well be offering a far from ideal level of transport provision and that the facilities which are available are not being used optimally even within the confines of these narrow markets.

The primary concern of the chapters in this book is to consider those elements of cost which do not fit into normal market regimes. The debate over the environment and how environmental factors should more fully be integrated into the way we make decisions obviously transcends the boundaries of transport. For instance, the whole question of sustainable development, raised by the World Commission on the Environment and Development (1987), is – and is likely to remain – a central concern of policy-makers and transport is but one element of this.

The various chapters in this book concentrate on the real problems which external environmental costs present to policy-makers and assess the contribution that social science can make to handling more effectively environmental considerations in transport decision making. Previously, environmental concerns in transport have been mainly restricted to local factors such as noise, severance and visual intrusion, but recent concerns over global warming, acid rain and a range of pollution-induced diseases have given importance to the regional, national and global implications of environmental degradation.

The aim of the remainder of this introduction is to provide a general background against which the chapters which follow may be set – a context for their various arguments and perspectives. It does not aim either to be comprehensive in its treatment of environmental policy and transport or to provide answers to the questions that it and some of the subsequent chapters raise. It is hoped, however, that it may flag some of the key issues where uncertainty remains and where subsequent research initiatives could prove beneficial.

The Scale and Nature of the Problem

Transport policy-makers have always appreciated that transport imposes environmental costs – the oft-cited example of 'time of day' chariot (or more exactly wagon) where chariots were banned from Rome at certain times of day gives some indication of how far back we can go in history to substantiate this point. However, the situation confronting policy-makers today is somewhat different to that of the past, both in terms of the scale of the problem and its nature.

With regard to the quantitative element, put quite simply there is much more transport today than ever before. At the crudest level, and without attributing cause and effect, as income grows so does the volume of traffic. Over the post Second World War period we have seen unprecedented economic growth in the Western industrialized economies and in parts of Asia. But even in the poorer countries of Africa, Asia and South America there has been, albeit uneven and often inconsistent, economic growth.

Despite the recent changes in Eastern Europe, with their accompanying economic reversals, income is now considerably higher than it was in 1945.

Transport has also taken on new dimensions as there have been modal shifts. For example, aviation represented a negligible element of the overall global transport market before 1939 but now dominates long-distance international passenger transport. Perhaps more importantly from the environmental perspective has been the very rapid growth in car ownership and use. The automobile offers considerable benefits in terms of enhancing mobility and affording greater flexibility in personal travel behaviour. It is, however, often seen as being particularly environmentally intrusive and harmful in terms of resource consumption from both the point of view of the costs of using the vehicle and of the resources used in the manufacturing process.

On the freight transport side, the increased dominance by trucking for short- and medium-distance carriage has emerged as both the nature of goods transported has changed and the overall logistics employed by manufacturers have become more sophisticated. While the volume of bulk commodities transported – especially raw materials – has not actually declined globally (indeed it has followed a gradual upward path) most of the growth in freight transport has been in manufactured goods. These are generally higher-value, final-consumption products where movements to end users require more direct modes of transport. In addition, major advances in such things as inventory control and data information exchange now permit greater exploitation of just-in-time production economies. Transport thus acts not only as a means of shipment but also as an important holder of inventories. Trucks usually offer the best portfolio of attributes to meet the requirements of this joint function. The difficulty is that road haulage, and in particular large lorries, are often seen as being more intrusive on the environment than are other modes of freight transport.

Linked with the trends in both passenger and freight transport has been the increased urbanization of societies. While this has taken several forms, ranging from the extremes of the migration of rural populations into many Third World cities to the counter-urbanization movements of Western cities (in the form of suburban growth around established cores and the growth of new developments in green field locations) the broad implications for transport are the same. People and industry have made more use of transport wherever possible. This means, however, that even if the absolute volume of transport had remained constant, the increased geographical concentration of population would have brought more people within the umbrella of the local environmental damage inflicted by transport.

One should perhaps add that while we have been talking about historic trends, the indications are that they are, in very broad terms, likely to continue into the future if current policies are retained. While, for instance, there are indications that car ownership and use is stabilizing in some parts of the United States as saturation levels of car ownership are approached, there are equally indications that there will be increasing demands for car ownership in the Third World and in the post communist nations of Europe. Continued exploitation of low-cost production locations will similarly add to the number of goods moved by road and the demand for travel by car.

Clearly the simple growth in transport, and especially road-based transport, poses environmental problems in itself but from the policy-making perspective these have been compounded by several important qualitative developments. Perhaps the most important of these is the appreciation that transport does not just have local implications for the environment. For many years transport policy had taken some account of local difficulties caused by traffic and of noise in particular. Road and airport design, for example, took it into account and many countries offered compensation in money or kind (for example, insulation) to those adversely affected. Also appreciated and, to some extent acted upon, were the particular problems of cities, such as Los Angeles, where the local geography leads to build ups of atmospheric pollutants and climatic factors create synergy effects amongst them which have serious adverse health implications. Aesthetics were also seen as important in locating and designing major pieces of transport infrastructure. Beyond this, very little was done.

However, concern over the damaging effects of 'acid rain' on forests and water life mounted in the late 1970s and early 1980s and the importance of NO_x and other gaseous emissions from automobiles was recognized as a major contributing factor. At about the same time, there emerged the issue of high level ozone depletion and the effects it might have for the long-term incidence of certain types of cancer. Transport contributes, albeit in a relatively minor way via the use of such things as CFCs in air-conditioning units, to the gases which may cause this problem. More recently, global warming has become an issue as many scientists have began to argue that the release of CO_2 and other gases is strengthening the greenhouse effect and causing a rise in average temperatures. While the effect is likely to be a long-term one, and the economic implications are by no means certain (Nordhaus, 1991), a natural desire to minimize the potential risk has gradually emerged within some national governments and the population as a whole.

It is not just the influence of new scientific evidence which is important but also the increased concern which people are showing in general with regard to environmental matters, even of the more 'traditional' variety.

In part this can be explained by the increased affluence in industrialized countries. This not only has afforded the growth in mobility, but also has meant that now that basic short-term 'material' needs are being met people have the time to become interested in the future of the planet and the surroundings in which they live. In the former context the rapid assimilation of the idea set out in the Bründtland Commission's Report (World Commission on the Environment and Development, 1987) of attempting to attain 'sustainable development' is indicative of the longer-term thinking which has permeated the environmental debate.

Of course, transport is only one element in this debate, but it is a very important element and one that in some ways attracts a disproportionate amount of attention. First, transport is an important contributor at three levels (local, transboundary and global) at which the debate is taking place. While our understanding of all the implications of transport activities is still far from complete, there is ample empirical evidence to substantiate this fact (for example, Button and Rothengatter, 1992, Linster, 1990). There is also evidence that in some areas, such as CO_2 emissions, transport is likely to pose increasing problems.

Second, and in many ways of far more importance from a policy formulation perspective, transport is *perceived* by the population to be a major intruder on the environment. In part this relates back to the point made earlier, transport comes into cities and is highly visible unlike, for instance, agricultural production, power stations or sewage disposal facilities which tend to be located away from concentrations of people.

Third, transport interacts with many other areas of activity which are seen as environmentally harmful. For instance, the motor vehicle is generally seen as a prime creator of suburbanization and, hence, the reduction of countryside. It is seen, at another level, as a key component of the rapidly growing international tourist industry which is resulting in the gradual destruction of traditional societies and values as well as intrusions into areas of natural importance. Equally, transport opens up new lands for agriculture, forestry and mineral extraction which, once again, can result in adverse consequences for the natural environment.

Fourth, transport is a sector which has traditionally, and for a diverse range of reasons, been the subject of considerable government intervention, regulation and planning, especially regarding infrastructure provision. The underlying rationale for this and questions of whether such involvement is actually desirable is not the issue here, but the fact that government intervention is standard is relevant. Transport supply is manipulated for a variety of reasons but frequently such interventions to achieve objectives such as mobility, regional development, equity, etc. have been at the expense of the environment. While such intervention failures are known in other sectors they are certainly severe in the transport field (Organisation for Economic Coordination and Development, 1991). Many of the current environmental problems, therefore, are not due to traditional market failures but are the by-products, albeit often accidental, of deliberate policy initiatives.

Bringing the Market more fully into Play: Pricing

In their influential book, *Blueprint for a Green Economy*, Pearce *et al.* (1989) argue strongly for bringing environmental matters more centrally within the realms of economics. In particular, they advocate the greater use of economic instruments, and especially appropriate pricing, to tackle environmental issues. For example, they argue that, 'Prices should reflect the true social costs of production and use. Essentially this means getting the true value of environmental services reflected in prices, rather than having them treated as "free goods".'

There is, in fact, a wide range of economic instruments which can be applied to bring environmental costs within the market although the evidence to date is that they are neither as effectively nor as widely used as they might be (Organisation for Economic Coordination and Development, 1989; Barde and Button, 1990) – a situation which applies to all sectors of the economy and not just transport. One case where some success has been claimed for using economic instruments is in the reduction of lead pollution from gasoline. Differential taxation for leaded and unleaded fuel has certainly had an effect but enthusiasm should perhaps be tempered when it is remembered that there have been increasingly tight legal limits on the actual degree of lead additive permitted over the years and in some countries, including the United Kingdom, legislation was also enacted to remove certain grades of leaded petrol to force retailers to stock unleaded fuel at their pumps. Therefore the decreased use of leaded petrol is not entirely due to economic factors.

Some of the more radical pricing strategies which have been advocated have also recently attracted considerable attention, such as carbon taxes to contain global warming gas emissions and road pricing to limit traffic congestion with all its adverse effects on the environment, but their public acceptance has been very limited. Although, for example, the European Commission environmental ministers have generally welcomed an EC Commission's discussion paper which proposes an energy tax to reduce CO_2 emissions, and thus combat global warming, there is already concern over whether the proposals could be made to work. In particular, the EC Environment Commissioner wishes to ensure the cooperation of the Japanese and Americans in such a scheme, as action taken only at a European level may reduce the competitiveness of European industries.

Traditional physical command and control instruments (for example, legislation causing new cars to be fitted with catalytic converters, controls over take-offs and landings at airports, tighter limits on benzene in fuel, safety standards relating to vehicle design and use, etc.) still play the largest role in environmental policy. As a second best measure subsidies, despite their demonstrable limited effectiveness and proneness to capture by the subsidized suppliers (Pickrell, 1989), are widespread in transport and are often justified as a means of encouraging the use of more environmentally friendly public transport modes. This is despite a fairly high degree of agreement amongst economists that pricing is a more flexible and potentially more efficient way of allocating scarce environmental resources (for example, Baumol and Oates, 1989).

While economic instruments are now gaining some limited political support in some countries this should be seen as much as an illustration of the TINA ('there is no alternative') phenomenon as any positive appreciation of their advantages (Common, 1989). One problem with adopting pollution pricing in the transport field is that it is often seen as inequitable and fears that 'motoring will become the prerogative of the wealthy' are often expressed. Subsidies, whereby revenues are raised from a dispersed electorate and seldom hypothecated, do not suffer from that image while there is a perception that regulations are somehow fairer than charges. The latter is, in fact, debatable since it costs money to meet rigorous environmental standards and the penalty for failing to conform is generally a financial one, namely a fine. The link between the punishments for evading standards and the actual social and environmental costs imposed on others by this evasion, together with the associated distributional implications, is one suspects a tenuous one and very little is known about it.

There is also the issue of the processes of policy implementation. The problem with introducing many measures, fiscal or otherwise, involving the environment is to develop appropriate strategies to minimize short-term disruption costs. Economists, for instance, are particularly good (or at least think they are) at defining optimal solutions but often less good at mapping out the appropriate path to these solutions. By nature most people are risk adverse and prefer immediate benefits to future benefits. In this context, it is important to look at the sequence in which reforms may be introduced and their implications. Environmental changes may offer optimal outcomes in the future but uncertainty about the transition effects of their phasing in, together with fears that they may be abused by the authorities, tends to dampen the degree to which they gain public acceptability. A particular problem in this context with regard to such things as carbon taxes is how the revenue of the fiscal regime is to be spent. This not only has current equity implications and but also raises inter-temporal distribution questions as well as having implications for economic efficiency.

Fiscal measures are also sometimes perceived to be less efficient than other instruments because their physical results are less certain – in contrast a requirement that a catalytic converter is fitted is definitive (even if the exact long-term implications for the environment are not). In some cases where there is the prospect of irreversible environmental damage *carte blanche* prohibitions are appropriate since an infinite price (reflecting the environmental damage cost) is nonsensical. But in other cases, standards can be rigid and it is not altogether clear that the environmental resources which are actually 'consumed' are used in the most efficient manner. The mechanisms for ensuring that they are consumed by those who would benefit most from them seldom exist with physical controls.

There are methods of circumventing this involving hybrid systems such as 'marketable permits'. These have been used in the United States and elsewhere but seldom in the context of transport. (However, marketable permits were successfully employed in the United States to allocate lead pollution rights to gasoline refineries when leaded fuel was initially being phased out – see Hahn, 1989.) What they involve is a decision based on the best available data and scientific evidence to draw a physical limit on the exploitation of certain aspects of the environment – say a limit on NO_x emissions – but then to allow potential users to trade the rights to this use of environmental assets. The theory is that those who are most efficient and economical in their use of the environment will sell their surplus rights to the less efficient and thus put pressure on the latter either to change the technology they use or to cease to be active in transport. A similar type of idea underlies the notion of an environmental bank which if applied to cars as, for example, suggested by Rothengatter (1990) would mean that each car produced would require an emissions certificate to be bought with it. A 'cleaner' than average car would have a cheaper certificate and a 'dirtier' one a more expensive certificate. Retro-fitting of environmentally friendly technologies would enable an owner to exchange a certificate for a cheaper one. There is an incentive here to reduce the level of environmental intrusion associated with individual vehicles beyond a fixed limit specification but, unlike a pure marketable permit regime, there is no automatic overall capping on the amount of emission released. Detailed research on the implications and feasibility of all these types of scheme is, however, currently lacking in the transport field.

Bringing the Environment into Investment Appraisal

Transport infrastructure tends to be long lived and dedicated in its use and thus it is important that correct investment decisions are made. It is also very environmentally intrusive, not only after its construction when it is being used for transport purposes but also during its building and after its useful transport life is over. Full-life costing and benefit assessment is, therefore, required. The problems arise from the difficulties in forecasting the overall environmental benefits of a project and the actual use which will be made of any new transport facilities. These two problems are not unrelated.

Most countries, and especially those within the EC where environmental impact assessment is a statutory requirement, do attempt to look at the environmental as well as the narrow transport implications of new infrastructure. The problem is that while most transport inputs are, albeit very imperfectly, traded in conventional markets or at least some indication of their value can be obtained by looking at quasi-market situations this is much more difficult with regard to many environmental factors. They are, often via a series of quite sophisticated and ingenious procedures, examined in a quantitative manner but are very rarely reduced to the common denominator of money which is the currency of the standard cost-benefit framework used for transport infrastructure appraisal. Further, the degree to which the environment is brought within the appraisal process and the ways in which it is brought in vary across modes which holds the inevitable danger of inconsistency even within the narrow confines of environmental impact assessment let alone between overall project appraisal or between inter sectorial alternatives.

Linked with this is a more technical issue of the role of investment policy in a situation where inappropriate prices are being charged for use. The users of transport infrastructure are generally seen as not paying their full costs when environmental factors are brought into the calculation and one adjustment which has been advocated in such a situation is actually to ration infrastructure supply to the point where the overall external cost of transport is more or less optimal. (Wheaton (1978) provides a simple economic model justifying this albeit exclusively in terms of road congestion externalities.) In other words, if there is inappropriate carbon pricing associated with road use and physical standards, and regulations are not correcting for this, then road building should be limited so that the aggregate emission of carbon is optimized. Of course, this may not be fully efficient in that those actually consuming the environment, in terms of emitting CO_2, may not be those who derive the greatest benefit but from an environmental perspective optimal preservation is attained. To what extent this type of investment restraint approach should, or could, be combined with adjustments to user charges and standards in a policy portfolio has been largely unexplored even at a theoretical level.

Questions, therefore, remain not only regarding the way that environmental factors are best treated in transport investment appraisal but also in terms of what is the appropriate strategic stance to take regarding infrastructure provision when its ultimate use is, from an overall social perspective, inevitably going to be sub-optimal.

The International Aspects

While many of the ways in which transport impinges on the environment are of a purely local and domestic nature, there are also significant spill-overs in terms of both transborder and global effects. Further, much of the growth in transport is in international transport which means that many local environmental problems stem from traffic generated in other countries. The noise and other problems at international airports and the marine pollution around many coast lines and many of the major river systems offer ample illustration of this.

How to handle international aspects of environmental damage is very much under explored. In many ways it is a question of political science and international affairs rather than a topic for the more usual social science disciplines involved in transport matters. Of course, those countries which are net exporters of pollution have a vested interest in retaining the *status quo* as far as many forms of environmental damage are concerned. In some instances, a single small country may not consider unilateral action of much help if its contribution to the aggregate impact is small – this is often said with regard to global warming gas emissions. One of the other reasons for what appears to be an official lack of interest in this area is the fear of adverse consequences for trade if all externalities were to be internalized.

However, some progress is being made. For example, the recent *Green Paper on the Urban Environment* (Commission of the European Communities, 1990*a*) argues for a high-density compact city where journey lengths would be short, public transport provision would be more effective, and land consumption would be minimized. This 'energy efficient' urban form would revitalize the city and permit greater use of energy-efficient transport (for example, walking and cycling). But traffic congestion would be increased, as could journey times, and more emissions together with higher fuel consumption may result.

As with much of the debate over the environment, there are no easy solutions and decisions have to be taken within a broad policy spectrum that balances environment against the other possible priorities of government such as economic growth, low levels of inflation, high levels of employment and competitive advantage in world trade. However, it is the role of government to give both industry and the general public clear signals as to their environmental intentions. In this respect, Europe lags behind California where industry is being forced to advance its technology.

Industry justly claims that advances need to be phased over time, but it must also realize that higher priorities should be given to research to speed up implementation. It is the role of government to find mechanisms to signal this fact.

A more basic question is whether there is a limit to technology. For many years, the electric car has been promoted as the ultimate clean vehicle. Certainly it would be a quieter vehicle (although for pedestrian safety reasons not silent) which would be pollution free at the point it operated, but it would not solve the associated problems of urban congestion and parking, unless it were substantially smaller than the existing stock of vehicles. Conversely, the electric car can still contribute to global environmental pollution as most of Europe's electricity is generated from fossil fuels and, hence, the electric car is likely to make a greater contribution to the greenhouse effect. In terms of emissions, electricity emits 2.75 times as much CO_2 as petroleum measured in kilogrammes per giga joule of delivered energy (Warren Springs Laboratory, 1990).

The policy choices also need to be placed against the growth which has taken place over the last decade in all forms of transport. The car and taxi stock within the EC has increased by 39 per cent and in the rest of Europe by 50 per cent. Growth rates in Japan and the USA are 49 per cent and 32 per cent respectively (Department of Transport, 1990). Travel distance has increased by a similar amount, and fuel consumption (petrol and diesel) has increased within the EC by 36 per cent, in the rest of Europe by 17 per cent, and in Japan and the USA by 40 per cent and 11 per cent respectively (1977–1987). In terms of environmental policy, this growth indicates a greater use of resources and an increase in all forms of environmental pollution (with the exception of lead and sulphur oxide) in these countries. If the purpose of international action on the environment is intended to reduce levels of pollution, it is against this background of growth in the transport sector. Transport now accounts for over a third of all energy consumption in many Western countries, and it is rapidly becoming the major contributor to many of the pollutants. Technological advances may only delay the point at which major decisions have to be taken.

With the breaking down of the political barriers between East and West, and with the Single European Market, these trends may be accelerated. The EC Commission's Task Force report on the environmental impacts of the Internal Market examined transport as one of the major sectors where action is required (Commission of the European Communities, 1990*b*). Significant increases in passenger vehicles and road freight would result from growth in economic activity. The completion of the Internal Market would also affect land use as a result of changes in industrial location, population distribution and transport and other infrastructure developments. This is likely to result in concentrations of population and industry at the heart of the Community, while encouraging a centrifugal expansion of urban areas unless countervailing measures are devised (Collins, 1991).

The Structure of the Book

There has been unprecedented growth in traffic, a growing awareness of the scale of the environmental problems facing the planet, and concern over the limitations of transport policy in responding to these changes. This book's purpose is to present an authoritative set of chapters on the theme of environmental policy and transport. Each paper was commissioned from an international expert and presented at a conference held in Oxford in September 1991. The timing of the event was opportune as it coincided with the UK Economic and Social Research Council's Global Environmental Change Initiative and a new transport research initiative which will include a substantial environmental input. It also links in with the UK Science and Engineering Research Council's review of transport research and education. We are grateful to these two Research Councils for their sponsorship of the conference. More generally, the environment is at the forefront of EC policy formulation and forms a key component of OECD discussions. It was also the theme for the United Nations Conference on the Environment and Development held in Rio de Janeiro in June 1992. It is there that national governments will attempt to agree on the global agenda together with the possibility of a carbon tax and various targets for reductions in the levels of pollutants, principally CO_2.

The focus of the book is on the main contributors in the transport sector to the use of resources and to the pollution of the environment namely road and air. These two modes are also those where the most rapid growth in consumption has taken place. Other transport modes such as rail and water also use resources and contribute to environmental degradation, but the scale of that impact is far more limited.

The book is in three parts. In Part I, four papers present an international overview of the current situation in the developed world. The chapter by Kenneth Button and Werner Rothengatter presents a definitive and synoptic view of past trends and the implications of these trends for future travel and consumption patterns. It also covers the increasingly important impact that the growth in levels of affluence in the central European and developing countries will have on car ownership levels and, hence, the environment. The following three chapters take national perspectives on the evolution of policy on transport and the environment in the UK (David Banister), the USA (Elizabeth Deakin) and the Netherlands (Piet Rietveld). Each country has allocated different levels of importance to the issue and have used different policy measures. Between them these three countries seem to cover the entire range of policy options for charging for the environment, through the use of tradeable permits, environmental impact assessments, and strict controls on the emissions from vehicles to a comprehensive statement on environmental policy together with explicit targets for reductions in energy consumption and levels of emissions.

In Part II, attention is switched to the role of the main actors with chapters on the important influence that both governmental and non-governmental organizations can have in influencing policy (Neil Schofield and David Cope). These two chapters are supplemented by short statements on the energy issues and the role of the European agencies (David Martin and Jack Short). The other two major contributions cover the response of the motor and aviation sectors (Bert Morris and Hugh Somerville). The limitations as to what can be achieved by the industry are apparent, particularly when this is set against the lead time for change and the continuous growth in demand for travel. Closer partnership between all actors, including the general public, is argued for. It seems that governments should give clear indications of proposed major changes in policy such as significant increases in the costs of motoring, carbon taxes and more stringent emission controls so that industry can respond. In market economies, such signals would maintain fair competition.

In Part III, the focus is switched to analysis issues with chapters on the problems of valuing the environment (Emile Quinet) and the current procedures used in the UK for major road investment decisions (Derek Woods). The difficult question of whether environmental factors can be measured and valued is tackled, together with the means by which environmental factors can be included more explicitly in the overall evaluation process. The role that design and control can have in improving the environment, together with the important links between transport and other policy areas such as land-use planning and the development process, is covered by Tony May. In each of these three chapters the unresolved issues in analysis are presented and some indication is given of the important research which still needs to be undertaken. Phil Goodwin's chapter provides the conclusion to the book and he argues that efficiency and environmental objectives are not exclusive. Policy can be implemented which both improves economic efficiency and has environmental benefits. Often in the past the environment and efficiency have been seen as alternatives and not as partners. The 'Green-Gold' alliance is seen as an important means to ensure environmental policies are politically acceptable.

Responsibilities for the environment cut across all society, locally, nationally and internationally. For vehicle and aircraft manufacturers it goes beyond the design, construction and marketing of their products. These must be extended to embrace the entire life cycle of the product (full-life costings). For governments it extends beyond the short-term horizons of the next election to the longer-term notions of sustainable development and the requirement to meet the needs of the present without compromising the ability of future generations to meet their own needs (World Commission on the Environment and Development, 1987). For individuals, it requires a change in attitudes from one based on high consumption and ever increasing use of non-renewable resources towards one based on the maximum efficiency in the use of resources and an explicit awareness of the full environmental consequences of individual actions. Quality of life, economic efficiency and environmental improvements can all be mutually reinforcing and operate in the same direction. Transport, as a major contributor to the quality of life, efficiency and the environment, must play an important role in achieving these objectives.

REFERENCES

Barde, J-P. and Button, K. J. (eds.) (1990) *Transport Policy and the Environment: Six Case Studies*. London: Earthscan.

Barde, J-P. and Pearce, D. W. (eds.) (1991) *Valuing the Environment: Six Case Studies*. London: Earthscan.

Baumol, W. J. and Oates, W. E. (1989) *The Theory of Environmental Policy*. Cambridge: Cambridge University Press.

Button, K. J. (1991) The development of East-West European transport in the 1990s, in *Evolution in Transportation* Quebec: CTRF.

Button, K. J. and Rothengatter, W. (1992) Global environmental degradation: The role of transport, Chapter 2 in this volume.

Collins, K. (1991) A community strategy for urban mobility, in *Mobility and the Urban Environment*, Sixth volume in series. Turin: FIAT Delegation.

Commission of the European Communities (1990a) *Green Paper on the Urban Environment*, EUR 12920. Brussels: EC.

Commission of the European Communities (1990b) *1992: The Environmental Dimension, Task Force Report on the Environment and the Internal Market*. Brussels: EC.

Common, M. S. (1989) The choice of pollution control instruments: why is so little notice taken of economists' recommendations? *Environment and Planning*, Vol. **21A**, pp. 1297–1314.

Department of Transport (1990) *International Comparison of Transport Statistics 1970–87, Part 3*. London: HMSO.

Hahn, R. (1989) Economic prescriptions for environmental problems: how the patient followed the doctor's orders. *Journal of Economic Perspectives*, Vol. **3**, pp. 95–114.

Linster, M. (1990) Background facts and figures, in *Transport Policy and the Environment*. Paris: European Conference of Ministers of Transport.

Nordhaus, W. D. (1991) 'The cost of slowing climate change: a survey. *Energy Journal*, Vol. **12**, pp. 37–66.

Organisation for Economic Coordination and Development (1989) *Economic Instruments for Environmental Protection*. Paris: OECD.

Organisation for Economic Coordination and Development (1991) *Market and Intervention Failures in Transport Policy*. Paris: OECD.

Pearce, D. W., Markandya, A. and Barbier, E. B. (1989) *Blueprint for a Green Economy*. London: Earthscan.

Pickrell, D. H. (1989) *Urban Rail Transit Projects: Forecast versus Actual Ridership and Costs*. Cambridge, Mass: US Department of Transportation.

Rothengatter, W. (1990) Economic aspects, in *Transport Policy and the Environment*. Paris: European Conference of Ministers of Transport.

Warren Springs Laboratory (1990) Investigation of Air Pollution. Standing Conference held at the Warren Springs Laboratory.

Wheaton, W. C. (1978) Price-induced distortions in urban highway investment. *Bell Journal of Economics*, Vol. **9**, pp. 622–632.

World Commission on the Environment and Development (1987). *Our Common Future* (Bründtland Commission's Report) Oxford: Oxford University Press.

PART I

Transport and the Environment:
International Policy Responses

2

Global Environmental Degradation: The Role of Transport

KENNETH BUTTON and WERNER ROTHENGATTER

The aim of this chapter is to examine the role which transport plays in causing environmental degradation. In this sense we are taking a fairly wide definition of the term global environmental pollution and do not limit ourselves to more narrow macro issues of global warming or higher-level ozone depletion. While it is true that these latter issues attract much media attention, for many individuals more immediate questions of higher noise levels, destruction of established social environments and perceptions of deteriorating aesthetics are equally global in their effects.

The chapter is not theoretical in its orientation nor does it attempt any form of policy assessment but rather seeks to examine the broad links between transport and environmental degradation, provide some information regarding the current quantitative impact that transport is having and look at some of the longer-term trends which are likely to affect the current situation.

Certainly the environmental question has come to the forefront of international debate in recent years. To a large extent this has stemmed from general comments about the prospects for longer-term sustainable development highlighted, in particular, but certainly not exclusively, by the publication of the Bründtland Commission's Report (World Commission on Environment and Development, 1987). Equally, however, there have been more specific global issues concerning such matters as the so-called 'greenhouse effect' (United Nations Intergovernmental Panel on Climate Change, 1990) and the depletion of the higher-level ozone layer.

These concerns for the global environment should not be divorced from rather more local, in a relative sense, issues. They represent rather a general 'greening' in the thinking of society, especially of societies in the industrial world where increased economic wellbeing (in the narrow sense) has given the opportunity for people to take a much wider view of both their life styles and the prospective life styles of future generations. This greening of attitude extends well beyond the issues of global warming and ozone depletion and is reflected in pressures to reduce transborder pollution (associated for instance with such things as acid rain, marine spillages, dangers of the spread of nuclear radiation etc.) and to contain more local forms of environmental degradation (associated, for instance, with such things as noise, local atmospheric pollution, amenity destruction, etc.).

These are obviously not exclusively transport issues but, nevertheless, on the global scene transport is a major user of scarce resources and a significant contributor to environmental degradation. What we are concerned with here, therefore, is to put the role of transport into some form of context.

Interestingly, the links between transport and environmental quality have been long recognized, although the perceived form of the underlying relationships has changed with time (Button, 1990a). The more traditional concerns have been at the local level and were often seen as matters falling within the ambit of urban and local planners. Noise, community severance and safety, with perhaps a lesser concern with aesthetics, dominated this phase. One can point, for instance, to the discussions contained in the Buchanan Report in the UK (Ministry of Transport, 1963) but the philosophy can equally well be seen in the urban traffic planning frameworks adopted in other industrial economies.

Wider concerns, especially regarding atmospheric pollution, began to emerge in the late 1960s and the 1970s as can be seen from the, quite often artistic, statements found in the academic literature of the time. In his leading textbook, for example, surface transport was described by Thomson (1974) as, 'an engineering industry carried on, not privately within the walls of a factory, but in public places where people are living, working, shopping and going about their daily business. The noise, smell, danger and other unpleasant features of large, fast-moving machinery are brought close to people, with potentially devastating consequences for the human environment.' Equally, Baumol and Oates (1979), in their seminal work on environmental economics, state that 'some of the most pervasive externalities are generated not by industrial operations, but by individual activities. The automobile is a notorious producer of detrimental spillovers. Automobile exhausts increase laundry expenses, make it more difficult to breathe, and even shorten lives. The heavy cloud of pollutants that hangs over crowded roadways, the widespread traffic delays, and the heavy accident rates in such areas again suggest that externalities created by the activities of consumers are not the exceptional phenomena.' While Mishan (1967) in his influential work on economic growth talks of, 'Hoarse beneath the fumes emitted by the endless swarm of crawling vehicles, today's city bears close resemblance to some gigantic and glamorous arsenal.'

But even here the concern fell short of what is being discussed in the 1990s. We have now moved on to an era where the impact of transport on local and transborder environmental matters has extended itself to embrace much more fundamental issues involving the survival of the global ecological system.

This change has come about in part, as suggested above, because in many countries for the vast majority of individuals the short-term needs for survival have been met, indeed in a physical sense more than met, and people's interests have switched to developing a better quality of life both for themselves and, of more importance perhaps in terms of the global environment, for future generations. This latter preoccupation has itself been stimulated both by increased scientific information about the implications of various forms of pollution (for example, the link between higher-level ozone depletion and cancer) and by improved methods of measurement. But in addition to this, there is now a much more thorough, albeit far from complete, understanding of the need to consider the whole ecosystem when looking at the environment implications of change.

Key Past Trends in Transport

Virtually all activities have environmental implications and certainly transport is no different in this respect. Where it does differ from many other sectors of the economy is perhaps in the diversity of ways in which it impacts on the environment. The matrix presented as table 1 offers some general, although not complete, guide to the main environmental effects of the various modes of mechanized transport. (Walking and cycling are perhaps less damaging, and are, therefore, omitted although both involve land take and do generate accidents.)

The verbal comments contained in the matrix obviously offer little by way of guidance either to the quantitative scale of the environmental damage associated with transport or to the implications (in money terms or otherwise) of this damage to the longer-term well-being of society. What they do suggest, however, is that developing policies to tackle the environmental damage associated with transport is a difficult task. Diversity of impact is almost inevitably associated with interactive effects and synergies. Pinpointing policies to tackle these environmental problems is made more difficult by these interactions and often policies aimed at ameliorating one particular form of degradation lead to a worsening elsewhere. For example, legal requirements to turn off automobile engines after a period of idling at, say, traffic lights may reduce CO_2 emissions and, possibly, noise but they effectively lead to engines cooling and as a

TABLE 1. The main environmental effects of the various transport modes.

Mode	Air	Water Resources	Land Resources	Solid Waste	Noise	Accident Risk	Other Impacts
Rail			Land taken for rights of way and terminals; dereliction of obsolete facilities	Abandoned lines, equipment and rolling stock	Noise and vibration around terminals and along lines	Derailment or collision of freight carrying hazardous substances	Partition or destruction of neighbourhoods, farmland and wildlife habitats
Road	Local (CO. C_xH_y, NO_x, fuel additives such as lead and particulates) Global (CO_2, CFC)	Pollution of surface water and groundwater by surface run-off; modification of water systems by road building	Land taken for infrastructure; extraction of road building materials	Abandoned spoil tips and rubble from road works; road vehicles withdrawn from service; waste oil	Noise and vibration from cars, motorcycles and lorries in cities and along main roads	Deaths, injuries and property damage from accidents; risk from transport of hazardous substances; risk of structural failure in old or worn road facilities	Partition or destruction of neighbourhoods, farmland and wildlife habitats; congestion

	Air Pollution				Air
Air	Modification of water tables, river courses and field drainage in airport construction	Land taken for infrastructures; dereliction of obsolete sites	Scrapped aircraft	Noise around airports		Congestion on access routes to airports
Marine and Inland Water	Modification of water system during port construction and canal cutting and dredging	Land taken for infrastructure; dereliction of obsolete port facilities and canals	Vessels and craft withdrawn from service		Bulk transport of fuels and hazardous substances

Source: Organisation for Economic Cooperation and Development (1988).

consequence the effectiveness of catalytic converters is considerably reduced in the subsequent acceleration period.

Further, environmental effects extend beyond the simple use of transport to the implications of providing the vehicles and infrastructure. Road building, for example, is disruptive of the natural environment and requires large quantities of stone, aggregate and bitumen, the extractions of which generate their own negative environmental effects. From a French study (cited in Lamure, 1990), it is also clear that maintenance of infrastructure is a major consumer of energy – accounting for as much as 30 per cent of the undiscounted total energy cost of road infrastructure, including construction and its use by vehicles, over a 25-year time horizon. Similar situations regarding environmental costs of construction and maintenance pertain with respect to railways. Equally, automobile manufacturing plants, railway workshops and ship construction yards are unsightly and their products require huge quantities of raw materials and energy. Excessive use of transport has, therefore, major backward multiplier linkages on the natural environment through the mechanical and civil engineering based industries and on back to the extractive industries. This again complicates policy-making.

No attempt is made to put a value on the various forms of environmental damage outlined in table 1, this is more expertly done elsewhere (Quinet, 1990) but rather some discussion is offered as to the scales of the various problems and their physical implications for society. This can conveniently be done according to the various forms of degradation which are set down in table 1. Initially, however, it is helpful to set out some of the key global transport trends which represent one of the major causes of the current upsurge of concern about environmental damage.

First it is important to recognize that transport is an integral part of any modern economy. It not only provides a vital input into manufacturing processes (indeed, some 1295 thousand million tonne-kilometres of freight were carried during 1987 in European Conference of Ministers of Transport countries) but also permits individuals to enjoy a wide range of geographically disparate, leisure activities. Transport use has grown with economic expansion being both a creative impetus to the economic development process and a consequence of it. Transport shapes urban form and is influential in determining the spatial distribution of many economic activities (see, for example, papers in Button and Gillingwater, 1983).

The importance of transport in the wider economy and in macroeconomic policy-making becomes apparent when it is realized that transport supply industries contribute 7 per cent directly to the Gross Domestic Product of the European Economic Community with further, far reaching, secondary links through personal consumption of transport services. The share of the private consumption budget devoted to transport and communications in North America has risen from 14.9 per cent in 1960 to 16.3 per cent in 1983 and is forecast to rise to as much as 18.6 per cent by the year 2000 (United Nations Economic Commission for Europe, 1987).

Transport expenditure also extends beyond the simple financial window. From a different perspective, for instance, at the personal level it has been estimated that travel accounts for one hour per individual per day in developed economies (Zahavi, 1979).

The 'hardware' required to meet this level of transport use has resulted in the growth of substantial automobile, aircraft and ship-building industries and in the maintenance of massive civil engineering construction activities. In the US, automobile production, for example, accounts for some 12 per cent of the country's aluminium consumption, 19 per cent of steel consumption, 20 per cent of machine tools manufactured, 50 per cent of the lead produced and 67 per cent of its rubber output. This in turn results in large-scale employment in transport related industries – prior to unification in Germany, for example, some 1.8 million jobs (7 per cent of the labour force) were dependent on the demand for and use of motor cars and in the US some 20 per cent of the labour force in 1980 was in jobs directly or indirectly related to automobile production.

Transport is also a major source of government revenue in many countries with fuel taxes representing 6.8 per cent of the Irish Republic's government revenue in 1983, 5.5 per cent of Italy's, 4.7 per cent of the UK's and 3.9 per cent on average across the European Community states. In total, road taxes amounted to some 6.2 per cent of the Netherlands's government revenue in 1982–84, 8.6 per cent of New Zealand's, 3.5 per cent of Japan's, 7.8 per cent of Switzerland's, 7.0 per cent of Australia's and 6.3 per cent of Sweden's.

While there has been increased use made of virtually all modes of transport in industrialized countries (for instance, freight transport grew, in tonne-kilometres, by 39.6 per cent between 1970 and 1986 and passenger movements, in passenger-kilometres, by 59.2 per cent in OECD Member States), quantitatively it has been land-based transport (and motor vehicles in particular) which have witnessed the greatest increase in usage. The numbers of both cars and goods vehicles have increased significantly in recent years (see tables 2 and 3). There has also been a corresponding increase in traffic volumes. For example, car traffic measured in vehicle-kilometres rose respectively by 79 per cent in France, 85 per cent in Italy, 49 per cent in the US, 82 per cent in the UK and 77 per cent in the former FRG between 1970 and 1987. Equally, goods movements by road have increased substantially, again between 1970 and 1987 vehicle-kilometres have risen by 93 per cent in France, 93 per cent in

TABLE 2. Selected transport and environment indicators.

		Canada	USA	France	Western Germany	Italy	UK	Japan	North America	OECD Europe	OECD
Infrastructure											
Motorways	% change[a]	170	55	323	95	55	182	513	61	146	81
Road vehicle stock											
	% change	92	66	87	104	151	68	198	68	111	94
Total ownership	Veh./1000 inh.	600	730	480	500	490	400	430	720	370	500
Traffic											
Total road traffic	% change	75	81	92	78	99	83[b]	113	80	92	86
Road freight traffic	% change	107	70	69	94	179	47	79	72	105	84
Rail freight traffic	% change	11	30	-23	-17	8	-26	-63	27	-6	21
Energy consumption											
Total final energy consumption by the transport sector											
Total	MTOE	42	482	40	49	32	43	66	523	254	868
of which: Air	%	11	15	9	10	5	15	4	15	11	13
Road	%	80	82	86	87	91	80	85	82	83	82
Rail	%	5	2	3	3	2	2	4	3	3	3
Diesel consumption by road transport	% change	447	191	233	112	279	86	210	203	172	191
Share of total	%	18	17	42	34	52	28	42	17	40	26

Noise from road traffic

	Million	2	17	9	8	10	6	37	19	63	120
Population exposed to > 65 dB (A)	Million	2	17	9	8	10	6	37	19	63	120

Air pollution
Share of transport emissions in total emissions

NO_x	%	61	41	76	65	52	49	44	43	60	49
CO	%	66	67	71	74	91	86	–	67	78	71
C_xH_y	%	37	33	60	53	87	32	–	33	50	39
SO_2	%	3	4	10	6	4	2	18	4	4	4

Notes: (a) All % change data cover the period 1970–1988. Other data refer to 1988 or the most recent year available.
(b) England and Wales only.

Source: Organisation for Economic Cooperation and Development (1990a).

TABLE 3. Trends in traffic, automobile ownership and motorway construction.

	Road Traffic			Motorways			Passenger Cars in Use			Vehicle Ownership
	10⁹ veh.-km		Change from 1970 (%)	km		Change from 1970 (%)	1 000 vehicles		Change from 1970 (%)	veh./100 persons
	1970	1989	1970–1989	1970	1989	1970–1989	1970	1989	1970–1989	1989
Canada	126	225	79	2 760	7 450	170	6 600	12 100	84	47
USA	1 787	3 307	85	53 700	83 960	56	89 200	143 700	61	58
Japan	226	521	130	700	4 410	531	8 800	32 600	272	27
Australia	79	153	94	1 030	1 100	7	3 800	7 600	98	46
New Zealand	13	22	63	100	140	40	900	1 700	97	51
Austria	22	54	147	480	1 410	194	1 200	2 900	143	38
Belgium	33	52	57	500	1 590	218	2 100	3 700	78	37
Denmark	23	36	56	200	600	204	1 100	1 700	54	32
Finland	19	39	101	110	220	99	700	1 900	166	38
France	208	414	99	1 550	6 950	348	12 300	23 000	87	41
West Germany	234	427	82	4 460	8 720	95	13 900	30 200	116	49
Greece	9	36	293	70	90	42	200	1 600	605	16
Ireland	11	23	114	–	10	–	400	800	96	22
Italy	146	297	103	3 910	6 080	55	10 200	26 200	157	46
Netherlands	48	89	85	980	2 070	113	2 500	5 400	118	36
Norway	11	21	98	80	290	272	700	1 600	132	38
Portugal	9	33	248	70	260	288	600	1 900	244	18
Spain	35	100	185	270	2 140	699	2 400	11 500	382	29
Sweden	35	61	73	400	1 000	148	2 300	3 600	56	42
Switzerland	25	48	90	380	1 500	297	1 400	2 900	111	44
Turkey	6	23	283	20	210	754	100	1 500	981	3
UK	179	357	99	1 060	2 990	183	11 800	21 600	83	38
Yugoslavia	11	37	243	10	810	8 856	700	3 200	340	13
OECD	3 288	6 343	93	72 800	133 300	83	173 200	339 800	96	41
World	–	–	–	–	–	–	193 500	2 114 700	993	41

Source: Organisation for Economic Cooperation and Development (1991*b*).

Italy, 49 per cent in the US, 45 per cent in the UK and 34 per cent in the former FRG.

This increased use of land-based transport has necessitated (and been facilitated by) the provision of extensive infrastructure. The amount of road, rail, sea port and airport capacity in most OECD member states is now considerable. Table 3 provides details of motorway networks but in addition countries such as Germany (the pre-unified states of the FRG had 35 thousand kilometres of rail), the UK (17 thousand kilometres), the US (240 thousand kilometres), France (35 thousand kilometres) and Italy (20 thousand kilometres) have extensive rail systems. The post-communist countries of Eastern Europe have, in relative terms, even larger rail systems with, for instance, Poland having 27 thousand kilometres of track, Czechoslovakia 13 thousand kilometres, and the old GDR 14 thousand kilometres.

In broad terms, recent years have seen a reduction in investment in new transport infrastructure but more resources being expended on maintenance. Indeed, the total length of rail network in OECD countries declined by 4.1 per cent between 1970 and 1985 although the proportions of electrified lines rose from 29.3 per cent to 38.6 per cent. The FRG had 12 thousand kilometres of electrified track prior to unification, for example, while France has 11 thousand kilometres, and Italy has 10 thousand kilometres. Future infrastructure plans for Europe, both on an EC basis and for individual countries (see Button, 1990*b*), suggest that there may, however, be something of an upsurge in investment in transport infrastructure expenditure into the next century, especially in terms of major, high-speed rail projects.

While the increased availability of land-based transport has brought unquestionable benefits to large sections of society, its positive impact on enhancing the general level of accessibility has not been evenly spread and large numbers of individuals have found themselves relatively disadvantaged. Changes in the nature of land-based transport modes have contributed towards this. In particular, the widespread growth in car ownership in many countries during the post Second World War period has been accompanied by a decline in the relative level of public transport provision. Studies of household travel behaviour (for example, Hillman *et al.*, 1976) suggest that this has had serious adverse implications for the mobility of those without easy access to an automobile. Equally, the advent of motorized road freight transport (the share of which, in tonne-kilometres, in European Conference of Ministers of Transport member states rose from 49.1 per cent in 1970 to 63.7 per cent in 1987) has resulted in shifts in the relative commercial advantages enjoyed by different geographical regions to the economic detriment of some.

The Environmental Implications of Transport

Any brief listing of the environmental implications associated with transport is inevitably inadequate. Further, the effects of transport on the environment are complex (Linster, 1989). For example, in the case of air pollution, there are direct short- and long-term effects which are caused by the particular pollutant before it undergoes chemical transformation in the atmosphere, while indirect effects occur after a mixture of pollutants has undergone atmospheric transformation. Traditionally, attention has tended to focus on single forms of pollution but there is a growing awareness of synergy effects and the damage done to the environment by cocktails of pollutants. The most serious problem is associated with photochemical oxidants which are formed by chain reactions between unsaturated hydrocarbons and other reactive organic compounds, nitrogen oxides and oxygen in the presence of sunlight. Ozone is the most prevalent photochemical oxidant.

One must also be somewhat careful in saying that all environmental problems are getting worse. While this is not the place to spend too much time on policy effects, it is certainly true that there have been major improvements in recent years in several areas where transport has been seen to pose particular environmental problems. Lead pollution has fallen considerably in most industrialized countries as fiscal and legislative measures have begun to exert an impact. In many places NO_x emissions have declined and are forecast to fall in several other countries. Equally, although this tends to be very area specific, issues of traffic noise nuisance seem to pose fewer problems for residents in some places (Organisation for Economic Cooperation and Development, 1991c). Many countries now also have fewer fatal and serious traffic accidents than in the past. The picture is not, therefore, altogether black.

Accepting the above caveats, the following items, each accompanied by a few notes on their importance, are widely accepted as being of importance as transport-based sources of degradation to the global environment. A summary of some of the key, quantifiable points, again, is also contained in table 3.

Noise

This is especially a nuisance in urban areas, alongside major trunk arteries, such as rail lines, and at locations around transport terminals, such as airports. Noise is, for example, often cited as the main nuisance in urban areas. For instance in the former FRG Frenking (1988) found 65 per cent of the population were adversely affected by road traffic noise with 25 per cent seriously affected – by way of comparison this represented twice the problem of noise from neighbours and three times the problem from industrial noise.

It has been estimated that about 110 million people in the industrial world are exposed to road traffic noise levels in excess of 65 dB(A), a level considered as unacceptable in OECD countries. While consistent data are somewhat sparse, there is also ample evidence that there are, in large part because of the nature of national land-use patterns but also because of differing national legal structures, quite considerable differences between countries in terms of the populations affected by transport related noise – see table 4. Equally it is difficult, because of data limitations, to discern exact trends in population exposure to high noise levels. International comparisons provide tentative evidence of a decline in numbers suffering from serious noise problems (i.e. over 65 dB(A)) in some countries but equally there are rises in others. There does, however, seem to be a pattern of significantly increasing numbers of people falling into the 'grey area' of between 55 and 65 dB(A). Equally, studies in the Netherlands suggest that the number of people claiming moderate disturbance from road traffic noise rose from 48 per cent to 60 per cent between 1977 and 1987.

Noise has several different effects on health and well-being. It affects activities such as communication (speaking, listening to radio and TV) and sleep. These effects further induce psychological and physiological disorders such as stress, tiredness and sleep disturbance. Noise can also contribute to cardiovascular disease and, at high and prolonged exposure, hearing loss.

Vibration
All large surface transport vehicles create vibrations as they move and aircraft at low altitude and on take-off and landing cause disturbances to the air. Road freight transport poses a particular problem in historic urban areas where buildings are particularly susceptible to damage from vibration. But in general, vibration can also have adverse effects on those living in houses affected in terms of disrupting their sleep which can have health implications as well as affecting their general enjoyment of life.

Accident Risk
Transport is an inherently dangerous activity. From a purely statistical perspective this is mainly seen in relation to road transport where there are, on a day-to-day basis, many fatal and serious accidents. Less frequent, but from a public perception perspective often more traumatic because of the degree of potential severity associated with each individual incident, are rail, maritime and aviation disasters.

Some indication of the order of magnitude of the risks involved in

TABLE 4. Exposure of national population to transport noise.

Unit: percentage[a,f]

Country	Year	Outside noise level in L_{eq} (dB(A))[b]													
		Road Transport Noise					Aircraft Noise					Railway Noise				
		>55	>60	>65	>70	>75	>55	>60	>65	>70	>75	>55	>60	>65	>70	>75
Australia	–	46.0	..	8.0	..	..	..	..	..	..	..	..	..	..	..	..
Japan[c]	1980	80.0	58.0	31.0	10.0	1.0	3.0	1.0	0.5	0.2	0.1	..	..	..	..	..
France[d]	1985	54.4	33.1	16.6	5.5	0.6	..	..	..	..	..	..	..	..	..	..
Germany	1985	45.0	26.7	12.5	5.1	1.1	..	..	1.0	..	0.2	18.0	8.4	2.9	0.8	0.1
Netherlands	1987	54.0	20.0	4.1	1.3	–	36.0	15.0	0.4	0.1	–	6.0	1.5	0.6	0.3	0.1
Switzerland[e]	1985	53.7	26.3	11.7	4.1	0.7	2.0	1.0	0.6	0.7	–	23.4	13.0	5.9	2.5	0.9

(a) The percentages are cumulative and not additive (e.g., the percentage of people exposed to over 55 dB(A) includes the figure for people exposed to over 60 dB(A), etc.).

(b) Daytime L_{eq} (06.00–22.00) measured in front of the most exposed facades of buildings.

(c) OECD estimates.

(d) L_{eq} (08.00–20.00); urban areas (over 5000 inhabitants); data refer to all facades of buildings.

(e) Aircraft: 1980 figures.

(f) .. not available

– nil or negligible.

Source: Organisation for Economic Cooperation and Development (1991c).

transport is the fact that road accidents cost some 48,800 lives in the US and 7,967 lives in the pre-unification states of the FRG during 1987 and 10,961 in France during 1986, while in the UK 5,052 people were killed on the roads in 1988 with a further 63,000 seriously injured. In Italy, between 7,076 and 9,308 people were killed in 1986 (the number depending upon whether deaths are measured at times of accidents or a week later – see Ponti and Vittadini, 1990) and 213,159 injured. It should be pointed out, however, that in many countries the number of fatal road accidents is decreasing – for example, the figure for the UK is the lowest since 1954 and that cited for the FRG for 1987 should be compared with 19,139 in 1970. The increased amount of hazardous waste transported in recent years has, however, added to the risks borne by third parties.

If one considers the accident rates by mode then road transport incidents dominate the statistics although, because of variations in modal split between countries, there are national variations in their relative importance. Some indication of the different accident rates by mode and over time for the US are, for example, given in table 5. Interpretation of such data does, however, pose some problems. In particular, there is the point of comparison against which numbers of accidents should be set. Commercial aviation is, from a statistical perspective, generally cited as the safest mode of transport but this may not be the case viewed in terms of time exposure. Perrow (1984) makes the point clearly,

> safety comparisons with other systems are hard to make. In many respects, commercial air travel appears to be much safer than automobile or rail travel. Many fewer people are killed in the first than in the other two. But an equally useful statistic would be the number of fatalities per hour of exposure, or per million miles travelled. Unfortunately, we do not have these statistics for automobile accidents . . . if we used the statistic of fatalities per 100,000 hours of exposure, highway travel would be the safest mode of transportation . . . One's chances of being killed while driving a car is only one per cent in fifty years of driving. We simply do a lot of driving and very little flying giving us the impression that the risk of the latter is much smaller.

Atmospheric Pollution
(a)　Fuel additive emissions. To enhance engine performances, additives are added to fuels. While some are relatively benign in their environmental effects others have caused increasing concern over time. 1,2 dibromoethane 1,2 dichloroethane are added to gasoline, together with tetraethyl lead, to increase volatility but have been found to be carcinogenic in animals and potentially so in humans. The organic lead compound added to gasoline as an anti-knock agent, especially when used by automobiles in confined urban spaces, has been singled out for particular attention. It is a metallic element which can be retained in the body and can have an

TABLE 5. Transportation accidents and resulting deaths and injuries by type of transport in the US, 1970–85.

Year and Casualty	Total (1000)	Motor Vehicles[1] (1000)	Railroads[2]	Air Carriers Total	Airlines[3]	Commuter Air Carriers[4]	On Demand Air Carriers[5]	General Aviation[6]	Waterborne[7]
Accidents:									
1970	16 013	16 000	8 095	(NA)	(NA)	(NA)	(NA)	(NA)	(NA)
1975	16 524	16 500	8 041	237	37	48	152	3 995	3 310
1980	17 925	17 900	8 451	228	19	38	171	3 590	4 624
1981	18 020	18 000	5 781	214	26	31	157	3 500	3 503
1982	18 118	18 100	4 589	178	19	27	132	3 231	3 174
1983	18 319	18 300	3 906	184	25	19	140	3 060	4 704
1984	18 817	18 800	3 900	185	18	21	146	3 008	3 275
1985	(NA)	(NA)	3 426	194	24	17	153	2 748	2 259
Deaths:									
1970	54.8	52.6	785	(NA)	(NA)	(NA)	(NA)	(NA)	(NA)
1975	48.2	44.5	575	221	124	28	69	1 252	243
1980	54.5	51.1	584	143	1	37	105	1 239	206
1981	52.5	49.3	556	132	4	34	94	1 282	154
1982	47.2	43.9	512	320	234	14	72	1 182	223
1983	45.7	42.6	498	89	15	12	62	1 081	289
1984	44.6	44.3	598	102	4	46	52	1 115	113
1985	44.1	43.8	454	638	526	35	77	944	69

Injuries:

1970	2 024	2 000	21 327	(NA)	(NA)	(NA)	(NA)	(NA)	(NA)
1975	1 858	1 800	54 306	109	71	6	32	728	97
1980	2 066	2 000	62 246	74	17	14	43	675	176
1981	1 956	1 900	53 003	82	21	24	37	597	141
1982	1 741	1 700	37 638	98	31	28	39	620	271
1983	1 636	1 600	32 196	49	8	12	29	566	209
1984	1 739	1 700	35 660	67	9	23	35	595	134
1985	1 735	1 700	31 617	73	10	12	51	497	57

NA Not available.

1. Data on deaths are from US National Highway Traffic Safety Administration and are based on 30-day definition.
2. Train accidents cover only those accidents which result in damage to railroad property exceeding amounts specified by the US Federal Railroad Administration. The reporting threshold was raised from $570 to $1750 in 1975; to $2900 in 1979; to $3700 in 1981; to $4500 in 1983; and to $4900 in 1985. Deaths exclude fatalities in railroad-highway grade crossing accidents.
3. Includes scheduled and non-scheduled (charter) air carriers operating under 14 CFR 121, 125, and 127, only serious injuries are included.
4. All scheduled services operating under 14 CFR 135; only serious injuries are included.
5. All non-scheduled services operating under 14 CFR 135; only serious injuries are included.
6. 1975–84 data exclude commuter and on-demand air taxis operating under 14 CFR 135.
7. Covers accidents involving commercial vessels which must be reported to US Coast Guard if there is property damage exceeding $1500: material damage affecting the sea-worthiness or efficiency of a vessel: stranding or grounding; loss of life; or injury causing a person's incapacity for more than three days.

Source: US Department of Transport, Transportation Systems Center (annual).

adverse effect on the mental development of children and affect the kidneys, liver and reproductive system.

In industrialized nations, transport is the single largest source of lead emissions, with some 50 per cent associated with transport, increasing to nearly 100 per cent in confined urban spaces. However, the tightening regulations on maximum lead content in gasoline (for example in the UK's case from 0.84 gram per litre to 0.40 gram per litre in 1981 and a further reduction to 0.15 gramme per litre in 1985) and the fostering of increasing use of lead free gasoline through fiscal measures has brought about major changes in recent years.

(b) Particulate matters. These embrace fine solids or liquid particles found in the air or in emissions such as dust, smoke or smog. Sources include the fine asbestos and other particles stemming from wear and tear of tyres and brakes as well as matter resulting from engine, and especially diesel engine, combustion. Transport is the major source of particulate emissions in many industrialized countries including the UK.

Particulate matter may be toxic in itself or carry toxic (including carcinogenic) trace substances absorbed onto its surfaces. It also imposes costs on physical structures, for example, in terms of the need to clean and repaint buildings.

(c) Carbon dioxide emissions. The environmental concern here is in relation to carbon dioxide's possible climatic impacts, for example, it is generally viewed by scientists as a major contributor to the exacerbation of the greenhouse effect and consequential global warming. CO_2 emissions are emitted by the combustion of fossil fuels. Estimates suggest that about 15 per cent of the world's total man-made emissions of CO_2 are generated by motor vehicles and in some OECD countries the figure may reach 70 per cent.

Since CO_2 is a natural constituent of air (although only about 0.03 per cent) it is not strictly a pollutant. Further, excess amounts of the gas have no direct detrimental effect on personal health. The problem is that there is mounting, although some would argue not yet conclusive, evidence that high levels of CO_2 in the atmosphere, by preventing heat from escaping from the planet, will lead to global climate changes. In particular, the retention of heat by the earth and atmosphere is due to CO_2 in the air being 'transparent' to incoming short-wave radiation but 'opaque' to the longer wave radiation back from the earth. It is called the greenhouse effect because the glass in a greenhouse acts in a (similar) heat retentive way (National Society for Clean Air, 1989).

The issue is not really one about the merits of the greenhouse effect *per se* – without it, estimates suggest, the global average temperature

TABLE 6. Contribution of gases to the greenhouse effect.

Greenhouse Gases	accumulated for the period 1860–1980	actual values: the period 1980–1990
Carbon dioxide (CO_2)	60%	50%
Chlorofluorocarbons (CFCs)	9%	22%
Methane (CH_4)	14%	13%
Tropospheric ozone (O_3)	10%	7%
Nitrous oxide (N_2O)	3%	5%
Stratospheric water (H_2O)	4%	3%

Source: Enquête-Commission (1990).

would fall to about −19°C – but rather about the desirability of the effects changes in its intensity will have. The exact geographical impacts of global warming and their timing are difficult to predict and the long-term economic consequences even harder to foretell (Nordhaus, 1991). After all, it is a global phenomena and little previous data exist to refine theoretical models.

The 'self-induced' greenhouse effect is caused by burning tropical woods (15 per cent), agriculture, in particular because of the methane emissions (15 per cent), chemical industries (20 per cent) and energy production/consumption (40 per cent). Table 6 shows the percentages of the greenhouse gases which contribute to the 'self-induced' greenhouse effect. If the trends continue until the year 2025 then the global average temperature on earth will increase by 2.5°C (Enquête-Commission, 1990). The warming up will be three times as fast as the ecological system is able to adjust to without negative consequences for mankind. The climatic zone changes will be faster than the zones of vegetation can follow. The probable effects are:

- rise of the sea level as a result of thermal expansion of the sea and the melting of land ice;
- changes of climatic zones, for example of desert regions or regions affected by tropical storms;
- global dying of woods due to climatic changes which are enforced by other pollutant emissions (NO_x);
- detrimental effects on water resources in many regions;
- increasing problems for agricultural production;
- changes in tundra, boreal forests and permafrost which can lead to further emissions of carbon dioxide and methane, and thus to a further enhancement of the greenhouse effect.

The Western and Eastern industrialized countries contribute 80 per cent to the global CO_2 emissions although their share of the world's population is only 25 per cent. Less developed countries, including the People's

TABLE 7. CO_2 – emissions of twenty countries caused by energy consumption in the year 1986.

Country	CO_2 Emissions (tonnes $\times$ 10^6)	Share of Worldwide Emissions (%)	Specific CO_2 Emissions (tonnes/ capita)
USA	4 766	23.8	19.7
USSR	3 737	18.6	13.2
PR China	2 030	10.1	1.9
FRG	1 067	5.3	13.7
West	715	3.6	11.7
East	352	1.8	21.2
Japan	914	4.6	7.5
U.K.	676	3.4	11.9
India	539	2.7	0.7
Poland	478	2.4	12.7
Canada	436	2.2	17.0
France	384	1.9	6.9
Italy	365	1.8	6.4
South Africa	293	1.5	7.7
Mexico	266	1.3	3.3
Australia	245	1.2	15.2
Czechoslovakia	244	1.2	15.7
Romania	212	1.1	9.2
Netherlands	203	1.0	13.9
Spain	189	0.9	4.9
Brazil	175	0.9	1.3
South Korea	162	0.8	3.9

Source: Enquête-Commission (1990).

Republic of China where 75 per cent of the world's population live, contribute only 20 per cent. Table 7 shows the twenty major emitters. From this comparison it follows that the US and the USSR are the biggest emitters followed by China and Germany. German unification has influenced the international CO_2 statistics negatively because the former GDR had reached the world record in energy consumption per capita. As the energy was produced by burning brown coal a tremendous level of air pollution followed. The pollution balance of the transport sector of the former GDR was much better. This was due to the comparatively low level of car ownership and the assignment of long-distance freight transport to the railways. Although the technologies of road and rail transport were antiquated it is estimated that an introduction of Western technologies *and* behavioural patterns in consumption and production would almost double the emissions of CO_2 and NO_x.

The German government decided in 1990 that the CO_2-emissions of all sectors in the year 2005 should not exceed 75 per cent of the 1987 level.

TABLE 8. Development of traffic and CO_2 – emissions under trend conditions.

Development under Trend Conditions					
Transportation Mode	Road	Rail	Air	Inland Waterway	Total
Share of emissions in 1987	88%	3%	8%	1%	
Pass./ton km (2005)	30%	20%	100%	0%	35%
Potential of reduction until 2005	−20%	−10%	−15%	0%	−19%
Change of emissions considering the growth of traffic	4%	8%	70%	0%	9%

TABLE 9. Development of traffic and CO_2 – emissions under conditions of strict environmental policy.

Development under Conditions of Strict Environmental Policy					
Transportation Mode	Road	Rail	Air	Inland Waterway	Total
Share of emissions in 1987	88%	3%	8%	1%	
Pass./ton km (2005)	10%	150%	10%	0%	14%
Potential of reduction until 2005	−35%	−30%	−30%	0%	−34%
Change of emissions considering the growth of traffic	−29%	75%	−23%	0%	−25%

Because of the rapid growth of transport activities, the transport sector can hardly contribute equally to the desired global reduction of CO_2. The Scientific Advisory Council of the German Ministry of Transport (1991) estimates, that, even using all technology available, under trend conditions CO_2-emissions would still increase by 9 per cent assuming the growth of road transport is about 30 per cent and of air transport is 100 per cent in the time from 1987 to 2005 (table 8).

The council has, however, underlined that it would be possible theoretically to reach the objective of 25 per cent CO_2 reduction (see table 9), but this would presuppose a dramatic change of the decision environment of all agents in the transport sector. Drastic rise of fuel taxes, road pricing, parking restrictions and further regulatory incentives to divert traffic to rail and ship are necessary conditions for such a development. The Council states that the environmental problems of the transport sector are mainly due to the fact that the prices for the use of environmental resources are too low and that the price structure leads to false signals. Therefore an active intervention policy of the government is regarded as inevitable to improve the quality of the environment.

(d) Nitrogen oxide emissions. These pose particular difficulties when combined with other air pollutants or in areas where residents already suffer from ill-health. In the latter case they can lead to respiratory difficulties and extended exposure can result in oedema or emphysema. At the transboundary level, NO_x emissions converted to nitric acid and combined with SO_2, form a significant component of 'acid rain' (or acid deposition) which has serious detrimental effects on ecosystems. The problems have been summarized by the Organisation for Economic Cooperation and Development (1988), namely,

> Decreases in the pH values of fresh water bodies, indicating higher acidity, have occurred throughout Europe and North America. As a result, there has been a decline in or an elimination of the fish population in acidified lakes. Some evidence suggests that essential nutrients can be removed from sensitive soils releasing metals that are toxic to plants. Based on a growing body of research, it has been suggested that this mechanism may be responsible for very substantial damage to the West German forests.

Although there are significant variations between countries, about 50 per cent of NO_x emissions stem from the transport sector, and the rest from the energy and industrial sectors although in many countries their output is falling. In the UK it is the fastest growing source of emissions, rising by about 2 per cent per annum.

(e) Carbon monoxode emissions. CO is an odourless and almost colourless gas. It can have detrimental effects on health because it interferes with the absorption of oxygen by red blood cells. This may lead to increased morbidity and adversely affected fertility and there is evidence that it affects worker productivity. CO is especially a problem in urban areas where synergistic effects with other pollutants mean it contributes to photochemical smog and surface ozone (O_3). Concentrations of O_3 at lower levels have implications for the respiratory system.

CO emissions result from incomplete combustion and some 90 per cent of all CO emissions in industrialized nations originate from the transport sector and about 85 per cent is associated with automobile use. The figure reaches 100 per cent in the centre of many built-up areas. Further, in countries such as the UK, if the trends of the 1980s continue, emissions will grow by about 2 per cent per annum.

(f) Sulphur dioxide emissions. Emissions of this colourless but strong

smelling gas can result in bronchitis and other diseases of the respiratory system and they are the major contributor to 'acid rain'. Transport is directly responsible for about 5 per cent of total SO_2 emissions (although in some countries it is as high as 17 per cent) with diesel fuel containing more SO_2 per litre than gasoline. More importantly, coal-fired electricity generation is a major source of this gas and thus there are further indirect environmental implications related to both the use of electric rail transport and the manufacture of transport vehicles.

(g)   Volatile organic compounds. These compromise a wide variety of hydrocarbons and other substances (for example, methane, ethylene oxide, formaldehyde, phenol, phosgene, benzene, carbon tetrachloride, chlorofluorocarbons and polychlorinated biphenyls). They generally result from incomplete combustion of fossil fuels, although evaporated gasoline from fuel tanks and the carburettor is increasingly contributing to releases of aromatic hydrocarbons such as benzene.

When combined with NO_x in sunlight, hydrocarbons and some volatile organic compounds can generate low-level ozone – the main component of photochemical smog. Besides producing respiratory problems and causing eye irritations, some of the compounds are suspected of being carcinogenic and possibly mutagens or teratogens (which can result in congenital malformations). For example, benzene emissions are both odorous and have been linked with certain forms of cancer such as leukemia. About 80 per cent of all benzene emissions originate from gasoline-powered vehicles.

Further, chlorofluorocarbons, containing both chlorine and fluorine atoms, are seen as partly responsible for depletions in the ozone layer which leads to increases in ultraviolet radiation and skin cancer. They also represent a significant factor in the greenhouse effect, and are potentially more damaging than CO_2. CFCs emissions are from foam used in vehicle construction and from mobile air conditioning systems. In the US, for example, transport air condition systems are responsible for about 25 per cent of CFC releases into the atmosphere. More generally, volatile organic compounds (VOCs) may also have adverse effects on plant growth and result in deterioration of other compounds such as rubber.

Excluding methane, emissions of which largely stem from agricultural sources, about half the volatile organic compound emissions in industrialized countries are generally associated with road traffic and the proportion, with the exception of the US, tends to be rising (OECD, 1991*b*). About 30 per cent of all hydrocarbon emissions are directly related to transport.

Excess Depletion of Natural Resources
While there is no economic reason not to exploit non-renewable resources

at an appropriate rate, distortions in the market and political framework suggest that many such resources (for example, hydro-carbon fuels, ecosystems, land, natural areas, etc.) are being over-exploited. Excessive exploitation of carbon-based fuels is often seen as the major problem. In OECD countries road transport in 1987 directly accounted for 682 million tonnes of oil equivalent (MTOE) of oil consumption or 47 per cent of the total – this represents a rise from 446 MTOE in 1970. This, however, takes no account of the full cradle-to-grave energy requirements of building and using an automobile or of providing and maintaining the associated infrastructure.

Urban sprawl reduces land for nature conservation, recreational and agricultural uses, and leads – because of increases in average trip length – to further high levels of travel demand with their associated environmental implications. Linked with this, transport infrastructure itself takes up considerable space – in the pre-unification states of the FRG 5 per cent of land was given over to transport and in the Rhine-Ruhr agglomeration 10 per cent of land is given over to transport infrastructure, although in some agglomerations the figure may reach 60 per cent (Rothengatter, 1989). Besides raising questions of exploitation of non-renewable land resources, this also has serious implications for such things as drainage and water ecology.

Community Severance
Communities are often divided by major infrastructure developments, especially in residential urban areas, which can result in social fragmentation. While some elements of the adverse effects this has on the local environment are encapsulated in such things as accident statistics and the state of the local atmosphere, there are also often significant social implications in terms of the quality of life which segmented communities can enjoy. Urban motorways or rail lines can make it difficult for members of the community to interact and participate fully.

Water Pollution
(a) Ground water. Transport affects ground water systems in two main ways. Firstly, transport infrastructure involves a substantial land take. This affects drainage patterns and the water table with consequential impacts on wildlife and, in the longer term, knock-on effects on agricultural patterns etc. Second, surface transport generates particulates and other matter which directly pollute water courses but can also, via drainage actions, lead to soil acidification and other forms of soil pollution.

(b) Maritime. Transport impinges on the marine environment not only through spillages of oils and chemicals and waste disposal but also via the

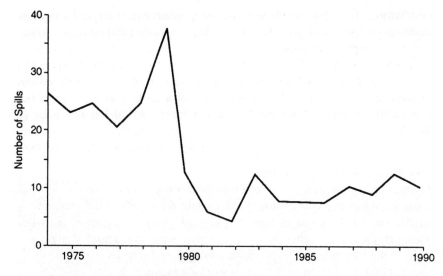

Source: International Tanker Owners Pollution Federation Ltd.

FIGURE 1. Accidental oil spills over 700 tonnes, 1974–1988.

coastal land take required for the construction of ports and other facilities. In terms of water pollution directly associated with shipping, globally about 1.5–2 million tonnes of oil pollution stems from maritime sources (both accidents and tank cleaning), although most of the major spills resulting in local scale environmental damage are associated with maritime accidents. These have serious effects on marine life. The evidence, however, is that the level of accidental marine spillage has stabilized, partly because of the reduction in the amount of oil carried and partly because of new legal requirements governing locations and methods of tank clearing (see figure 1).

Ports require significant land takes but, in addition, dredging poses problems both for the immediate marine life and also at dumping sites. The latter is becoming an increasing problem as bigger ships (for example, the post-Panama container vessels) mean that dredging requirements are more extensive than in the past.

Congestion

Although congestion is primarily an urban transport issue, it is also becoming an increasing problem at ports and airports where inefficient use is made of valuable time and environmental damage caused by atmospheric pollution, accidents, noise, excessive fuel use, etc. is compounded. Strictly, excessive traffic congestion, while an externality in the economic sense, really involves a lack of internal efficiency of the transport operations rather than being a form of environmental problem as conventionally understood. It is the fact that it is closely associated with and generally highly correlated with pollution and other environmental concerns which makes it a topic of interest.

Quantifying levels of excess congestion is not easy given the difficulty of defining the optimal level to use as a bench-mark. The traffic speeds in some cities (for example, Athens) are now as low as 7 to 8 km per hour while in Paris it is only 18 km per hour and 20 km per hour in London.

Visual Intrusion and Aesthetics
Problems here can stem from both transport infrastructure and the vehicles using it. While the two concepts are closely entwined, visual intrusion is strictly the blocking out of light or pleasant views by transport activities while aesthetics is rather more concerned with the actual design and style of the transport facilities. Both concepts embrace an entire life-cycle concept and in addition to the actual working facilities themselves embrace such things as the eyesores often associated with the disposal of old 'hardware' including disused infrastructure such as docks and railway lines and scrapped vehicles.

Developing Trends in Transport

While it is not too difficult to highlight the current contributions of transport to global environmental pollution, it is rather more difficult to decide which of a number of future possible trends are going to be of greatest importance.

We focus on broad economic trends in three categories of geographical area rather than any possible changes or developments in transport technology. The latter are particularly difficult to forecast not only in terms of the possible forms they might take but also with regard to the willingness of society to take them up. Clearly, there are important developments occurring which not only affect the environmental costs of transport (for example, developments in vehicle guidance, greater fuel efficiency, electric cars, etc.) but also the attractiveness of alternatives to transport (for example, telecommuting, videoconferencing, distance learning, remote banking, etc.) but their exact impacts are difficult to foresee (Button, 1991a).

We also say little about policy responses but assume that policies will evolve much as in recent years (i.e. reactive in their orientation and generally of a 'firefighting' nature). This is clearly unrealistic in that any successful initiative to achieve sustainable development must inevitably require new policy initiatives.

ECONOMIC GROWTH IN THE INDUSTRIAL ECONOMIES

Although there are inevitable trade-cycle effects, there is every indication that, if existing economic policies are continued, economic growth will continue in the Western world. Indeed, the movement towards the Single Internal Market within the European Communities and agreements such as the Free Trade Agreement between the US and Canada are likely to foster even more rapid growth. This growth is likely to lead both to more demand for transport *per se* as a result of high income levels and also to more transport as the removal of trade barriers enables the economies of greater spatial specialization to be reaped. It is forecast, for instance, that cross-border traffic within the EC will grow by 30–50 per cent as a result of the creation of the Single Internal Market.

At national levels, the forecasts are that, with the continuation of existing policies, road traffic growth will continue and in the case of, for example, Great Britain may rise by up to 142 per cent between 1988 and 2025 (Department of Transport, 1989). Predictions made on a similar basis for the Netherlands suggest a 72 per cent growth between 1986 and 2010. More aggregate studies of the EC have forecast significant growth in road haulage, especially international traffic, as manufactured goods take an ever increasing share of the overall amount of goods transported (Gwilliam and Allport, 1982).

Changing patterns of settlement which come with the higher incomes and different aspirations which come with economic growth influence personal travel behaviour, while changes in production management influence freight transport trends the more towards 'just-in-time' approaches and whole-quality management in the 1980s increased the role of transport in the overall production process. Although recent developments have refined the nature of the logistics process, there is still a considerable way to go in many countries before JIT management reaches the 70 per cent or so found in Japan – the US is at about a 40 per cent adoption level with the UK at well below 20 per cent. This has implications for domestic freight traffic growth and future modal split.

Equally, if one looks at European aviation a similar picture of traffic growth emerges with traffic growing from 321.3 thousand million passenger-kilometres in 1978 to 507.9 thousand million by 1988 and forecast, by the International Civil Aviation Organisation, to rise to some 850.0 thousand million by the end of the century. We also already find that of the forty-six largest airports in Western Europe, twelve are currently operating at or around their physical capacity and a further eleven will, it is predicted, reach capacity by 1995 (Association of European Airlines, 1987). Further, the EC Commission and others have identified a series of major bottle necks in the European surface transport networks and if traffic grows as forecast this number will expand and the problems intensify.

The underlying problem is that under current policies the efficiency of the transport system will inevitably deteriorate in Europe as congestion develops. The implications of this are summarized in a recent report submitted to the EC Commission (Group Transport 2000 Plus, 1991), *viz*: '. . . a general deterioration in transport conditions due to inefficient use of the networks and the saturation of certain infrastructures (especially road and air). Also – albeit not so immediately noticeable – there is an on-going increase in the nuisance caused by transport. The culprit here is not so much network saturation as the actual increase in traffic.'

The pressures will clearly be to remove such bottle necks and capacity constraints with potentially serious consequences for the environment.

DEVELOPMENTS IN EASTERN EUROPE

The Gorbachev era initiated a transformation of Eastern Europe. The political and economic changes – and especially *perestroika* – which are taking place in the post-communist states are inevitably resulting in widespread economic ripple effects throughout the rest of the Continent. The changes are as pronounced in the transport sector as any other (Button, 1991*b*). Indeed, emphasis is being put on improving communications, in the widest sense, between the East and West as a key ingredient in a broader integration process. The implications involve, however, not just immediate issues of handling changes in international freight flows across the Continent but also longer-term matters which extend into issues of reinvestment in the transport infrastructure of most Eastern European countries, the containment of environmental degradation associated with the transport technology employed, the problems of redeploying many hundreds of thousands of currently unproductive workers, and management questions concerning the efficient operations of transport systems.

At present the post-Communist Eastern European economies are characterized by a heavy reliance on rail freight transport (see table 10) compared to Western industrialized economies which, to a large extent, reflects both the nature of trade patterns in the former COMECON system and the types of goods produced. With regard to passenger transport, the post-Communist countries have significantly lower levels of car ownership than in the West (for example, in 1988 it was 0.132 car per capita in Bulgaria, 0.119 in Poland and 0.169 in Hungary, compared to 0.400 in France, 0.349 in the UK, 0.472 in Germany and 0.356 in the Netherlands).

As trading patterns involving the post-Communist countries change and their economies move away from heavy industrial products and raw materials to manufacturing so one can anticipate a switch away from

TABLE 10. Mode split for freight carriage (thousand tonnes/kilometres in 1988).

Country	Road	Rail	Inland Waterways
European Community			
Belgium	26.00	7.00	6.35
Denmark	9.10	1.66	–
France	111.80	52.30	7.35
Germany	151.40	58.50	52.80
Greece	14.00	0.60	–
Ireland	5.00	0.55	–
Italy	169.00	19.60	0.14
Luxemburg	0.40	0.64	0.36
Netherlands	22.10	3.20	33.85
Portugal	9.00	1.56	–
Spain	133.00	12.00	–
United Kingdom	124.80	18.20	2.30
Eastern Europe			
Bulgaria	14.70	17.60	–
Czechoslovakia	13.10	69.40	5.20
GDR	16.40	59.40	2.50
Hungary	13.20	20.20	2.00
Poland	38.80	120.70	1.40
Yugoslavia	20.90*	25.40	4.60

* Public transport only.

Source: Taken from United Nations, European Conference of Ministers of Transport, International Road Federation and International Union of Railways data sets.

rail transport and towards road haulage. New trade patterns will emerge requiring new infrastructure as well as leading to more truck and vehicle movements. Inevitably the average length of haul will rise as greater international specialization develops. These changes have clear implications both in terms of atmospheric pollution and noise nuisance.

Additionally, as the economies of the post-Communist countries expand and personal incomes rise so the demand for private car ownership will, if unrestrained, grow. Figure 2 provides an indication of the levels of car ownership in a selection of countries, including some post-Communist states, set against their relative income levels. The positive relationship is clear. Even this picture may, however, understate the speed at which private car ownership will grow in Eastern Europe. There already exists pent-up demand brought about by the physical difficulties of obtaining a vehicle even if money were available (for example, someone taking delivery of a Lada 2107 on 1 September 1987 in East Germany would have ordered it in November 1972). One could well anticipate an explosion of car ownership as people on lower incomes than in the West seek vehicles

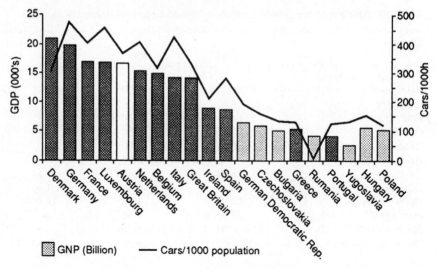

FIGURE 2. Per capita GDP and cars per 1000 population.

TABLE 11. Estimates of NO_x emissions (10^3 tonnes per annum).

Country	All Modes 1980	Road Transport 1980	Road Transport Forecast 2000
Bulgaria	89	88	185
Czechoslovakia	91	88	95
GDR	–	81	144
Hungary	100	75	142
Poland	190	185	201
Romania	–	85	105

Source: Laikin, *et al.* (1987).

quite simply because of social pressures and the status that car ownership provides.

Even accepting this there are other considerations to be taken into account. While there are national differences, the environments of Eastern Europe are all heavily polluted. Energy production, raw material extraction and heavy industry are the major culprits but transport is also a contributor (Russell, 1990). Data on the exact state of the environments in Eastern Europe, let alone the factors causing their degradation, are sparse but some indications are available. Table 11, for instance, gives some calculations regarding nitrogen oxides (NO_x), an atmospheric pollutant associated with acid rain, which in the West is being countered by the fitting of catalytic converters and is in most countries stable or falling. The vintage and technology of the vehicle stock in Eastern Europe also means that the NO_x and similar atmospheric pollution problems are increasing and not abating. Growth in car ownership can only add to these effects.

ECONOMIC CHANGE IN THE THIRD WORLD

The third element concerns low-income nations. At present the transport systems of these countries contribute relatively little to the total global pollution picture, mainly because car ownership etc. is so low. There are, for instance, less cars in Africa than in Germany. However, if incomes rise and economic activity expands in the way the World Bank and other international agencies anticipate, it is forecast that car ownership and use and freight traffic in less developed countries will rise even more dramatically during the next thirty-five years than is predicted for either the West or post-Communist nations. This very considerable increase in transport will also require large amounts of additional infrastructure. There are clear and potentially major implications of this for the global environment as well as the various national environments of the countries concerned. Infrastructure expansion, in particular, in many of these countries is almost inevitably going to have additional impacts on wilderness areas and species protection.

Obtaining even moderately reliable information on the existing car stocks of low-income countries is difficult and any predictions about the future must be surrounded with caveats. However, deploying the types of forecasting model used in industrial countries predictions can be made (Button and Ngoe, 1991). As can be seen from a sample of results in table 12, the indications are that vehicle ownership, and particularly at the higher end of the spectrum of low-income countries, will increase substantially over the coming decades, assuming existing transport policies remain in place. Much of the resulting environmental pressure will be felt in urban areas because, unlike recent trends in industrialized countries, there is often a high correlation between vehicle ownership growth and urbanization. Further, given the quality of vehicle maintenance in these countries, coupled with the projected age profile of fleets, then vehicle for vehicle the environmental damage which will result will be significantly higher than, say, in OECD nations.

The relevance of this traffic growth in the Third World for the rest of the world is that, on the assumption that there is no intention of forcibly restricting these countries in their desire to enjoy the material living standards now available in the West, there will be a need for the West to reduce significantly the global environmental impacts of its transport even if a steady state situation regarding such things as CO_2 emissions is to be achieved.

TABLE 12. Forecast levels of car ownership in low-income countries.

Country	Annual Rate of Per Capita Income Growth (%)	Forecast National Car Stock		
		1986	2000	2025
Burkina Faso	1	100	143	286
	4	100	183	394
Rwanda	1	100	177	499
	4	100	224	951
Togo	1	100	149	335
	4	100	205	751
Haiti	1	100	96	161
	4	100	128	351
Pakistan	1	100	148	340
	4	100	196	739
Cameroon	1	100	162	440
	4	100	255	1 309
Gabon	1	100	215	632
	4	100	355	1 922
Algeria	1	100	141	341
	4	100	232	1 000
Mauritius	1	100	146	209
	4	100	219	544
Malaysia	1	100	149	284
	4	100	216	628

Source: Button and Ngoe (1991).

Conclusions

Concerns about the environmental effects of transport have grown in recent years and given some of the transport trends which are evolving, are unlikely to fade away in the future. Some of the concern is driven by firm scientific evidence and immediately apparent adverse effects (for example, high traffic noise levels) and has been the subject of policy debate for some time. Other concerns are more recent and in many cases the exact links between transport and environmental degradation are still being explored. The problem with some of these latter problems (for example, higher level ozone depletion) is that if the worst current scenarios materialize then there is little scope for reversing the situation in the short or medium term. Concern is, therefore, rather more immediate and heavily tinged with notions of risk aversion.

Equally the picture is not one of complete gloom in that the reactive policies adopted in the past few years have, in a number of instances, virtually removed some forms of transport-related pollution or are at least in the process of doing so (for example, fiscal policies regarding leaded petrol), while in others the adoption of technological developments such as catalytic converters have given something of a breathing space both to conduct further research and seek out longer term policy options. Having said this serious problems remain.

At one level our understanding of the longer-term implications of many of the impacts transport has on the environment is relatively scant. The macroeconomic cost-benefit calculations associated with, for instance, assessing the implications of global warming are far from complete, let alone the specific equations which relate to transport's contribution to this process.

At the other level, the diversity of the environmental impacts of transport, coupled with the fact that most of the items involved (for example, clean air and water, peace and quiet, etc.) are not directly traded in markets, makes policy formulation difficult. Inevitably trade-offs must be made both between the various forms of environmental damage and between the various groups in society involved. This chapter has not directly addressed these latter issues but rather sought to provide guidelines to both the nature and the scale of the problems involved.

REFERENCES

Association of European Airlines (1987) *Capacity of Aviation Systems in Europe. Scenario on Airport Congestion*. Brussels: AEA.

Baumol, W. J. and Oates, W. E. (1979) *Economics, Environmental Policy and the Quality of Life*. Englewood Cliff: Prentice-Hall.

Button, K. J. (1990a) Environmental externalities and transport policy. *Oxford Review of Economic Policy*, Vol **6**, pp. 61–75.

Button, K. J. (1990b) Infrastructure plans for Europe, in Gidlund, J. and Tornqvist, G. (eds.) *European Networks*. Umea: CERUM.

Button, K. J. (1991a) Transport and communications, in Rickard, J. H. and Larkinson, J. (eds.) *Longer Term Issues in Transport: A Research Agenda*. Aldershot: Avebury.

Button, K. J. (1991b) The development of East-West transport in the 1990s, in *Evolutions in Transportation*. Quebec: CTRF.

Button, K. J. and Gillingwater, D. (1983) *Future Transport Policy*. London: Routledge.

Button, K. J. and Ngoe, N. (1991) Vehicle Ownership and Use Forecasting in Low Income Countries, Transport and Road Research Laboratory, Contract Report 278.

Department of Transport (1989) *National Traffic Forecasts (Great Britain)*. London: HMSO.

Enquête-Commission of the German Parliament (1990) Protection of the Atmosphere. Third Report, Bundestagsdrucksache 11/8030, Bonn.

Frenking, H. (1988) *Exchange of Information on Noise Abatement Policies. Case Study on Germany*. Paris: Report prepared for the Environment Directorate of the OECD.

Group Transport 2000 Plus (1991) *Transport in a Fast Changing Europe* (no place of publication).

Gwilliam, K. M. and Allport, R. J. (1982) A medium term transport research strategy for the EEC: Part 1. *Transport Reviews* Vol. **2**, pp. 305–346.

Hillman, M., Henderson, I. and Whalley, A. (1976)*Transport Realities and Planning Policy*. London: Political and Economic Planning.

Laikin, R. E., Chadwick, M. J. and Cooke, J. G. (1987) Energy-based emission inventories for modelling cost-effective SO_2 and NO_x abatement strategies in Europe. Paper presented at the International Workshop on Methodologies for Air Pollution Emission Inventories, Paris.

Lamure, C. (1990) Environmental considerations in transport investment, in *Ministerial Session on Transport and the Environment: Background Reports*. Paris: ECMT and OECD.

Linster, M. (1989) Background facts and figures, in *Ministerial Session on Transport and the Environment: Background Reports*. Paris: ECMT and OECD.

Ministry of Transport (1963) *Traffic in Towns*, London: HMSO.

Mishan, E. J. (1967) *The Costs of Economic Growth*. Harmondsworth: Penguin.

National Society for Clean Air (1989) *Pollution Glossary*. London: NSCA.

Nordhaus, W. D. (1991) To slow or not to slow: the economics of the greenhouse effect. *Economic Journal*, Vol. **101**, pp. 920–937.

Organisation for Economic Cooperation and Development (1988) *Transport and the Environment*. Paris: OECD.

Organisation for Economic Cooperation and Development (1991*a*) *The State of the Environment*. Paris: OECD.

Organisation for Economic Cooperation and Development (1991*b*) *Environmental Indicators*. Paris: OECD.

Organisation for Economic Cooperation and Development (1991*c*) *Fighting Noise in the 1990s*. Paris: OECD.

Perrow, C. (1984) *Normal Accidents: Living with High Risk Technologies*. New York: Basic Books.

Ponti, M. and Vittadini, M. R. (1990) Case study of Italy, in Barde J.-P, and Button, K. J. (eds.) *Transport Policy and the Environment: Six Case Studies*. London: Earthscan.

Quinet, E. (1990), *The Social Costs of Land Transport*, Environment Monograph No. 32, Paris: OECD.

Rothengatter, W. (1989) Economic aspects, in *Ministerial Session on Transport and the Environment: Background Reports*. Paris: ECMT and OECD.

Russell, J. (1990) *Environmental Issues in Eastern Europe: Setting an Agenda*. London: Royal Institute of International Affairs.

Scientific Advisory Council of the German Ministry of Transport (1991) Reduction of Pollutant Emissions of the Transport Sector, Report for the Ministry, Bonn.

Thomson, J. M. (1974) *Modern Transport Economics* Harmondsworth: Penguin.

United Nations Economic Commission for Europe (1987) Consumption patterns in the ECE region: long-term trends and policy issues. *Economic Bulletin for Europe, Vol.* **39**, pp. 245–482.

United Nations Intergovernmental Panel on Climate Change (1990) *Climate Change: The IPCC Scientific Assessment*. Cambridge: Cambridge University Press.

United States Department of Transportation, Transportation Systems Center (annual) *Transportation Safety Information Report*. Cambridge: USDOT.

World Commission on Environment and Development (1987) *Our Common Future* (Bründtland Commission Report) Oxford: Oxford University Press.

Zahavi, Y. (1979) *The 'UMOT' Project*, DOT-RSPA-DPB-2–79–3. Washington: US Department of Transportation Report.

3

Policy Responses in the UK

DAVID BANISTER

The environment is likely to be one of the main issues concerning society in the 1990s and as such will influence policy into the next century. The 1988 Toronto conference proposed a reduction in greenhouse gases by 50 per cent in the long term and by 20 per cent before 2005. The UK was not party to that agreement, resisted a more modest proposal at Nordwijk to stabilize emissions at current levels by 2000, and only accepted a target to stabilize levels of carbon dioxide emissions by 2005. This means that some EC countries (for example, the Netherlands and Germany) will have to seek higher reductions so that the overall aim to stabilize EC levels by 2000 is achieved. The end of the last decade has proved a watershed in thinking in the UK on certain aspects of the environment. The crucial test of the next decade will be to see whether this thinking can be translated into positive action.

Concern over the environment is not a new problem, but is one that has been thrown into sharp relief by the realization of the global dimension to pollution and the irreversibility of climatic change. In the UK, eight of the warmest ten years of the twentieth century have been in the 1980s. Global warming is now taking place and concepts such as sustainable development and the principle that the polluter pays are high on the political agenda (for example, World Commission on Environment and Development: The Bründtland Commission, the World Conservation Strategy, and the UN Conference on Environment and Development).

The environment has also been perceived by the electorate to be the second most important political problem within the European Community (1988) after unemployment (cited in Pearce *et al.* 1989). In addition to this greater awareness of the problems and heightened public concerns, there are other trends which make sustainable development difficult to achieve. The growth in demand for transport is proceeding at unprecedented rates and this means that difficult choices may have to be made. To accept the arguments for sustainability will mean a reduction in consumption and a much higher price for travel. It will also mean striking an appropriate balance between growth, the distribution of that growth and the environment. Environmental issues only form part of the political spectrum, and politicians have to balance economic growth with sustainable growth. Transport revenues form a significant part of total exchequer revenues and raising the cost of transport to the user to reflect the full social and environmental costs of travel may affect exchequer revenues. Even if the price elasticity is low and people are prepared to pay more for travel, expenditure patterns in other sectors may be affected, causing in turn a fall in demand, reduced growth and possible unemployment.

The interpretation of the environment taken in this chapter is a broad one (table 1) covering air pollution, the use of resources, environmental and development factors. Decisions taken to improve benefits along one dimension may be likely to increase costs along another dimension or in another sector. The complexity of decision making in environmental policy cannot be underestimated but as in transport, these difficult choices must now be faced by all governments.

Ironically, many of the potential effects of climate change in the UK may be beneficial to transport. Under the heading of transport, the UK Climate Change Impacts Review Group (Department of the Environment (DoE), 1991) listed eight specific conclusions relating to transport if the mean global surface temperature in 2030 increases by 1.4 deg C and the atmospheric content of carbon dioxide increases to 450 parts per million by volume (the 1990 level is 350 ppmv).

– Sensitivity to weather and climate change is high for all forms of transport, but especially for road and air transport.
– A reduction in frequency, severity and duration of winter freeze would reduce disruption to transport systems. Winter maintenance would be reduced as would road damage.
– Snow and ice present the most difficult weather related problems for the rail system: reductions in these problems would lead to savings in locomotive design, point heaters and de-icing equipment. There would be similar reductions in the costs of aircraft operations, although changes in wind direction could affect runway operations and redistribute noise impacts in urban areas.
– Any increase in the frequency of severe gale episodes could increase disruption from fallen trees, masonry and overturned vehicles, and interrupt flight schedules.
– Sea level rise and more frequent coastal flooding could cause structural damage to roads, bridges, embankments and other transport infrastructure.
– If precipitation increased, this would exacerbate road flooding, landslips and corrosion of steelwork on bridges.

TABLE 1. Environmental factors and transport in UK.

		Importance of Transport	Effects
1.	*Pollutants*		
	Carbon dioxide	16%	Global warming
	Nitrogen oxides	45%	Acid rain
	Sulphur dioxide	5%	Acid rain, bronchitis
	Carbon monoxide	85%	Morbidity, fertility
	Benzine	80%	Carcinogenic
	Lead	50%	Mental development
	Hydrocarbons	28%	Toxic trace substances
2.	*Resources*	Consumption	
	Oil	47%	Depletion of natural resources
	Land take		6 ha of land per km of motorway
	Ecology		Landscape and SSIs destroyed
	Ecosystems		Water quality, flood hazards, river systems modified
	Accidents	5 000 Deaths 63 000 Serious Injuries	Pain, suffering, grief
3.	*Environment*		
	Noise		Stress, concentration, health
	Vibration		Historic buildings
	Severance		Dividing communities
	Visual impact and aesthetics		Changes in physical appearance
	Conservation and townscape		Preservation
4.	*Development*		
	Regional development		Location of industry
	Local economic impacts		Income levels, employment, social impact
	Congestion		Delay, use of resources
	Urban sprawl		Traffic generation, induced development
	Construction effects		Blight, property prices, compensation

- Changes in demand for some goods (for example, perishables), coupled with higher ambient temperatures, may affect the pattern and frequency of distribution of goods to wholesalers and retailers.
- Changes in demand for travel, such as increased leisure journeys, may result from perceived 'better' summer weather.

However, all forms of powered transport, particularly road and air, are serious contributors to global warming and acid rain. The purpose of this contextual review of UK policy on transport and the environment is to trace the evolution of policy over the last thirty years and to present the range of options which are available and which have been used by the government. The chapter then draws certain conclusions and proposes research under four broad headings.

Evolution of National Policy in the UK

ROADS AND THE ENVIRONMENT IN THE 1970S

There has been a tradition of intervention in transport for the whole of the twentieth century, with most infrastructure investment in transport being publicly financed and most operators publicly owned. The 1960s marked a change in this emphasis with increasing concern over the efficiency of nationalized industries, the growth in car ownership and the problems of reconciling congestion with the environment. The famous Buchanan Report on Traffic in Towns (Ministry of Transport, 1963) highlights many of these problems including the links between land use and transport and the concept of environmental capacity. However, at that time, these ideas promoted an expanded programme of urban road construction even though it was realized that there were significant environmental disbenefits caused by traffic. The concept of road pricing was also first raised at this time (Ministry of Transport, 1964).The Smeed Report argued that people should be charged for the congestion they cause. Even though the economic arguments were accepted, the possibility was rejected for technical reasons given the unreliability of metering systems and the costs of implementation.

It was only in the 1970s that the environment again featured, with the rise in environmental movements and the encouragement given by the Skeffington Report (1968) to the public and pressure groups to get more involved in planning issues. The general public had become much more aware of the question of whether a road should be built, the weaknesses in established analysis and evaluation procedures, and the presumption that redevelopment and blight were the inevitable consequence of progress.

The opening of Westway in July 1970 epitomized public concerns. This section of elevated motorway in West London passed through communities, very close to housing and seemed to typify the insensitivity of highway engineering to existing urban structures. It was partly as a response to public concern about schemes such as Westway that the Urban Motorways Project team was set up (1969)

- to examine current policies for fitting major roads into the urban fabric;
- to consider changes that would improve the integration of roads with their environment;
- to examine the consequences of such changes for public policy, statutory powers and administrative procedures.

However, even in 1969, the government reaffirmed its commitment to 'devote a substantial, and growing part of the programme to road works in urban areas' (Ministry of Transport, 1969) and the 1970 White Paper on Roads for the Future required an investment programme of £4000 million (at 1970 prices) to be spent over fifteen to twenty years. The broad objective of this programme was to 'check and then eliminate the congestion on our trunk road system' (Ministry of Transport, 1970), and as part of that general aim the environment aim was to divert long-distance traffic, and particularly heavy goods vehicles, from a large number of towns and villages, so as to relieve them of the noise, dirt and damage which they suffered at present.

The early 1970s marked a sudden change of priority brought about by events at all levels of decision making. At the national level the Urban Motorways Committee recommended integration in the design of roads with the surrounding areas and the inclusion of the costs of remedial measures as part of the total construction costs of a scheme (DoE, 1972). The report was published at the same time as a review of the land compensation aspects of road construction, and together they formed the input to the 1973 Land Compensation Act, but even here the direct effects were limited to a distance of 200 m from the road (Starkie, 1982). The second influential report was that of the House of Commons Expenditure Committee on Urban Transport Planning (1973) which reinforced the general trend away from investment in roads to better management and the use of existing resources.

At the local level, political opposition to urban road building was growing. The most celebrated case outside London was the decision in Nottingham to abandon much of their highway strategy and to look at the possibility of controlling traffic entering the city centre. The zone and collar scheme was introduced in the western part of the city on an experimental basis in 1975. Private cars would have limited access to the city centre and would be delayed by traffic lights at peak periods. Long-stay city centre car parking was reduced and prices raised. The intention was to get car users to switch to public transport for city centre trips and to use the park and ride schemes. The Nottingham Scheme was not a success and was abandoned shortly afterwards (1976). However, its significance was that it reflected public concern over urban road building and it demonstrated that alternatives did exist.

In London, the London Amenity and Transport Association (LATA) produced its own report on Motorways in London (Thomson, 1969) which made a strong case against any urban motorways in the capital. This report coincided with the Greater London Development Plan inquiry set up to consider objections to that plan. These objections exceeded 28,000 and mainly related to the transport proposals for a series of orbital motorways. The Panel recommended scaling down the orbitals to the M25 (substantially outside the GLC areas and in green belt countryside) and the most controversial inner ring road. However, it was the political changes in London that marked the end of these urban road schemes. The London Labour Party, after much debate, decided to fight the 1973 elections on an anti-motorway platform. This decision won them power and London's motorway plans were effectively abandoned for the next ten years.

Although some cities, such as Glasgow, Newcastle, Leeds and Liverpool, maintained urban roads programmes, the majority abandoned (at least temporarily) most schemes. The philosophy of the Buchanan Report which had been the standard for policy in the previous decade was also abandoned. Cities would no longer be subjected to substantial road building programmes to allow unrestricted access to private cars. In the autumn of 1973, John Peyton the Minister of Transport announced in a short speech to the House of Commons 'that he proposed a switch in resources in the transport sector away from urban road construction'. This statement was made exactly ten years after the unveiling of the Buchanan Report on Traffic in Towns (Starkie, 1982).

The public inquiry was the forum within which many of these debates were held. The government maintained that the public inquiry could not question public policy on roads or the basis on which traffic forecasts were made to justify the schemes. The protestors claimed that they should be able to question the need for a road, and they were also concerned about the independence of the inspector and the treatment of those protestors with legitimate cases at the inquiry, including the availability of information to them and the costs of being represented at an inquiry. Their success was not so much in getting decisions reversed, but in raising public concerns over roads and in delaying the road building programme. It was now taking over twelve years for a road to complete the process of preparation, inquiry and construction.

Two major initiatives were taken by the government in the mid-1970s. In December 1976, the Advisory Committee on Trunk Road Assessment was set up to review the Department of Transport's Trunk Road Assessment methods, including the procedures used in traffic forecasts and the relative importance it attached to economic and environmental factors. The second inquiry was concerned with the procedures surrounding the conduct of public inquiries into highway proposals (Department of Transport [DTp], 1978), which recommended independent inspectors, a pre-inquiry stage, greater access to information and an agreed programme for representation at the inquiry. Objectors were still not allowed to question government policy, but they could debate whether national forecasts were appropriate to that particular local situation. These changes did much to dissipate public concern, but the changes coincided with a move away from a network of long distance motorways and urban motorways to small town bypass construction. The environmental concerns of protestors were less focused at this level.

The environment as an issue was a public concern throughout the 1970s, both in terms of the increased land take required for new roads and urban development, and the externalities created by noise and pollution from road traffic. The economic benefits of a high speed motorway and primary road network for industry and other users had to be balanced against the loss of land and a general reduction in the quality of the environment for others. In parallel with the revision of the roads programme, assessment and forecasting procedures, and public inquiry procedures, there were additional studies undertaken on the impact of the heavy lorry.

The Armitage Inquiry on *Lorries, People and the Environment* (DTp, 1980) concluded that heavier lorries offered large and continued economic benefits through reduced transport costs. However, the assessment of the impact of the lorry on people and the environment is more problematical. The case hinged on the argument that heavier lorries would mean fewer lorries, and that if stringent noise and braking standards were introduced the lorry would be both quieter and safer. A reduction in heavy vehicle mileage resulting from fewer lorries would mean fewer accidents. The main conclusion reached was that heavier lorries should be allowed up to a gross weight of 44 tonnes, with a variety of axle configurations to distribute the load. Evidence submitted by environmental groups to the Inquiry on the increasing average journey lengths for lorries and the fact that vehicle utilization rates for the heaviest lorries were falling in the 1970s did not make much impact (Starkie, 1982).

For a decade, environmental groups had been successful in delaying and blocking the powerful industrial interests who wanted to increase the gross weight and dimensions of lorries. It was only at the end of the decade that the argument for heavier and larger lorries was won, and even then it seemed that this victory was because of recession and low economic growth brought about by the oil crisis of 1979. In times of economic

recession and hardship, environmental issues became of secondary importance. A lesson which may still be true a decade later!

LONDON'S THIRD AIRPORT

The Roskill Commission Inquiry (1968–70) into London's Third Airport
initially examined a list of seventy-eight possible sites, and within seven
months had reduced this list to four: Thurleigh (near Bedford), Cublington
(Buckinghamshire), Nuthampstead (in northern Hertfordshire) and Foulness (later known as Maplin on the Essex coast). Stansted was missing as
it had been excluded as being inferior to Nuthampstead on grounds of air
traffic control, of noise impact and of poorer surface access. Similarly,
Foulness had been included as it ranked best on noise, defence and air
traffic control, but it was a very expensive site to develop and was furthest
from London with a high surface access cost. Logically, this option should
not have been shortlisted, but was included so that the Commission had
a yardstick against which it could compare the three 'best' sites.

A comprehensive evaluation was carried out on the four shortlisted
sites with comparisons being drawn with the cheapest overall alternative
(Cublington). Thurleigh was £70 million more expensive than Cublington
whilst Nuthampstead and Foulness were £129 million and £159 million
more, respectively, in terms of the full social costs and benefits. Sensitivity
analysis suggested that the rankings would not change, even if substantially
different values of time were used. There was criticism at the time of the
exclusive use of monetary valuations, the values of time and noise, and
the omission of many planning and economic development factors.

Despite the undoubted environmental disadvantages, the Roskill team
opted for Cublington. However, one of the team members, Colin Buchanan, could not agree with that decision and argued that Foulness was
the only acceptable site despite the higher development costs. Apart from
his distrust of the cost benefit analysis of the four shortlisted sites, he
argued for the preservation of open space around London. He concluded
'that it would be nothing less than an environmental disaster if the airport
were to be built at any of the inland sites, but nowhere more serious than
at Cublington where it would lie athwart the critically important belt of
open country between London and Birmingham' (Commission on the
Third London Airport, 1971). The public quickly reacted to the dissension
among the Roskill Commission members and pressure groups from the
Cublington areas became instrumental in switching the economic arguments for Cublington to the environmental arguments for Foulness. In
April 1971, the government announced that the Third London Airport
would be built at Maplin Sands (or Foulness) in Essex.

The Maplin Review (Department of Trade, 1974) modified some of the demand estimates and concluded that the existing London terminals (Heathrow, Gatwick, Stansted and Luton) could accommodate the reduced demand now expected. The main constraint was terminal capacity, not runway capacity. This evidence allowed the government to abandon the decision to build at Maplin Sands (July 1974). The environmental arguments were instrumental in overturning the recommendations of the most comprehensive evaluation ever undertaken on a transport investment project. But even those arguments were not strong enough to see the development completed as global recession in the mid–1970s resulted in optimistic demand forecasts being reduced and there was considerable pressure to reduce public expenditure budgets. It is ironic that many of the same arguments are again being rehearsed as the Civil Aviation Authority is forecasting a doubling of demand for air travel (1987–2005) with a 13 million shortfall expected in the capacity of the London area airports. The recent report by the Airports Policy Consortium (1991) argues for expansion at regional airports together with major new investment in the London region. Stansted could be expanded as a 'Europe One' airport with new terminals and runways, or a new airport could be built in the Thames estuary. This second option would obviate the need for any expansion at Heathrow, Gatwick or Stansted. It seems possible that the same arguments will be rehearsed in the 1990s as were presented in the 1970s to the Roskill Commission.

ROADS AND THE ENVIRONMENT IN THE 1980s

The 1980s were characterized by a general withdrawal of government from transport decision making in the sense that there was extensive privatization of transport industries and the establishment of new regulatory regimes to allow greater competition between operators. Part of the rationale for this radical change in policy was a desire to introduce greater efficiency in transport, but equally important was the concern over increasing levels of public funding for both capital investment and revenue support. As part of this move, the government has encouraged private sector investment in transport infrastructure, but this has only taken place in particular instances. The overall objective of the roads programme is still seen as providing sufficient capacity to meet expected growth in demand (DTp, 1989*a,b*).

In terms of environmental factors, the main debates in the first part of the 1980s were over their inclusion in evaluation procedures (table 2). Evaluation procedures for trunk roads were changed as a result of the Leitch Committee's Report on Trunk Road Appraisal (DTp, 1977). The cost benefit analysis was broadened into a framework for assessment which would include monetary and non-monetary valuations. It was acknow-

TABLE 2. Major government publications on the environment and on transport and the environment in the UK and EC.

	Environment
1968	Clean Air Act
1985	EC Directive on Environmental Impact Assessment
1986	Single European Act
1988	Town and Country Planning (Assessment of Environmental Effects) Regulations
1989	Air Quality Standard Regulations
1989	Control of Smoke Pollution Act
1989	Water Act
1990	Environmental Protection Act
1990	White Paper: This Common Inheritance
1991	Climate Change Impacts Review Group Report on the Potential Effects of Climate Change in the UK

	Transport and the Environment
1963	Buchanan Report on Traffic in Towns
1971	Roskill Commission Report on London's Third Airport
1972	DoE Report on New Roads in Towns
1973	Land Compensation Act
1973	Heavy Commercial Vehicles (Controls and Regulations) Act
1976	Jefferson Committee Report on Noise and Other Environmental Issues
1977	Leitch Committee Report on Trunk Road Assessment
1980	Armitage Committee Report on Lorries, People and the Environment
1983	Manual of Environmental Appraisal
1986	SACTRA Report on Urban Road Appraisal
1991	Road Traffic Act
1992	SACTRA Report on the Environmental Effects of Proposed Road Schemes and Their Assessment

ledged that both environmental and regional development factors were important in evaluation and that methods were available to rank these factors. Increased consultation and public participation would help in explaining the options and the implications of each. Leitch (DTp, 1977) also concluded that the range of environmental factors covered in the Jefferson Report (DTp, 1976) was basically sound. However, that list would only include those headings listed under environment, land take, accidents and construction effects (table 1). Assessment of pollutants, resources and development effects was very limited.

The *Manual of Environmental Appraisal* (DTp, 1983) develops this list of environmental factors and adds to it assessment of heritage and conservation areas as well as ecological factors. The Standing Advisory Committee on Trunk Road Appraisal's (SACTRA) own report on Urban Road Appraisal (DTp, 1986) interpreted these factors within the urban environment.

In June 1985, the EC issued the Directive on the assessment of the effects of certain public and private projects on the environment, including the construction of motorways and express roads – interpreted in the UK as trunk roads over 10 km in length (Article 4(1)), and other roads or urban development projects at the discretion of individual Member countries (Article 4(2)). The Directive took effect from July 1988 (EC Council Directive, 1985). The SACTRA report (DTp, 1986) concluded that their recommendations are compatible with the requirements of the Directive. However, the Directive is explicit in specifying a much wider range of factors that should be included in any Environmental Impact Assessment. Article 3 requires an assessment of the direct and indirect effects of a project covering the following factors:

– human beings, fauna and flora;
– soil, water, air, climate and landscape;
– the interaction between the factors mentioned above;
– material assets and the cultural heritage.

Article 5 requires the developer to supply information on the following topics and to have regard to current knowledge and methods of assessment:

– a description of the project comprising information on the site, design and size of the project;
– a description of the measures envisaged in order to avoid, reduce and, if possible, remedy significant adverse effects;
– the data required to identify and assess the main effects which the project is likely to have on the environment;
– a non technical summary of the above information.

The EC Directive provides clear guidance on how a comprehensive Environmental Impact Assessment (EIA)[1] can be prepared. The *Manual of Environmental Appraisal* meets the requirements of the EC Directive and public inquiries are held for all major schemes to which there are objections, at which the environmental assessment will be considered.

In the UK, the Town and Country Planning regulations (July 1988) make it compulsory for some types of project to have an EIA to accompany the planning application. This requirement is in line with the EC Directive and ensures the EIA's compatibility with existing planning procedures. Schedule One includes major transport infrastructure proposals and aerodromes with runways over 2100 metres as projects requiring an EIA. If the proposed development is of sufficient size or is in an environmentally sensitive area the local authority may require an Environmental Impact Statement (EIS) – a summary document. Once the EIS has been submitted, the normal planning procedures are followed with the exception that the local authority has sixteen weeks to make a decision rather than the normal eight weeks. The recent report of SACTRA on the environmental effects of proposed road schemes and their assessment (DTp, 1992) comments on the full implementation of the EC Directive and on the possibilities for the valuation of environmental factors in assessment.

The government has now undertaken a major programme of new road building, including many bypasses. It is argued that this £12 billion investment for the 1990s will take traffic away from towns, help to protect local communities and buildings, and make life tolerable for residential areas and shopping streets (DTp, 1989a, para 44). This programme is partly determined by a cost benefit appraisal which covers, in monetary terms, the main effects of alternative options with regard to road users. This appraisal is coupled with an Environmental Impact Statement which expresses the impact of the proposals, in quantitative and qualitative terms, on the natural and built environment. The effects of road investment options on different groups of people are essentially 'colour coded' on the map. There is an inherent bias in the procedure which favours schemes with high user benefits but also have significant environmental costs. The House of Commons Committee of Public Accounts (1989) concluded 'we regard the evaluation of environmental effects as important in arriving at sound decisions on the roads programme and we recommend that the department should address this issue more determinedly.'

Other forms of transport infrastructure investments are also normally subjected to environmental impact assessments, although with schemes initiated under the Private Bill procedures, it seems that they do not comply fully with the EC Directive (Barde and Button, 1990). With the move to reduce public subsidies for rail services it seems that the financial appraisal of the viability is always likely to be more important than environmental considerations. Two procedures can be followed. Parliamentary procedures require promoters to consult local communities before depositing their Bills and objections to schemes are considered by Select Committees. Alternatively an order-making procedure could be authorized by the Minister, and a full public inquiry might be necessary and the EC Directive on EIA would then apply.

Compensation can be paid to people who suffer the adverse affects of noise. This principle, for example, has been incorporated in a number of Civil Aviation Acts with regard to airport noise. Insulating those affected from local environmental intrusion can be expensive as the recent experience of British Rail has shown with respect to the construction of the high speed rail link between the Channel Tunnel and London. Here, some £1.2 billion of the £3.5 billion cost of the 68-mile proposed link announced in 1989 was earmarked for environmental protection (Button, 1990). This view conforms to the notion that environmental costs should be internalized within the decision-making process. For example, in evidence to the House of Lords European Communities Committee, the Department of Transport stated 'as in the case of new road schemes, new railway developments are expected to bear their own environmental protection costs.'

Apart from the environmental evaluation of the roads programme and other investment decisions, the 1980s were also characterized by improvements in other environmental policy areas, principally in reducing emissions and in road safety. The government has set the target of reducing road deaths by 50 per cent over the current decade, seat belt wearing for both front and rear passengers is now compulsory, the drink drive laws have been tightened, there is a more rigorous test for motorcyclists, and the most recent Road Traffic Act (1991) has introduced new offences for causing death by careless driving when under the influence of drink or drugs and for causing danger to road users.

Vehicles are also subject to an annual inspection (if over three years of age) and this test now includes emissions standards (Road Vehicles (Construction and Use) Regulations, 1990). Regulations covering vehicular emissions levels and the eventual introduction of catalytic converters have been introduced. All new cars will be fitted with catalytic converters from January 1993 and new standards for emissions for heavy goods vehicles will be in force by 1996.

However, it is at the urban level that the main problems of traffic have to be addressed, and it is here that environmental benefits must be balanced with other objectives such as minimizing congestion. The government still has a strong desire not to limit an individual's freedom and to allow people to fulfil their aspirations to own and use a car.

All three major political parties have recently published statements on the environment, and there is full agreement on both the importance of the issues and the need for action. The government's Environment White Paper, *This Common Inheritance*, the Labour Party's environmental policy statement, *An Earthly Chance* and the Liberal Democrats' agenda for environmental action, *What Price Our Planet?* all recognize the role that transport and planning can play in achieving environmental and energy policy objectives. There also seems to be pressure from local authorities for more guidance and a framework within which to operate, perhaps through a planning policy guidance (PPG) on energy and land use (Owens, 1991). Owens comments that 'a transport policy which genuinely integrated an environmental dimension as opposed to considering the environment as an afterthought, would have to begin with a ceiling on the amount of pollution from traffic by specific dates: achieving these targets would almost certainly involve controlling the growth of traffic as well as improving the energy efficiency and environmental performance of individual vehicles.'

COMMENT

Just as policy priorities have changed over the last twenty years so have the range of environmental factors in transport. Environment as an issue has always been important, particularly in terms of how the car and urban road construction impacts upon urban areas in terms of land take, noise, visual intrusion, severance and blight. These problems were highlighted by the energy crises in the 1970s which added the use of non-renewable resources to the list of environmental factors. However, in all policy-making during the 1970s it seems that environmental factors were interpreted narrowly and they always seem to be a poor second best to the economic arguments for a particular investment. However, as we have illustrated, it was often the environmental factors which caused delay and eventual abandonment of several large-scale projects. These decisions were often justified on environmental grounds, but the influence of public protest (often by environmental groups) and shortages of public monies should not be underestimated.

The late 1980s has been marked by a significant broadening of the debate with international conferences and agreements playing an important role. This development has been brought about by the realization that there is a global dimension to environmental change, principally the issues of global warming and acid rain. Over the next few years, apart from the major road building programme, plans for the Channel Tunnel rail link, for the new Cross London rail lines, for the thirty or so proposals for light rail projects in cities will all require environmental assessments, as will the more speculative proposals for new runway capacity or even new airports. However, for the first time there also seems to be a remarkable consensus, among the general public within the UK and between the political parties, that there is a need for a national policy on the environment.

Policy Options

In September 1990, the Department of the Environment published a White Paper, *This Common Inheritance*, which claimed to present the first comprehensive review of every aspect of Britain's environmental policy. Conservation of energy was identified as an issue in development plans, as was the need to reduce the emission of greenhouse gases. It was suggested that locations should be selected which reduced the need for long car journeys and distances driven or which permitted the choice of more energy efficient public transport (para 6.34). Walking and cycling should be added to that list of more energy efficient modes. It was also suggested that the planning of transport routes should take account of the potential impact on settlement and development plans. It also acknowledges that good transport is vital to the well being of our towns. Many of the proposals require action by the European Community and other international agencies, whilst others need the cooperation of industry. The detailed options are presented and discussed elsewhere in this book, and here just a summary is presented (table 3).

Two points should be noted. Firstly, road pricing is explicitly ruled out for the next few years and secondly the view is taken that public transport is not a panacea for controlling CO_2 emissions, even in the transport sector. More generally the White Paper proposes regulation, guidance and encouragement but does not make any commitment to environmental taxes at present. Equally, it recognizes the possible need for such intervention in the longer term. The overall direction of environmental policy concentrates on the role of market mechanisms to encourage producers and consumers to act in environmentally beneficial ways. A secondary focus concentrates on prevention and on international cooperation, particularly within the EC. In the 1970s the environment meant using less energy, but now the environment means much more. Energy consumption in transport has increased over the last decade by some 34 per cent, with people making more journeys overall, more by car and longer journeys. The total passenger-kilometres has increased by some 50 per cent and the total tonne-kilometres by about 30 per cent (DTp, 1990), and levels of pollution, noise and other environmental factors have also increased (Transnet, 1990). The considerable volume of research has been summarized in the Transnet report where the 'solutions' are subdivided under five headings (table 4).

In each case the contribution to reductions in energy consumption and consequent reductions in pollution are assessed. Action is required at all levels of decision making.

- For local government it includes land-use planning and traffic management policies.
- For central government it includes pricing and taxation policies to assist in the development of alternative fuels, improvements in efficiency and intermodal shift, as well as reducing unnecessary travel.
- For European government, recommendations comprise the imposition of 'environmentally optimal' community-wide policies involving fuel and tax harmonization, vehicle speed limits and heavy vehicle weights.

Yet all of these options seem to be limiting and limited in their scope as they restrict themselves to the transport sector and primarily to reducing

TABLE 3. Transport policy options proposed in the White Paper *This Common Inheritance*.

---

1. Vehicle Standards

Tax incentives to reduce emissions
Standards for cars
Standards for heavy diesel vehicles
Road planning
Public transport

2. Taxation

Vehicle excise duties
Tax on company cars
Duties on petrol and diesel

3. Car Manufacturers and Consumers

Pressure on EC to tighten fuel efficiency standards on large cars
Support for EC proposals to require catalytic converters on all new cars by the end of 1992
Government encouragement for fleet operators and individuals to buy cars fitted with catalytic converters
Extension of MOT testing to cover emission of carbon monoxide, other polluting gases and possibly noise
Stricter enforcement of speed limits and possible lower limits in the long term

4. Heavy Diesel Vehicles

Pressure for stricter EC standards on particulate emissions from new vehicles
Support for US style restrictions on NO_x emissions by 1996/97
Possible application of tighter standards to existing vehicles which may necessitate retrofitting
Extension of MOT tests to include emissions of polluting gases, smoke and possibly noise, with proposals to increase the frequency of roadside tests
Encouragement to local authorities to control lorry movements in urban areas
Consideration of environmental benefits in the award of grants for rail or water-borne freight schemes

5. Road Planning

Reduction in congestion through the creation of red routes
Construction of by-passes and trunk roads, in conjunction with local authorities where appropriate
Support for local authority parking schemes
Research into design to reduce road noise

6. Public Transport

Continued financial support for British Rail and London Transport
Local authority action on priority bus lanes/traffic lights
Increased provision of cycle networks
Research into noise from public transport

Source: Based on Coopers and Lybrand, Deloitte (1990).

TABLE 4. 'Solutions' to transport and pollution.

---

1. Technical Fixes 1: Pollution Reduction and Energy Efficiency

---

Pollution reduction technology	– oxidation catalysts
	three-way catalysts
	catalytic trap oxidisers
Improving energy efficiencies	– engine changes (e.g. lean burn)
	weight reduction
	aerodynamics
	other technological modifications (e.g. transmission changes, rolling resistance)

---

2. Technical Fixes 2: Alternative Fuels and Power Sources

Diesel
Electricity
Hydrogen
Alternative power sources (e.g. nuclear power, gas from power stations, renewable sources)
Gas (e.g. liquefied natural gas, liquefied petroleum gas)
Methanol and ethanol

---

3. The Role of the Driver

Lower average engine size: the vehicle purchase decision
The vehicle replacement decision
Increasing car occupancies
Better driving practices
Better maintenance

---

4. Transport Planning Policies

Intermodal shift
Road traffic management – improving traffic flow
　　　　　　　　　　　　reducing excessive speeds
　　　　　　　　　　　　discouraging car traffic
Land-use planning
Other policies　　　　　　– public information campaigns encouraging telecommuting

---

5. Transport Pricing Policies

Road pricing
Fuel pricing and taxation policies
Company car tax policies
Vehicle pricing and taxation

Source: Based on Transnet (1990).

levels of energy consumption. The environment must be interpreted much more broadly as transport affects all our lives in a variety of ways. Here are just two examples of the complexity of the interactions and the breadth of the transport and environment links.

In the past, demand forecasts have been made for traffic and networks have been defined to meet that demand. It has now been realized that it may not be socially efficient, or desirable or possible to meet unrestricted demand and so restraint and management have become key concerns of transport planners. Alternative means of forecasting are being used such as scenario building, where alternative strategies are tested against possible future scenarios (Department of Energy, 1990). Alternatively, simulation studies have been developed to establish energy efficient forms of urban settlement patterns (Rickaby, 1987). In most cases these studies have taken one or two sectors (transport and land use) and examined the environment in terms of one variable (energy). Yet no one has established the conditions under which a settlement pattern is energy efficient, let alone environmentally efficient. Transport factors have to be balanced against other energy costs such as the energy used in the construction and maintenance of the infrastructure (including buildings) together with the costs of space heating and ventilation. The energy factors have to be balanced against the economic costs of development, the availability and price of land, and labour costs. The qualitative factors which make up the environment add to this complexity. The research issue here is whether it is worthwhile to unravel these complexities and measure the interactions, or whether it is more sensible to take a modest perspective and examine policy questions individually.

The second example is that of health and stress as it relates to transport. In recent surveys carried out at the Marylebone Centre Trust (Tennyson, 1991) it seems that transport is now a major cause of stress both for users of the system and for those who live near to major transport routes. Transport raises people's anger and aggression at one time through such factors as the delays in traffic and actions of other drivers, whilst at another time transport creates fear and worry through the difficulties of crossing roads or travelling in very crowded conditions. The qualitative factors of the travelling environment seem to have deteriorated, yet little research has been carried out on the effects of this on people's health, their absenteeism from work, their performance at work and their job satisfaction. In addition to the stress factors, public transport and certain spaces (tunnels and some roads) are perceived to be unsafe and questions of security can help explain why some people are reluctant to travel after dark on their own (Atkins, 1990).

These two examples illustrate the range and complexity of issues as they relate to the environment. The list of options given in the White Paper (1990) and by Transnet (1990) is comprehensive, but a narrow perspective is taken, and the broader environmental objectives are subsumed by the desire to reduce energy consumption or to ease congestion. Part of any research initiative on transport and the environment must decide where the boundaries should be set. Similarly, if the purpose of the research is to have some useful input into the decision-making processes, then both the analysis and the output should be transparent.

There are three basic options for government action:

- *Command and control* where maximum levels are set for levels of pollution. However, these levels may result in these maximum levels becoming minimum levels as the polluter will seek to produce to this level.
- *Taxes or levy* where pricing is used to affect demand. When a price differential was introduced on lead free petrol in the UK making it 12 pence per gallon cheaper than leaded petrol, the market share rose from about 2 per cent to 30 per cent in a year (1989–1990). The level in 1991 was 40 per cent of the market.
- *Pollution permits* where the holder is allowed to produce a certain amount of pollution. The total amount of pollution is thus controllable, and companies can trade their permits which in turn would favour the cleaner companies.[2]

There are different arguments for and against each of these options depending on whether the pricing mechanism is seen as most appropriate or whether enforceable standards should be introduced. Charges enable the polluter to choose whether to pay the charge or to lower the levels of pollution. Some pressure groups are against even the recognition that a price can or should be placed on environmental pollution and degradation, or whether any level of pollution is acceptable. For example, the deep greens (for example, Greenpeace) believe in maintaining global stability by deemphasizing economic growth and concentrating on earth survival (Andersen Consulting, 1990).

Conclusions

Over the last twenty years there has been a considerable widening of perceptions on the environment and how it relates to transport. Four stages can be identified.

1. Early concerns over the links between land use and transport with efforts being made to minimize local environmental impacts on residents.
2. The modal split issue then became important with efforts being made to get people to switch to less environmentally intrusive public transport through priority schemes and subsidy.
3. Attempts to restrict the access of cars to environmentally sensitive areas and to use traffic calming where car access was still necessary.

Programmes of ring road construction were initiated to take traffic away from many city centres.

4. The globalization and the internationalization of the problem with concerns over pollution levels and the use of non-renewable resources becoming more important than local environmental measures.

Many of the local measures have encouraged longer journeys and the movement of activities out of the city centres, thus exacerbating the wider environmental impacts. By focusing on the manifestation of the problem, one is ignoring the causes which are essentially political and economic. There also seems to be a consensus in society as a whole that the environment is an important issue and that action is required at different levels. The role that environmental pressure groups played in the 1970s was crucial in that it put the issue on the agenda and questioned the underlying rationale of providing roads to meet the demand of car owners for increased mobility. To the green lobby have been added green consumers, green investors, green politics together with an unprecedented level of scientific research into environmental change (for example, Pearce *et al* 1989; DoE, 1991; Department of Energy, 1990). Initiatives have been taken at the global, international, national and local levels. Rather than developing detailed transport related research activities, this review will end by focusing on four of the broader, more general research problems.

1.   THE PRINCIPLES

The main focus of the recent Environmental Protection Act (1990) was to require the polluter to have the responsibility to ensure that the waste produced can be disposed of without causing harm to the environment. This 'duty of care' is tied in with the 'polluter pays principle' which means that the costs of pollution prevention and clean up fall on the originator of the pollution. The third facet is that the polluter has this responsibility for the lifetime of the product, the 'cradle to grave responsibility'. The precautionary principle shifts the burden of proof to the polluter giving him the obligation to demonstrate that his activities are not harmful to the environment. The question here is how can these principles be interpreted with respect to transport.

The notions of sustainable development and sustainability have been much debated, but these concepts are often at odds with each other as development is often interpreted as increased production and consumption, but sustainability must also be ecologically and socially benign. Many researchers (for example, Pearce *et al.*, 1989; Goodwin, in this volume) argue that a sustainable environment can be valued and that economic and environmental objectives are compatible. Indeed, a transport policy can be developed which combines the best aspects of economic growth, whilst at the same time ensuring widespread environmental benefits – the *Green Gold Alliance*. The Bründtland Commission Report (1987) firmly established the concept of sustainable development as the basis for an integrative approach to economic policy and transport should be an integral part of that strategy.

2. ENVIRONMENTAL AUDITS

Audits range from studies of the complete operation of business to detailed investigations of sites or the competitive market. In each case the aim is to provide information on the current environmental position (table 5). The environmental audit has been long established in the US, where a fairly narrow definition is used to ensure that there is compliance with environmental legislation and checking that sites which are bought or sold have no unexpected liabilities (Andersen Consulting, 1990). Their importance is likely to increase with the growth in environmental legislation, with the growth of multinational companies and with the growing concern that companies have over their public image. Environmental audits in Europe are likely to be broader based to cover company policies, plants, manufacturing, processes, products and distribution processes (Elkington, 1990). Vehicle manufacturers will be subject to these audits,

TABLE 5. A management tool to assess the performance of all or any part of the business from an environmental stand point.

Full Environmental Audit	Complete detailed environmental audit of the complete business
Compliance Audit	Ensuring that the current operations comply with current and potential immediate changes in environmental legislation
Site Audit	Detailed environmental audit of a particular manufacturing site
Corporate Audit	Overview of the business focusing on environmental issues
Product Stewardship Audit	Review of the cradle to grave implications for a particular product
Competitive Audit	Review of the environmental stance of key competitors
Organizational Audits	Review of policies and procedures for handling environmental issues, waste and processes

Source: Andersen Consulting (1990).

but there is no reason why they cannot be extended to public transport operators and freight distribution companies. Local authorities may be the appropriate level at which such command and control activities can take place.

In addition to the transport industries being subject to an environmental audit, individual schemes can be examined in the same way as part of the environmental assessment. Bypass schemes often alleviate traffic congestion in the centre of towns, but this narrow view omits at least two important effects. The first is the opportunity for the town centre to be made more attractive environmentally through traffic calming and pedestrianization. The UK government has initiated a bypass demonstration scheme covering six towns in England in which bypass construction can be combined with local traffic management measures. The second effect is the growth in speculative development along the line of the new road (for example, the M40) where intense pressure for development pushes up land prices. Both these factors need to be included as part of the environmental assessment and the environmental audit processes.

3. PARTNERSHIP

Environmental issues impact on all people, at all levels of government and there is considerable advantage for companies to make their products 'environmentally friendly'. Action should involve cooperation between all three parties – people, government and industry. There has often in the past been a tendency to view industry and commerce as the main enemy of the environment while local government has been placed in the role of controller. A survey of 100 European chief executives by Business International Ltd, showed that 92 per cent felt environmental issues were either central or important to their company and that 48 per cent of companies had published an environmental policy. Many firms employ people whose main responsibility is to look at the environmental side of the company's business, for example the Automobile Association, the Royal Automobile Club and British Airways. Although there is an element of self-interest, there is also a genuine desire to be more environmentally informed in internal policy formulation. What is lacking is a clear framework within which to operate. Each of the three parties (people, government and industry) is operating separately and there are different levels of involvement in different industries. One problem is the lack of guidance from central and local government, and there is often an absence of relevant information (Button, 1991).

4. INTERNATIONALIZATION OF THE ENVIRONMENT

One of the main reasons why concern over the environment is likely to remain as a key policy issue is its new global dimension. Reducing levels of carbon dioxide, nitrogen oxides and sulphur dioxide emissions will limit the increases in global warming and acid rain. Pollution of the atmosphere, of the sea and rivers and of the soil does not end at national boundaries. Consequently, many of the initiatives have come from international conferences and agencies.

The Single European Act (1986) has confirmed the legal status of the European Community's environmental policy and has set out the following objectives:

- wider use of taxes and charges to ensure the reduction of pollution;
- implementation of the polluter pays principle;
- improved information at the local level so that local authorities can assess more effectively the environmental risks;
- compulsory environmental assessment of projects;
- environmental labelling of goods and produce.

To achieve these objectives a European Environmental Agency[3] was set up in May 1990 to gather information on the state of the environment within the EC. More generally the EEA will encourage harmonization of environmental measurement methods, to stimulate the development and application of environmental forecasting techniques, including the assessment of the costs of environmental damage and preventive, protective and restorative policies, and to stimulate the exchange of information on the best technologies available.

Within the transport sector the Chicago Convention made recommendations on aircraft noise, there are OECD guidelines on vehicle noise and the EC Directive on Environmental Impact Assessment is now in operation. To allow fair competition and free trade it is necessary to have a common set of ground rules. Failure to cover the full environmental costs of transport should be seen as equivalent to a subsidy on the costs of production of a commodity. However, on a global scale, there are problems of fairness as ability to meet stringent environmental standards relates to each country's stage in economic development. Such standards must be acceptable to all countries or they will not be adhered to. There is a conflict between development objectives and those relating to transport and the environment on a global scale, but this does not reduce the responsibilities of the developed countries to take the lead. Within each developed country, transport must play an important role in achieving those objectives as it is both a major consumer of resources and a major polluter of the environment.

NOTES

1 EIA refers to the evaluation of the environmental improvement or detriment likely to arise from a major project significantly affecting the environment. Consultation and participation are integral to this evaluation, the results of which must be available in the form of an environmental impact statement (EIS), before a decision is given on whether or not a project should proceed (Wood and Jones, 1991).
2 From 1998 in California any company wanting to sell more than 35,000 cars must make sure that 2 per cent of them are 'zero-emission vehicles', and this figure will rise to 10 per cent by 2003. Companies not developing their own zero-emission car can sell another company's car at a subsidized price and cover those losses through raising the price on petrol cars. Similarly, if a company sells more than the magic 2 per cent, credit can be claimed and those credits can then be sold on the open market to other companies to fulfill their quotas.
3 It should be noted that the EEA has not yet been set up (Summer 1992) as the location of the new agency is still in dispute.

REFERENCES

Airports Policy Consortium (1991) Europe One: Meeting London's Long Term Airport Needs. A discussion paper prepared by Terence Bendixson for the APC, London.

Andersen Consulting (1990) The Impact of Environmental Issues on Business – A Guide for Senior Management. London: Andersen Consulting.

Atkins, S. (1990) Personal security as a transport issue: a state of the art review. *Transport Reviews* Vol. 10, No. 2, pp. 111–124.

Barde, J.-P. and Button K. (1990) (eds.) *Transport Policy and Environment: Six Case Studies*. London: Earthscan.

Button, K. (1990) Environmental Keys to the 21st Century: Interurban and Regional Transport. Paper presented to the UKCEED Seminar at Gatwick Airport, February.

Button, K. (1991) Sustainable Development at the Local Level. Paper presented to the members seminar on Sustainable Development at the Local Level, East Sussex County Council, Lewes.

Commission on the Third London Airport (1971) *Report*. London: HMSO.

Coopers and Lybrand, Deloitte (1990) The Environmental White Paper: This Common Inheritance, Briefing Digest. London: Cooper and Lybrand, Deloitte.

Department of Energy (1990) *Energy Use and Energy Efficiency in UK Transport up to the Year 2010*, Energy Efficiency Office, Energy Efficiency Series 10. London: HMSO.

Department of the Environment (1972) *New Roads in Towns*. London: HMSO.

Department of the Environment (1973) *Urban Transport Planning: Government Observations on the Second Report of the Expenditure Committee* Cmnd 5366. London: HMSO.

Department of the Environment (1990) *This Common Inheritance: Britain's Environmental Strategy*, Cmnd 1200. London: HMSO.

Department of the Environment (1991) *The Potential Effects of Climate Change*

in the UK. First Report of the UK Climate Change Impacts Review Group.
London: HMSO.

Department of Trade (1974) *Maplin: Review of Airport Project.* London: HMSO.

Department of Transport (1976) *Report on the Location of Major Inter-Urban Road Schemes with Regard to Noise and Other Environmental Issues* (Chairman J. Jefferson). London: HMSO.

Department of Transport (1977) *Report of the Advisory Committee on Trunk Road Assessment* (Chairman Sir George Leitch). London: HMSO.

Department of Transport (1978) *Report on the Review of Highway Inquiry Procedures,* Cmnd 7133. London: HMSO.

Department of Transport (1980) *Report of the Inquiry into Lorries, People and Environment.* London: HMSO.

Department of Transport (1983) *Manual of Environmental Appraisal.* London: HMSO.

Department of Transport (1986) *Urban Road Appraisal: Report of the Standing Committee on Trunk Road Appraisal* (Chairman Professor Tom Williams). London: HMSO.

Department of Transport (1989a) *Roads for Prosperity,* Cmnd 693. London: HMSO.

Department of Transport (1989b) *National Road Traffic Forecasts (Great Britain).* London: HMSO.

Department of Transport (1990) *Transport Statistics Great Britain 1979–1989.* London: HMSO.

Department of Transport (1992) *Assessing the Environmental Impact of Road Schemes: Report of the Standing Committee on Trunk Road Appraisal* (Chairman Derek Wood QC). London: HMSO.

EC Council Directive (1985) On the assessment of the effects of certain public and private projects on the environment. *Official Journal of the European Communities,* L175, pp. 40–48.

Elkington, J. (1990) The Environmental Audit – A Green Filter for Company Policies, Plants, Processes and Products. Paper for the World Wildlife Fund.

House of Commons Committee of Public Accounts (1989) *Fifteenth Report: Road Planning,* House of Commons Papers Session 1988/89, HC101. London: HMSO.

House of Commons Expenditure Committee (1973) *Urban Transport Planning,* Vols I-III. London: HMSO.

House of Lords European Communities Committee (1989) *Transport Infrastructure,* Session 1989–90 House of Lords Paper 88. London: HMSO.

The Labour Party (1990) *An Earthly Chance: Labour's Programme for a Cleaner, Greener Britain, a Safer, Sustainable Planet.* London.

Liberal Democrats (1990) *What Price Our Planet?* London.

Ministry of Transport (1963) *Traffic in Towns: A Study of the Long Term Problems of Traffic in Urban Areas.* London: HMSO.

Ministry of Transport (1964) *Road Pricing: The Economic and Technical Possibilities.* London: HMSO.

Ministry of Transport (1969) *Roads for the Future: A New Inter-Urban Plan.* London: HMSO.

Ministry of Transport (1970) *Roads for the Future: The New Inter-Urban Plan for England,* Cmnd 4369. London: HMSO.

Owens, S. (1991) Energy-Conscious Planning: The Case for Action. A Report Commissioned by the Council for the Protection of Rural England.

Pearce, D. W., Markandya, A. and Barbier, E. B. (1989) *Blueprint for a Green Economy*. London: Earthscan.

Rickaby, P. (1987) Six settlement patterns compared. *Environment and Planning B*, Vol. 14, No. 3, pp. 193–223.

Starkie, D. (1982) *The Motorway Age: Road and Traffic Policies in Post-War Britain*. London: Pergamon Press.

Tennyson, R. (1991) Interactions between Changing Urban Patterns and Health. Paper presented at the Solar Energy Conference on Architecture in Climate Change, RIBA, February.

Thomson, J. M. (1969) *Motorways in London*. London: Duckworth.

Town and Country Planning (1988) Statutory Instrument Number 1199: Assessment of Environmental Effects.

Transnet (1990) *Energy, Transport and the Environment*. London: Transnet.

Wood, C. and Jones, C. (1991) *Monitoring Environmental Assessment and Planning*, Report by the EIA Centre, Department of Planning and Landscape, University of Manchester for the Department of the Environment, London: HMSO.

World Commission on Environment and Development (1987) *Our Common Future* (The Bründtland Commission Report). Oxford: Oxford University Press.

4

Policy Responses in the USA

ELIZABETH DEAKIN

The United States has long placed great stock in fast, safe, efficient transportation systems and, with some exceptions, it has succeeded in having them. The importance of transportation to Americans is reflected in its economic statistics: transportation accounts for some 18 per cent of US GNP, is a major part of both business investments and consumer expenditures (approximately 13 per cent in each case), and employs one person in ten. Transportation's roles go far beyond its economic impacts, however. Transportation has been a major shaper of growth, a catalyst in social change and social opportunity, a symbol of opportunity.

By most indicators the American transportation system would be considered reliable, flexible, and responsive to consumer wants and needs. However, the US transportation systems also continue to be a source of a number of urban and national problems. Over 40 thousand people are killed each year on highways and streets, and many more are injured. The transport of hazardous materials creates public safety and security problems. Transportation remains heavily dependent upon petroleum; despite significant increases in vehicle efficiencies, some two-thirds of the nation's annual petroleum usage is by transport vehicles. Auto- and truck-related air pollutants continue to exceed national ambient air quality standards in at least 100 urban areas. Water pollution from transportation occurs from routine shipping and port activities, run-off from airports and highways, and occasional but highly visible spills. High-growth areas suffer increasingly from severe traffic congestion at a time when capital for infrastructure is sharply limited. Negative effects attributed to transportation extend to noise, fumes and soot, vibration, community severance, glaring lights, abandoned cars, blocked views, visual intrusion, construction and manufacturing impacts, waste disposal problems, depletion of scarce resources, acceleration of urban sprawl, and loss of farmlands and other open space.

Transportation's effects on the natural, social, and economic environment are, of course, positive as well as negative. The mobility and access provided by transportation systems are widely recognized as beneficial, as are the contributions to the built environment of well-designed facilities. But environmental problems are increasingly visible to many, and today both citizens and public officials are searching for ways to make transportation less environmentally damaging and more supportive of environmental preservation and enhancement.

In addition to the concern over transportation's immediate environmental impacts, there is growing interest in transport's role in shaping growth patterns and supporting lifestyle choices and business decisions. These patterns and choices in turn impact the environment by triggering additional transportation needs in the urban and metropolitan system and indeed in the economy as a whole. Increasingly, transportation planners and analysts are being challenged to examine these impacts and, indeed, to intervene in them.

Faced with this complex set of issues, there are sharp divisions of opinion on how to proceed. Transportation officials have tended to deal with environmental problems as largely unavoidable consequences of otherwise socially beneficial activity, and to pursue mitigation and amelioration strategies. Environmental programmes, on the other hand, have increasingly demanded affirmative action to avoid environmental harm and to correct existing deficiencies, as illustrated by the 'no net loss' policies on wetlands and the transportation control policies in response to air pollution. Conflicts over these programmes have been widespread.

The debate over transportation and the environment reveals a variety of diagnoses of the problem and prescriptions for change. Some advocate reductions in transportation use and restraints on the deployment of additional transportation facilities (especially highways) as the only way to save the environment. Others argue that the best way to alleviate at least some of transportation's environmental problems is through increased spending on transportation vehicles and facilities and their design, operations, and management. Some favour certain modes over others: transit over auto, rail over truck. Yet another group places its hopes on technological substitution and technological innovation: smart cars and smart highways, magnetic levitation and people-movers. Still others call for a rethinking of the basic approaches to transportation and the environment, to tap market mechanisms and provide signals which will lead to efficient and effective choices.

Because of transportation's critical roles, which of these choices are made, the success with which they are implemented, and their ultimate efficiency and effectiveness will surely have major impacts not only on transportation and on environmental quality, but on the economic performance and the social wellbeing of the nation and its citizens as well.

In this chapter, I review key dimensions of the US approach to transportation and the environment. I first review the scope, framework, and assignments of responsibility for transportation environmental impact, then describe the general approach taken to environmental analysis and environmental policy. I then present the case of transportation and air quality planning under the federal Clean Air Act, which illustrates many of the problems raised by current approaches. I conclude with comments on the implications for policy development and for research.

Regulatory Scope, Framework and Assignments of Responsibility

Regulation of transportation's environmental impacts at both federal and state levels grew rapidly in the 1960s and 1970s, and after somewhat of a hiatus in the 1980s is once again occupying a major position on the policy agenda. Interventions range from broad requirements for environmental impact assessments of all major actions to specific admonitions to avoid taking parklands for highways unless there is no technically feasible alternative. Laws which impose procedural requirements (such as a public hearing) as conditions of funding assistance are common as well.

The impacts of environmental regulation of transportation have been substantial. Federal auto emissions controls, safety requirements, and fuel efficiency standards have affected both vehicle manufacturers and users, and have spawned the development of new industries. Pollution standards, noise limits, and equity provisions (such as those governing transit service for the elderly and disabled, and others calling for local government involvement in state highway programme decisions) have steered the direction of planning efforts and have led to the establishment of new agencies and offices. State laws on these matters, which often parallel those at the federal level and sometimes surpass federal requirements, have had similar impact.

Probably the most controversial laws and regulations are those that include technology-forcing requirements. The Clean Air Act, as well as energy efficiency standards for vehicles and much safety legislation, falls under this classification. The Clean Air Act created a regulatory approach involving both industrial and vehicle emissions controls, plus a complex State Implementation Plan for achieving ambient air quality standards; the Energy Policy and Conservation Act spelled out sales-weighted fuel efficiency standards to be met by all manufacturers. Similar laws have been adopted in many states.

Government-required changes in the automobiles produced have particularly affected the auto industry. Safety, energy conservation and environmental regulations have significantly added to the costs of producing a vehicle. The Motor Vehicle Manufacturers Association reports that cumulative costs of safety and emissions requirements had reached some $1,700 per average new vehicle by 1983. The technologies needed to comply with these requirements have absorbed considerable resources, especially because of the short time frames in which compliance was due. At the same time, they have produced improvements in the product, at least some of which accrue to the manufacturers as well as the general public (for example, safety requirements presumably have reduced certain liability risks).

Most observers agree that these laws and regulations have produced results – for example vehicle emissions have been reduced some 80–90 per cent from precontrol levels, and automobile fuel economy has more than doubled. The issues are whether the benefits are worth the costs, and whether a different style of control might be preferable. Most interventions are of the command and control variety, whereas it is argued, principally by economists, that the use of pricing mechanisms would be more efficient and effective.

Command and control regulatory approaches are particularly complex in combination with the decentralized planning and decision-making characteristic of the US. Perhaps the most salient feature of policy on transportation and the environment in the US is the tendency toward multiple assignments of responsibility for a particular matter. At the federal level, the US Department of Transportation and its administrative units (such as the Federal Highway Administration, the Federal Aviation Administration, and the Urban Mass Transportation Administration) have major responsibility for development and implementation of policy on transportation and the environment. But other federal agencies also have major regulatory responsibilities which have important effects on transportation. The Environmental Protection Agency's responsibilities for air pollution control and the US Army Corps of Engineers' responsibilities for wetlands are prime examples.

State-level responsibilities for environmental factors in transportation also tend to be located both in transportation administrative agencies and in counterpart environmental regulatory units. Moreover regional transportation agencies and city and county engineering and planning agencies often play major roles in transportation decision-making and regulation, as do special purpose operating agencies such as for transit and airports. The sharing of responsibilities has at very least clouded the picture on policy implementation.

General Approach: The Environmental Impact Statement Process

While specific regulatory aspects vary with the environmental problem, the general planning and analysis approach used in the US is rooted in the identification, analysis, and documentation of environmental impact. The approach is exemplified by the environmental impact statement (EIS) process; there are numerous federal and state legislative provisions which require specific actions if particular aspects of the environment are affected (ranging from parklands preservation to historic preservation requirements), but the EIS process remains the basic approach framing environmental assessment.

EISs are required by the National Environmental Policy Act of 1969 (NEPA) for every major federal action significantly affecting the quality of the human environment. While NEPA applies only to projects in which the federal government is involved, many states have their own environmental quality laws that call for similar impact reporting on state and local projects. Some of these state laws are broader in scope and more detailed than NEPA. For example, the California Environmental Quality Act applies not only to state and local government actions but also to those private projects which require contracts, loans, grants, leases, permits, or licenses from a public agency, and it mandates mitigation of significant negative impacts under most circumstances.

NEPA itself neither mandates nor prevents specific outcomes. Rather, it establishes policy favouring respect for and enhancement of the environment, and prescribes planning and analyses intended to assure that environmental quality is carefully weighed in programme and project decisions. EISs and related documents are intended both to document the findings of those planning and analysis efforts, and to serve as the basis for responsible, fully-informed decision-making.

How well have these intentions been met? For transportation programmes and projects, the evidence is mixed. Most areas can document cases where environmental studies have provided important information that has helped shape better projects, or where unintended harm has been avoided. In many other cases, however, environmental impact statements have come to be regarded as tedious paperwork exercises, consuming valuable resources and adding to the amount of time required to deliver projects without producing anything of substantive value. Indeed, transportation staff, community and environmental groups, and elected officials often agree that transportation EISs and their state and local parallels are reactive, fragmented, partial, unrealistic, and perfunctory. There is growing concern that the environmental impact statement is a costly, time-consuming, but ineffectual document destined to collect dust, or serve as a focus for litigation, rather than to influence programme and project development.

Examination of these criticisms reveals the problems. Environmental documents are reactive largely because they are typically done late in the development of a programme or project, in many cases not commencing until a preferred alternative is fully fleshed out. Other alternatives may not have been considered, or may have been given only limited attention. In some instances so many resources have been committed to the development of the preferred alternative that it is hard, financially, politically, and for staff, emotionally, to give serious thought to major revisions or new options, even when environmental studies reveal serious problems, or previously overlooked opportunities. Thus the environmental assessment may merely react to the proposal at hand; significant changes in direction are seen as too costly, and even mitigation measures are constrained.

Second, environmental impact assessments have tended to be fragmented. For transportation, this problem stems in large part from the current emphasis on individual projects rather than systems or programmes, and has been exacerbated by funding shortages which have sometimes necessitated the splitting up of projects into small, fundable pieces – successive widenings of a few miles of a highway at a time, for example. The focus on 'pieces' of projects makes it difficult to assess the overall effects of a series of improvements, and limits the consideration of significantly different approaches. Improvements along a parallel arterial might deliver equivalent benefits to a series of freeway ramp improvements, at less cost; but when the ramp improvements proceed one at a time over a period of years, the arterial improvement option may not be apparent.

Another criticism of environmental assessments is that they tend to be focused on the immediate and direct impacts, sometimes providing only a partial view of the overall significance of the project under study. Cumulative impacts, positive and negative, are hard to discern or are so contingent on uncertain future projects that they are set aside as mere speculation. Areawide effects similarly receive little attention, since the effects of small projects taken individually do not show up well from an areawide perspective. Concern about the cost of the assessment relative to the size of the project further limits the investigation of alternatives and impacts.

A lack of realism in the impact assessments also may result. Low-cost but simplistic analysis methods are often used; analysis may be based on whatever data are available. Mitigation opportunities, limited by cost considerations and short-term focus, may be overlooked altogether or, especially when the project is controversial, may be presented in glowing terms unsupported by previous experience or analysis of the case at hand.

Issues of incidence – who will benefit from the project, and who might lose – are dismissed or downplayed.

Finally, environmental assessment may be carried out in a perfunctory manner. Increasingly, assessment documents are stored on the computers of the lead agencies or their consultants and, with a quick editing and a few pages of additional text, a completed draft is produced. Pages and pages of an EIS may be devoted to the discussion of impacts that are not at issue for the project at hand; little more effort may be devoted to the major concerns raised by the project. Fat documents are produced, but they may have little relevance to the project decisions, which may already have been made, in fact. Indeed, it is becoming common for EISs to be produced years after the basic project development was completed. The resulting document may satisfy a narrow interpretation of one particular section of NEPA or related state laws, but more fundamental policy intentions are not well served.

For many projects, review of environmental documents is the first significant opportunity for community groups to comment on the proposed action. Confronted with a document that seems to them to be incomplete or even misleading, and met with resistance to proposals which would require substantial amounts of additional study, these groups are increasingly fighting back. For some environmental documents, the comments on the drafts are lengthier than the documents themselves. Additional analyses may be necessitated; supplementary EISs and revisions are more and more frequent. In California, for example, it is becoming commonplace for several competing analyses to be carried out. In addition to the 'official' analyses by the sponsoring agency, separate analyses of the special concerns of affected local governments, community groups, and development interests are being produced. The official document is viewed as an advocacy piece; consequently, the other groups commission their own studies to defend their interests. Out of this process some compromises may be produced, but usually at significant monetary and time costs. These costs, in turn, eat up funds that might be more productively used to address both transportation needs and environmental concerns. Lawsuits are another negative by-product of the current EIS process. Transportation agency staff report that they feel under siege whenever an EIS for a controversial project is undergoing review; project opponents comb the document for any error or omission, however minor or irrelevant to the issues they are concerned about, which could be used to stop or delay the project. To 'protect' the transportation agency, legal advice commonly is to carry out worst-case analyses, in order to block possible claims of failures to disclose. As a result, the analyses may describe situations that have only a remote chance of actually occurring, and may emphasize negative effects while ignoring beneficial ones. Community groups also find the litigiousness of the EIS process problematic. They say that in many cases, concerns about lawsuits lead to an early hardening of sponsoring agencies' positions, out of fear that admitting to the possible need for further study would be turned against them.

A number of specific reforms to streamline the EIS process, make it more useful, and clarify responsibilities have been suggested. For example:

- Greater use could be made of focused EISs – ones that deal in detail with those impacts anticipated to be significant, and sharply reduce discussion of impacts of minor or uncontroversial import. Screening procedures, carried out with public review, would provide the basis for selecting the impacts to be analysed in detail.

- System-plan, corridor-level, and programme EISs could allow review of the broad implications of a long-term plan or set of related projects, permitting an assessment of cumulative and areawide impacts. Such EISs would usually not eliminate the need for project EISs, but would permit focused EISs to be used at the project level (since impacts sufficiently dealt with in the 'master' document would not need to be discussed again). Changes in the system or corridor-level plans or programmes would require an update to the EIS, but this need not be a major undertaking unless the change in the plan or programme is itself major. An important advantage of such broader, if more general, EISs is that they can help in the identification of overall benefits, rather than just negative impacts.

- Establishment of ground rules on 'acceptable professional practice' in EIS preparation may be appropriate. Analysis methods for impact prediction need further development, but guidance could be provided on what constitutes a reasonable approach given the state of the art. Requirements for timely production of environmental documents, and for major updates if project delays cast doubt on an earlier study's continued validity, also may need review and clarification. Procedures for handling minor updates and revisions perhaps could be streamlined.

Changes such as these could reduce some of the 'game' aspects of the EIS process and redirect it back toward its original policy intentions. Such reforms, however, are unlikely to address the root problems unless they are accompanied by more fundamental changes in attitude and approach. Transportation agencies in the US remain largely antagonistic to environmental concerns, viewing them as constraints rather than an integral part of programme and project development and treating them accordingly. How to change this perspective remains a puzzle, though the institutional redesigns being contemplated as the era of Interstate highway building draws to a close may offer important opportunities to make such changes.

Transportation and Air Pollution

The United States regulates air pollution through the federal Clean Air Act, as well as through state and local laws and regulations. Under the framework first laid out in the Clean Air Act Amendments of 1970 and the subsequent amendments of 1977 and 1990, the Environmental Protection Agency (EPA) is charged with setting national ambient air quality standards for pollutants considered harmful to public health or welfare. The states then are responsible for meeting the standards with EPA assistance.

Harm due to air pollution includes adverse effects on human health, crop damage, damage to paints and other surface coatings, and damage to vegetation. EPA has set standards for six major pollutants, ozone (O_3, carbon monoxide (CO), nitrogen dioxide (NO_2), lead (Pb), suspended particulates (TSP, now measured by particulate matter of less than 10 microns in diameter, PM10), and sulphur dioxide (SO_2). Specific effects vary with the pollutant, its concentration, and whether other pollutants are present, as well as the underlying condition of the person or thing suffering exposure. Dose-response rates are not well understood, and there is some evidence that certain otherwise healthy individuals are particularly sensitive to pollutants.

Estimates of the social costs of air pollution are problematic, given the uncertainties in the scientific evidence, and many of the estimates must rely on heroic extrapolations of limited data. Kanafani in 1983 reported air pollution total social cost estimates ranging from $4 billion to $20 billion a year, with a 'consensus' figure of $9.7 billion (1981 $), or around $14 billion in current dollars. In view of that figure it is interesting to note recent EPA estimates that crop damage alone could be costing the US $2.5–$3 billion, and Los Angeles estimates that damages to health and agriculture in that air basin alone sum to $3.65–$7.3 billion – sharply higher costs than the 'consensus' figure would tolerate. One reason for the substantially higher estimates of pollution costs is the recent scientific evidence which suggests ozone may be more harmful than was earlier thought. Indeed, based on its own studies, California has adopted an ozone standard of 0.08 parts per million, sharply lower than the federal 0.12 ppm standard. If social costs are even roughly proportional to the standards, earlier estimates could have been substantially too low, perhaps by a factor of two. Moreover, none of the cost estimates account for the damages due to acid rain, in which transportation volatile organic compounds (VOC) and NO_x emissions are thought to play a contributing role, nor do the estimates consider possible global warming effects due to emissions of CO_2, which are very roughly proportional to overall emissions.

Of the six pollutants, transportation sources are responsible for much of the total emissions except for SO_2. For example, EPA in 1988 estimated that on a nationwide average, highway vehicles produced some 58 per cent of the carbon monoxide, 34 per cent of the NO_x, and 30 per cent of the ozone precursor hydrocarbons (VOC) emitted in 1986. Data from urban air basins suggest that transportation's role in their air quality problems is even more severe. In Los Angeles, for example, mobile sources are responsible for 96 per cent of the CO, 72 per cent of the NO_x and 52 per cent of the VOC emissions (SCAQMD, 1989.). Within transportation, gasoline powered automobiles and trucks are estimated to produce more than 80 per cent of the VOC emissions. Personal travel accounts for roughly 75 per cent of these emissions and freight about 25 per cent.

Major strategies used to reduce air pollution include controls of emissions from new motor vehicles, emissions controls on stationary sources (factories, power plants, etc.) and various other measures which the states select, including measures which control or restrict operations and use of polluting devices and processes. Significant progress has been made in reducing both emissions and ambient air pollution concentrations. Between 1977 and 1987 EPA estimates that auto emissions dropped some 90 per cent, while ozone levels dropped 21 per cent, CO dropped 32 per cent, NO_x declined 14 per cent, SO_2 37 per cent, and lead fully 87 per cent (due to the phase-out of leaded gasoline.)

Nevertheless, some 100 metropolitan areas still have not met the federal air quality standards. In fact, the number of metropolitan areas exceeding the allowable one-hour ozone level of 0.12 part per million increased from sixty-two to sixty-eight in the late 1980s. Prospects of worsening air quality were a major reason why Congress tightened auto emissions standards in the 1990 Amendments. Congress also substantially revamped the transportation sections of the Act to require transport plan, programme, and project conformity to air quality plans and programmes, as well as detailed monitoring and forecasting of population and employment growth and vehicle-miles travelled (VMT) increases, and achievement of specific interim emissions reduction targets. At the same time, deadlines for attainment were extended and altered to vary with the severity of the problems faced (severely polluted areas get more time.) Nevertheless many areas, especially the larger and faster-growing ones, will need to develop transportation control measures (TCMs) to meet the air standards by the legislated deadlines.

It is not obvious that the reasons for past difficulties in attaining the standards are cleared up by the new legislation. Uncertainties over the costs of pollution and the benefits of control, disagreements about air quality's importance in comparison to personal mobility and convenience, and conflict among agencies with different missions all have been barriers to achievement. Problems also have been exacerbated by faster than anticipated growth and lower than expected fuel prices. A more rigorous planning process may provide a better evidentiary base for planning, but will not necessarily address the other issues.

From a transportation planning and policy perspective, a major consideration is whether the measures proposed for air quality improvement have any real promise. The case of the San Francisco Bay Area illustrates the issues. The Bay Area's pollution problems are considered moderate, but it remains one of some 100 metropolitan areas across the country which have not yet attained federal air quality standards. Like most of these areas, the Bay Area will be required to develop a revised State Implementation Plan showing the measures to be taken to reduce air pollution, in accordance with the Clean Air Act Amendments of 1990. Significant emissions reductions will be produced by tougher emissions controls on new cars, vehicle inspection-maintenance programmes, cleaner fuels, and industrial controls, but growth in per-capita and total trip-making and vehicle-miles of travel (VMT) will partially offset these gains.

The Bay Area has faced two additional requirements for transportation-air quality planning not present in most metro areas. First, litigation stemming from the Bay Area's failure to attain federal standards by the 1977 Clean Air Act Amendments' 1987 deadline forced a search for measures which could bring the area back into compliance with federal requirements for annual emissions reductions. An immediate 6 per cent reduction of hydrocarbons was required for the federal plan. Second, state air quality legislation, the California Clean Air Act of 1988, set forth a series of requirements for TCM development and implementation in non-attainment areas; companion legislation called for the Bay Area to draft its air quality plan a year earlier than other areas in the state, in part to serve as an example and test case. For the state plan, the regional air quality management district set a target reduction in mobile source hydro-carbons, to be accomplished by 1997, of fully 35 per cent – over and above improvements due to vehicle turnover, inspection-maintenance, and cleaner fuels. Because of these mandates the Bay Area has undertaken a comprehensive look at transportation emissions and possible measures to control them, not only including conventional TCMs such as ridesharing and transit improvements but also covering such items as road pricing, parking pricing, and retirement of older, high-emissions vehicles (table 1). The analysis has been greatly aided by the availability of high-quality travel survey data and advanced modelling capabilities developed for the Metropolitan Transportation Commission, the regional transportation

TABLE 1. Transportation air quality strategies.

---

1. Improving traffic flow conditions through road improvements and better utilization of existing capacity

* new roads; added lanes
* intersection widenings; over- or underpasses
* provision of left- and right-turn lanes
* peak period on-street parking bans
* efficient signal timing
* freeway ramp metering and flow metering
* timely accident removal

2. Shifting trips to less congested routes

* route guidance
* route restrictions
* corridor management

3. Shifting trips to less congested times of day/days of week

* flextime programmes
* staggered work hours
* staggered work weeks
* congestion pricing
* peak period restrictions on travel, deliveries

4. Shifting travel to less polluting modes

(a) provision of/improvements to commute alternatives:

* better transit: denser networks, increased frequency, direct service, express service, timed transfers
* specialized services (shuttles, club buses, shared taxis)
* programmes to market, promote, and assist carpooling, vanpooling, bicycling, walking

(b) provision of related facilities:

* HOV lanes, bypasses on freeways and local streets
* HOV signal preemption on on-ramps, major intersections
* improved transit stops, shelters, stations
* park-and-ride lots
* parking facilities for carpools, vanpools
* bike paths and parking
* walking paths and sidewalks

(c) subsidies/other incentives:

* transit passes, employer provided or subsidized vehicles for pooling, mileage payments for bike, walk use
* preferential parking allocation, location, and price for HOVs
* guaranteed rides home; midday transportation; short-term auto rentals

5. *Reducing auto use and removing auto subsidies:*

* promotion of voluntary no-drive days
* vehicle-free zones, transit malls
* area entry licenses
* parking by permit only
* congestion tolls, entry tolls
* parking pricing
* control of parking supply, location, use, rates
* no free employee parking for solo commuters

6. *Eliminating some trips altogether*

* telecommuting
* teleconferencing
* delivery services
* automatic payroll deposits

7. *Technology substitutions*

* new emissions control devices
* clean fuels
* clean engines

8. *Other*

* restrictions on idling
* retirement of older vehicles

---

planning agency for the area. A 1981 household travel survey is currently being used in the analyses; another major survey was conducted in 1990 and is now available for use. Modelling tools include formulations implemented in the Urban Transportation Planning System (UTPS) framework as well as a quick-response package called STEP (Short-Range Transportation Evaluation Package), both of which incorporate state-of-the-art submodels for trip generation, trip distribution, and mode choice. Analyses also drew upon studies applying traffic operations models such as TRANSYT and NETSIM to example corridors.

A first step in the analysis was to review trip-making patterns in the nine-county region, in order to develop a clearer understanding of the sources of air pollution emissions and the potential of various TCMs to reduce them. Since many TCMs are oriented toward work trips, one item that proved to be a surprise to many local officials (though not to transportation staff) is that work trips are only about 33 per cent of the VMT and less than 25 per cent of the trips made by vehicle in the region on the typical workday. Of these trips, on a regional average, some 12 per cent are made by transit and about 16 per cent are shared rides. Thus measures which attempted to lure drive-alone commuters to other travel modes would be aimed at only 18 per cent of the region's trips and about 24 per cent of the VMT. In addition, over 25 per cent of work trips are made outside of peak periods (6 am–10 am and 3 pm–7pm), so that measures which are available (or practical) only during conventional commute periods would target an even smaller share of travel.

Success in converting work trips to alternate modes might have somewhat larger overall effects than the work trip numbers imply, since an additional 17 per cent of the VMT are work-related, for example mid-day business trips. The commuter who leaves the car at home may make these trips by an alternative mode as well. On the other hand, the need to make such trips by car appears to be a reason for auto use on the primary commute in some cases.

Mode shares for work trips vary substantially over the region – from 60 per cent by transit in downtown San Francisco and 35 per cent in downtown Oakland, to only 1 or 2 per cent in outlying suburban areas. Analyses indicated that some increases in transit ridership would be possible even in the core areas, if fare incentives and service improvements could be provided. However, the places with the biggest 'target' of drive-alone commuters are also, for the most part, places where transit service ranges from poor to non-existent. In these areas ridesharing will be the only practical commute alternative for some years to come.

Model results indicated that the measures most often proposed for commuters, including transit system expansion, improved routes and schedules, and fare discounts, would produce reduced VMT and emissions just over 3 per cent. Additional ridesharing efforts and incentives would add half a per cent. Institutional measures to increase implementation frequency and effectiveness, including programmes to assist employers wishing to establish commute alternatives and manage parking, and a rigorous trip reduction ordinance, were judged to boost the effectiveness of the transit and ridesharing efforts by another half a per cent. Overall, then, reductions of about 4 per cent in VMT, trips, and emissions were judged feasible using conventional demand-side TCMs. The most effective of these TCMs were ones that improved travel times for alternative modes – transit service improvements and high-occupancy vehicle lanes.

Traffic operations measures also were analysed, extrapolating the results of studies conducted for specific corridors in the Bay Area. The most effective TCM in this category was freeway incident management; that is fast removal of accidents and other lane blockages. While the resulting improvement in highway level of service was estimated to somewhat increase VMT (both through induced trips and mode shifts), the reduction in highly polluting stop-and-go driving more than offset this impact, producing net hydrocarbon and carbon monoxide reductions in the order of 2 per cent. Traffic signal timing on arterials would further reduce these emissions by just over 1 per cent. One advantage of the traffic operations measures, in particular signal timing, is that they affect trips of all sorts, at many times of day.

Social, recreational and personal trip purposes account for nearly as much VMT as do work trips – 31 per cent – while shopping trips add another 13 per cent. The auto is the primary mode of travel for these trips, accounting for 90–95 per cent of the trip total (walking is the second most frequent mode). Auto occupancy tends to be high, in the 1.4–1.6 range, largely because family members make the trips together. Yet most of these trips also are short, and relatively few use freeways or other facilities likely to offer priority treatment to high-occupancy vehicles.

Few conventional demand-side TCMs are likely to affect these non-work trips over the short-run, although for some origin-destination pairs better transit may attract riders. In the longer run some impact was estimated to accrue from measures to develop higher densities around transit stations and encourage mixed-use development, such as shopping and social-recreational facilities and services within walking distance of housing and places of employment. Still, the effect on non-work travel emissions would be likely to be smaller than that resulting from better signal timing and incident management – especially considering that well over half of the trips in the eight-hour 'peaks' are for non-work purposes.

Trips to school and to accompany passengers (most of which also are school trips) account for the most of the remaining VMT, about 6 per cent. The serve passenger-school trips have increased since the mid–1970s largely because budget restrictions and liability concerns led to a loss of school busing services. Here again, few conventional TCMs are likely to affect this component of daily travel and emissions. A programme to encourage reinstatement of school bus services was deemed worth trying on a demonstration basis.

Together, the package of conventional TCMs considered for the Bay Area was estimated to produce reductions in emissions in the order of 7–8 per cent. This is enough, with some margin for error, to meet the immediate court-ordered reduction requirement, but it falls far short of the state mandated reductions. Moreover, available funding fell short of the levels needed to implement the TCM package by over $500 million. Hence the analysis turned to a search for TCMs which would be sufficiently revenue-generating to fund the other elements of the package, as well as to strategies which could explicitly use price to reduce VMT and emissions.

Three measures were considered as ways of raising revenues while reducing emissions. These measures are of particular interest in that, if adopted, they could represent first steps toward a 'polluter pays' strategy for controlling air pollution rather than the current approach which regulates largely independent of cost or efficiency considerations.

The first pricing measure was an increase in tolls on the Bay's many bridges, to $2.00 a crossing (tolls are collected only in one direction). This would produce additional revenues in the order of $94 million per year, while cutting trips and emissions by about half a per cent. The second revenue measure was a gas tax increase of $0.14/gal (3.7 cents/litre), an amount equivalent to an emissions charge of roughly half a cent per mile (0.3 cent/km) the low end of estimated costs to health and property due to air pollution. This gas tax increase was estimated to produce annual revenues of about $420 million while reducing emissions by about 0.7 per cent. Finally, a vehicle registration fee of $4.00 per year was estimated to produce an annual $24 million, but the amount was deemed too small to affect travel behaviour or emissions levels.

All three pricing measures required state legislation, and in the case of the bridge tolls this was, in fact, secured. Whether legislative authorization for the other measures will eventually be forthcoming is uncertain.

A bundle of additional pricing measures was considered as a means of accomplishing the substantial emissions reductions required by state law. Regionwide congestion pricing on all facilities, sufficient to attain a target level of service or better, was estimated to reduce emissions by nearly 7 per cent. (There was neither time nor sufficient data to determine the economically efficient level of emissions reduction.) VMT was estimated to drop by only 1 per cent, largely because travellers could choose alternate routes or alternate times of day; the emissions reduction was largely due to speed increases and other operational improvements. In comparison, a regionwide employee parking charge of $3.00/day was estimated to reduce emissions by just under 1.5 per cent (no additional charge would be imposed in areas already charging at least $3.00/day for parking under this scheme). Expanding the parking charge to all trips (at a rate of 1 cent a minute) would have a much larger effect, reducing emissions by some 5 per cent or more. Finally, a European-style gas tax of $2.00/gallon ($0.53/L) was estimated to reduce emissions and VMT by some 8 per cent, and a mileage- and emissions-based registration fee was estimated to cut emissions by 4.5 per cent (with little effect on VMT, since the most polluting cars soon would be replaced with cleaner ones).

The significant revenues generated by these pricing schemes could support substantial improvements in, and subsidies to, transit and ridesharing, designed to offset impacts on low and moderate income households. (Indeed, enough revenues would be generated that a transportation allowance of some $500.00 per year for households earning less than $25,000 year would be possible.) The transit and ridesharing enchancements in turn would produce further reductions in emissions, by some 3–4 per cent. Overall, the package would produce emissions reductions in the 20–25 per cent range while substantially eliminating severe congestion and providing mobility options via transit.

But the pricing proposals also created substantial controversy. Support came from some business leaders and some environmentalists, particularly those in the inner parts of the region. Strong opposition was voiced by shopping centre developers and operators and outer-suburban interests. At present, the pricing package has been tentatively included in the air quality plan for 'future' implementation, but additional state authorization appears to be need to proceed, and there is considerable doubt that state legislators will be willing to act on this.

Several other measures were evaluated but did not make it into the plan largely because they are not conventional TCMs. For example, an analysis of emissions by vehicle age and ownership suggested that targeted retirement of older vehicles would be an effective emissions reduction strategy. Some 30 per cent of total emissions in the Bay Area are from vehicles that are eight years old or older. While nearly half of the vehicles owned by low-income households fall into this age group, low-income people produce only about 12 per cent of the VMT and 15 per cent of the trips made in older vehicles. Indeed, the majority of older vehicles are owned by households with incomes of $25,000 and up, and these households account for three-quarters of the VMT and trips made in older vehicles. In many cases these are second, third, or even fourth cars.

Retirement of older vehicles that cannot meet modern emissions standards – some can – would be a highly effective strategy for overall air pollution reduction. Low-income owners of such vehicles could be provided with newer, cleaner cars at far less cost than that of many other TCMs, particularly those that require the construction of new transportation facilities. Yet this strategy was never seriously considered for implementation.

The Bay Area's transportation-air quality planning efforts are still underway, and it remains to be seen what is actually implemented. The work to date, while incomplete, offers several insights. The analyses indicate that conventional transportation control measures are likely to produce but modest results, assuming funds could be found to implement them effectively. Pricing measures might produce more substantial results but probably would require new legislative authority and are likely to be controversial. Other potentially effective measures may lack an institutional home and may not even qualify as TCMs. Overall, these findings suggest that effective transportation-air quality planning is likely to be a challenge for the many other metropolitan areas now facing TCM requirements.

Table 2 summarizes the full range of TCM measures available, to be

TABLE 2(a). Summary of state TCM plan emissions reductions: Phase 1 (reasonably available measures).

State Plan Transportation Control Measure	Percentage Change in:								Annual Cost Per Ton ($)
	VMT	Trips	C_xH_y	CO	NO_x	PM10	CO_2	Fuel	
STCM 1 Expand employer assistance programmes	-0.2	-0.14	-0.18	-0.17	-0.18	-0.20	-0.20	-0.20	0
STCM 2 Adopt employer-based trip reduction rule	-3.27	-4.06	-3.57	-3.76	-3.67	-3.27	-3.27	-3.27	$50 000
STCM 3 Improve areawide transit service	-0.48	-0.43	-0.46	-0.44	-0.46	-0.48	-0.48	-0.48	0
STCM 4 Expedite and expand regional rail agreement	-0.07	-0.05	-0.06	-0.06	-0.06	-0.07	-0.07	-0.07	0
STCM 5 Improve access to rail	-0.02	-0.03	-0.02	-0.03	-0.02	-0.02	-0.02	-0.02	0
STCM 6 Improve intercity rail service	-0.05	-0.04	-0.05	-0.04	-0.05	-0.05	-0.05	-0.05	0
STCM 7 Improve ferry service	-0.015	-0.01	-0.015	-0.011	-0.012	-0.015	-0.015	-0.015	0
STCM 8 Construct carpool/express bus lanes on freeways	-0.23	-0.22	-0.23	-0.20	-0.22	-0.23	-0.23	-0.23	0
STCM 9 Improve bicycle access	-0.01	-0.01	-0.01	-0.01	-0.01	-0.01	-0.01	-0.01	0
STCM 10 Youth transportation	0	0	0	0	0	0	0	0	0
STCM 11 Install freeway traffic operations	+0.02	+0.01	-0.42	-0.65	-0.35	+0.02	-0.45	-0.45	0
STCM 12 Improve arterial traffic management	+0.01	+0.01	-0.20	-0.30	-0.25	0	-0.15	-0.15	0
STCM 13 Reduce transit fares	-0.11	-0.11	-0.11	-0.09	-0.11	-0.11	-0.11	-0.11	0
STCM 14 Vanpool liability insurance	0	0	0	0	0	0	0	0	0
STCM 15 Provide carpool incentives	0	0	0	0	0	0	0	0	0
STCM 16 Adopt indirect source control programme	-0.7	-0.7	-0.7	-0.7	-0.7	-0.7	-0.7	-0.7	0
STCM 17 Conduct public education	0	0	0	0	0	0	0	0	0
STCM 18 Zoning plans for higher densities near transit	0	0	0	0	0	0	0	0	0
STCM 19 Air quality element for general plans	0	0	0	0	0	0	0	0	0
STCM 20 Conduct demonstration projects	0	0	0	0	0	0	0	0	0
STCM 21 Implement revenue measures	-0.62	-0.55	-0.60	-0.57	-0.60	-0.62	-0.62	-0.62	0
Total	-5.64	-6.22	-6.48	-6.86	-6.54	-5.64	-5.64	-5.64	

TABLE 2(b). Summary of state TCM plan emissions reductions: Phase 2 (mobility and incentives measures).

State Plan Transportation Control Measure		Percentage Change in:								Annual Cost Per Ton ($)
		VMT	Trips	C_xH_y	CO	NO_x	PM10	CO_2	Fuel	
STCM 1	Expand employer assistance programme									
STCM 2	Adopt employer-based trip reduction rule									
STCM 3	Improve areawide transit service	-1.0	-0.9	-1.0	-0.9	-0.9	-1.0	-1.0	-1.0	
STCM 4	Expedite and expand regional rail agreement	-0.7	-0.8	-0.8	-0.8	-0.7	-0.7	-0.7	-0.7	
STCM 5	Improve access to rail	-0.3	-0.25	-0.3	-0.25	-0.3	-0.3	-0.3	-0.3	
STCM 6	Improve intercity rail service	-0.04	-0.03	-0.04	-0.03	-0.04	-0.04	-0.04	-0.04	
STCM 7	Improve ferry service	-0.03	-0.02	-0.03	-0.02	-0.03	-0.03	-0.03	-0.03	
STCM 8	Construct carpool/express bus lanes on freeways	-0.45	-0.35	-0.41	-0.38	-0.4	-0.45	-0.45	-0.45	
STCM 9	Improve bicycle access	-0.02	-0.03	-0.02	-0.03	-0.02	-0.02	-0.02	-0.02	
STCM 10	Youth transportation	-0.11	-0.17	-0.14	-0.16	-0.14	-0.11	-0.11	-0.11	
STCM 11	Install freeway traffic operations	+0.13	+0.09	-1.4	-1.8	-1.1	+0.13	-1.2	-1.2	
STCM 12	Improve arterial traffic management	-0.01	-0.02	-0.23	-0.33	-0.27	-0.01	-0.17	-0.17	
STCM 13	Reduce transit fares	-0.17	-0.22	-0.21	-0.22	-0.21	-0.17	-0.17	-0.17	
STCM 14	Vanpool liability insurance	-0.02	-0.01	-0.02	-0.01	-0.02	-0.02	-0.02	-0.02	
STCM 15	Provide carpool incentives	-0.3	-0.2	-0.2	-0.2	-0.3	-0.3	-0.3	-0.3	
STCM 16	Adopt indirect source control programme	0	0	0	0	0	0	0	0	
STCM 17	Conduct public education									
STCM 18	Zoning plans for higher densities near transit	-0.05	-0.05	-0.05	-0.05	-0.05	-0.05	-0.05	-0.05	
STCM 19	Air quality element for general plans	0	0	0	0	0	0	0	0	
STCM 20	Conduct demonstration projects	0	0	0	0	0	0	0	0	
STCM 21	Implement revenue measures	-1.3	-1.2	-1.2	-1.2	-1.3	-1.3	-1.3	-1.3	
	Total	-4.29	-4.09	-5.90	-6.21	-5.64	-4.29	-5.72	-5.72	

TABLE 2(c). Summary of state TCM plan emissions reductions: Phase 3 (market-based measures).

State Plan Transportation Control Measure	Percentage Change in:								Annual Cost Per Ton ($)
	VMT	Trips	C_xH_y	CO	NO_x	PM10	CO_2	Fuel	
STCM 1 Expand employer assistance programmes									
STCM 2 Adopt employer-based trip reduction rule									
STCM 3 Improve areawide transit service	NA	NA	NA	NA	NA	NA	NA	NA	
STCM 4 Expedite and expand regional rail agreement									
STCM 5 Improve access to rail	NA	NA	NA	NA	NA	NA	NA	NA	
STCM 6 Improve intercity rail service	NA	NA	NA	NA	NA	NA	NA	NA	
STCM 7 Improve ferry service									
STCM 8 Construct carpool/express bus lanes on freeways									
STCM 9 Improve bicycle access									
STCM 10 Youth transportation	NA	NA	NA	NA	NA	NA	NA	NA	
STCM 11 Install freeway traffic operations	NA	NA	NA	NA	NA	NA	NA	NA	
STCM 12 Improve arterial traffic management									
STCM 13 Reduce transit fares									
STCM 14 Vanpool liability insurance									
STCM 15 Provide carpool incentives									
STCM 16 Adopt indirect source control programme									
STCM 17 Conduct public education	0	0	0	0	0	0	0	0	
STCM 18 Zoning plans for higher densities near transit			0	0	0	0	0		
STCM 19 Air quality element for general plans									
STCM 20 Conduct demonstration projects									
STCM 21 Implement revenue measures									
STCM 22 Implement market-based measures	−13.72	−14.6	−20.62	−22.54	−15.53	−13.72	−18.93	−18.93	
Total	−13.72	−14.6	−20.62	−22.54	−15.53	−13.72	−18.93	−18.93	

TABLE 2(c). Summary of state TCM plan emissions reductions: All phases.

Description	Percentage Change in:								Annual Cost Per Ton ($)
	VMT	Trips	C_xH_y	CO	NO_x	PM10	CO_2	Fuel	
Phase 1: Reasonably Available Measures (target year 1994)	−5.6	−6.2	−6.5	−6.9	−6.5	−5.6	−5.6	−5.6	
Phase 2: Mobility Improvements and Incentives (target year 1997)	−4.3	−4.1	−5.9	−6.2	−5.6	−4.3	−5.7	−5.7	
Phase 3: Market-Based Measures (target year 2000)	−13.7	−14.6	−20.6	−22.5	−15.5	−13.7	−18.9	−18.9	
Total change	−22.1	−23.2	−30.1	−32.3	−25.5	−22.1	−27.9	−27.9	

phased in over the next decade, together with their expected impact on the range of travel and environmental factors considered.

The Bay Area case also illustrates the difficulties in implementing either command and control regulations or market-oriented approaches in cases where the regulated activity is one in which nearly all citizens regularly are engaged.

Concluding Remarks

Unwanted environmental impacts of the US transportation system are addressed through a variety of federal, state, and local programmes. Key programmes, in particular the EIS process set forth by the National Environmental Policy Act and comparable state laws, place a heavy emphasis on production of information on environmental impacts. However, the evidence on the utility and effect of this information is mixed at best. As illustrated by the critique of EIS process and substance, current approaches tend to treat environmental considerations as constraints on projects rather than as initial design criteria, and may lead to little or no substantive response to noted problems. Changing the approach from one of mitigation to one of integrated transportation and environmental planning is a major challenge.

In programmes where specific interventions are mandated, command and control regulatory approaches are widely used. This has produced major benefits in a number of cases, but the costs may also be high. The case of transportation air quality planning illustrates the difficulties such approaches may entail. Considerable effort is expended on analysis, but implementation depends less on the analysis results than on the presence or absence of legal, institutional and political support. How such support can be mustered is an open question.

Current debates over US policies affecting transportation and the environment provide mixed signals regarding future directions. The US has been reluctant to commit itself to an aggressive greenhouse gas reduction programme; indeed, while continuing to caution about the uncertainties in the data and forecasts, recent assessments argue that the problem (at least for the US) will not be as bad. as some have implied it might be. On the other hand, the country has adopted a very aggressive 'no net loss' policy concerning wetlands, apparently overriding concerns about efficiency. (Note, however, that the policy is in flux.)

Whether 'polluter pays' pricing strategies will eventually take hold remains an open question. In the Bay Area, current debates reveal considerable opposition to the concept on equity and other grounds, but at the same time important support for the concept has developed. Attention to the distributional consequences of pricing strategies, and development of strategies to compensate low- and moderate-income people harmed by price increases, seems imperative if further progress is to be made.

REFERENCES

Deakin, E. A. (1990) The United States [case], in Barde, J. P. and Button, K. (eds.) *Transport Policy and the Environment*. London: Earthscan Press.

Deakin, E. A. and Garrison, W. L. (1986) *The Status of the American Transportation Industries*, prepared for the U. S. Congress Office on Technology Assessment.

Harvey, Greig, and Deakin, E. A. (1990) *Mobility and Emissions in the San Francisco Bay Area*. prepared for the Metropolitan Transportation Commission.

Horowitz, J. (1982) *Air Quality Analysis for Urban Transportation Planning*. Cambridge, Mass: MIT Press.

Kanafani, A. 1983, *The Social Costs of Road Transport*. Paris: OECD.

Metropolitan Transportation Commission (1990*a*) *Final Transportation Control Plan*. Oakland, CA: MTC.

Metropolitan Transportation Commission (1990*b*) *Bay Area Travel Forecasts: Year 1987 Trips by Mode, Vehicle Miles of Travel, and Vehicle Emissions*. Oakland, CA: MTC.

Motor Vehicle Manufacturers Association (MVMA) (Various years) *Facts and Figures*.

South Coast Air Quality Management District (SCAQMD) and Southern California Association of Governments (1989) Draft 1988 Air Quality Management Plan. California.

Transportation Planning Associates (TPA) (1980–1988) *Transportation in America*.

US Environmental Protection Agency (1982) *Compendium of Noise Documents*. Washington, DC: EPA.

US Environmental Protection Agency (1988) *Trends in the Quality of the Nation's Air*, OPA 87019. Washington, DC: EPA.

5

Policy Responses in the Netherlands

PIET RIETVELD

Transport is an important and rapidly growing activity in modern society. It is an essential element of many production processes where movement of goods or labour is required (freight transport, business travel, commuting). But it also plays an important role in consumptive activities of households in the form of shopping, social visits, etc. Moreover, transport itself is an important industry in many countries. In the Netherlands for example, it contributes 8 per cent to the GDP. Road transport is considered as one of the main export sectors of the Dutch economy: the share of Dutch companies in international freight transport by road in the EC is near to 25 per cent.

There are several reasons why a further growth of mobility may be expected during the next decades. First, the general trends in transport and logistics are in the direction of a reduction of average stock size, which makes production and distribution processes more transport intensive. Another reason is that income levels are expected to continue to grow. This will exert an upward pressure on car ownership and car use. The growing number of one person households will lead to an increase in the number of cars per capita, and also the number of households with more than one car is expected to grow rapidly. A further influence is the process of internationalization of the economy, especially in the EC, which will lead to an increase of average transport distances.

Transport is an important source of external effects such as air pollution, noise, casualties and congestion. Table 1 gives some data on the contribution of road transport to total air pollution in the Netherlands. For certain categories such as NO_x, C_xH_y and CO the contribution of road traffic is about 50 per cent; for specific pollutants such as lead, transport is the major source.

As shown in table 2, air pollution caused by road traffic has decreased substantially for certain categories such as lead and CO. For categories such as C_xH_y, NO_x and SO_2 the level of total pollution caused by road

TABLE 1. Contribution of road traffic to air pollution in the Netherlands, 1988 (in %).

	Passenger Cars	Total Road Transport	Other Sources
CO	41	51	49
C_xH_y	29	43	57
SO_2	2	6	94
CO_2	11	17	83
NO_x	30	54	46
Pb	82	87	13
Particulates	8	22	78
Smog	28	50	50
Acid rain	11	20	80

Source: Vleugel and Van Gent (1991).

TABLE 2. Emissions of road traffic (in kg $\times 10^6$).

		1979	1984	1988	Index 1988 (1979=100)
CO:	total	1 123	818	723	64
	passenger cars	942	674	581	62
C_xH_y:	total	236	202	198	84
	passenger cars	175	145	135	77
NO_x	total	265	278	299	113
	passenger cars	159	164	165	104
Particulates:	total	24.9	28.3	38.0	153
	passenger cars	5.6	8.5	12.2	218
SO_2:	total	16.0	11.4	15.6	98
	passenger cars	3.5	3.9	5.2	149
Pb:	total	1.40	1.27	0.34	24
	passenger cars	1.30	1.18	0.32	25

Source: Vleugel and Van Gent (1991).

traffic has been rather stable. It must be noted however that road use has grown substantially during this period (about 4 per cent per year). It may be concluded therefore that the level of pollution per vehicle-kilometre has improved substantially for the above-mentioned pollution categories. This favourable development does not hold true for all pollution categories, however: for particulates a substantial increase in pollution levels can be observed. The favourable development with lead shows that it is possible to achieve substantial reductions in some polluting emissions in a relatively short period. Major efforts will, however, be needed to achieve comparable results for other pollution types. Part of the trends in table 2 relates to changes in the choice of fuel. The relatively fast increase of SO_2 and particulate emissions by passenger cars can be explained by the increase in the use of diesel motors for fiscal reasons. Another important point revealed by table 2 is that the share of passenger cars in total pollution caused by road traffic varies strongly between different pollutants. For pollutants such as NO_x, SO_2 and particulates, freight traffic plays an important role.

The present level of pollution and of other external effects caused by transport is generally considered as too high. Especially in view of the expected rapid growth of transport, the Dutch government has formulated a long-run transport plan for the period to 2010 to bring the external effects back to acceptable levels. A review of the policies will be given in the next section, while goals achievement is discussed in the third section and an evaluation of the policy proposals is carried out in the fourth section. The final section is a discussion of some recent developments which are not covered by the long-run policy proposals.

Proposals for Long-Run Transport Planning and the Environment

During the period 1988–1990 the Dutch government formulated its long-run policies for transport and the environment till the year 2010. (The most important documents are the Second National Transport Structure Plan SVV-II parts a and d, and the National Environmental Policy Proposal NMP, followed by an extended version NMP+.) Important parts of the planning documents are based on a rational planning model, where targets, intermediate variables and policy instruments are linked to each other (see figure 1).

We start with a presentation of the main targets for external effects.

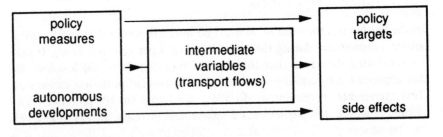

FIGURE 1. Policy analysis of long-run transport planning.

TABLE 3. Target values for external effect in transport (indexed 1986=100).

	1994/5	*2010*
Air pollution road traffic		
– NO_x passenger	61	25
– NO_x freight	90	20
– C_xH_y passenger	–	26
– C_xH_y freight	–	26
– CO_2 total traffic	115	90
Noise		
– total area with noise level higher than 50 dB(A) as a consequence of interlocal traffic	100	100
– total number of dwellings with noise level higher than 55 dB(A) as a consequence of local traffic	95	50
Traffic safety		
– number of persons killed in traffic	85	50
– number of persons wounded in traffic	90	60
Energy use		
– use of fossil fuels	100	90
Mobility: passenger car kilometres	–	130
Congestion on highway network		
– congestion probability on main corridors	–	2%
– congestion probability on other parts of highway network	–	5%

Source: SVV-IId (1990) and NMP+(1990).

These are presented in table 3. The table shows ambitious targets for the emission of NO_x and C_xH_y a reduction to a level of about 25 per cent of the 1986 value. Also for safety rather ambitious targets have been formulated: a reduction to about 50 per cent of the 1986 value. The targets for CO_2 and fossil fuels are more modest: a reduction is aimed at of about 10 per cent. Clearly, the Dutch government gives priority to reducing acid deposition problems compared with the CO_2 and energy problems. For congestion on the highway network, maximum acceptable congestion probabilities of 2 per cent on main corridors and 5 per cent on other parts of the highway network have been formulated.

Several models have been used to link the various types of factors mentioned in figure 1. The most important models include general economic models for long-term forecasts developed by the Dutch Central Planning Bureau (CPB), and the LMS, a system of models mainly dealing with passenger transport at a fairly detailed spatial level with about 350 zones covering the whole of the Netherlands (Rijkswaterstaat, 1990). The

TABLE 4. Outcomes of Central Planning Bureau scenarios for the year 2010 (indexed 1986=100).

	CPB low	CPB middle	CPB high
Employment	119	129	164
Number of passenger cars	156	172	194
Number of vehicle kilometres of passenger cars with unchanged policy	160	170	184

Source: Bovy (1991).

degree of uncertainty on the long-run forecasts of the economy is high, as can be seen from table 4, where three scenarios have been formulated. According to the high scenario, the number of passenger cars in 2010 is about 25 per cent higher than according to the low scenario. Proposed government policies are based on the middle scenario. Model simulations indicate that, for the middle scenario, when government policies remain as they are, passenger-car mileage will increase by about 70 per cent and the targets for external effects will not be met. There is a clear need for additional policy measures.

The Dutch government has proposed a package of policy measures to enable the policy targets to be achieved.

Fiscal measures concerning car use are a main element of the policy measures proposed. The most daring proposal concerns the large-scale introduction of electronic road pricing (or of tolls) in the Randstad, the most urbanized part of the Netherlands which includes the major cities of Amsterdam, Rotterdam, the Hague and Utrecht (see figure 2). Another proposal concerns an extra increase in real fuel prices of about 30 per cent (on top of an increase of 25 per cent which is already foreseen in the unchanged policy variant). It is expected that these measures will have a significant effect on the fuel efficiency of cars. A third proposal is the abolition of tax allowances on commuting costs for distances over 30 km if commuting is done by car. A fourth group of fiscal policy measures concerns parking and includes among things a doubling of real parking tariffs.

These four policies all lead to a reduction of car use, either in the form of shorter trips, or by a substitution towards other transport modes. Nevertheless, even with these measures, car use will continue to grow during the next decades. Therefore, investments are needed in highways in order to satisfy the restrictions on congestion formulated in table 3. The proposed increase in the length of the network is modest (about 15 per cent in 25 years). The actual increase in network capacity is higher,

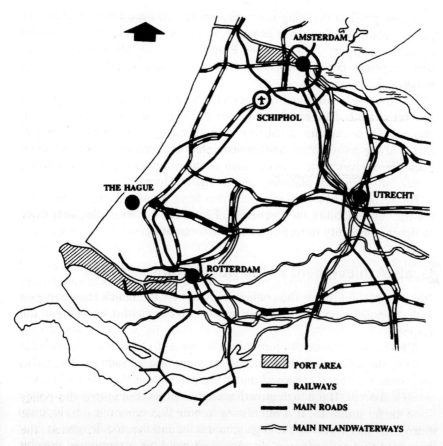

FIGURE 2. The main towns of the Randstad.

however (about 30 per cent), since lanes will be added at certain congested links. Later, it is expected (hoped?) that technological developments in the sphere of telematics will lead to an increase in the capacity per lane of 15 per cent. The resulting change in the total network capacity is about 50 per cent during the 25-year period (Bovy, 1991).

The government has proposed several measures to stimulate the use of public transport. The most important plans concern efforts to improve the speed of public transport, especially by a relatively large infrastructure investment plan for the Dutch railways. Tariffs on public transport will increase in real terms to avoid further budgetary problems for the government.

Next to public transport, the government also addresses car pooling and bicycle use. Car-pooling will be stimulated by, among other measures, special tariffs on tollroads and by the construction of special lanes on certain highway segments.

A new physical planning instrument proposed concerns restrictions on parking places for firms. For example, firms with an 'excellent accessibility by public transport' located in the Randstad are only allowed to have ten parking places per 100 workers. At other locations higher numbers of parking places are allowed.

In two fields institutional changes have been proposed which are new to the Netherlands. The first concerns the introduction of so-called transport regions. These regions, consisting of cooperating municipalities, have to carry out the coordination and implementation of regional transport plans. Such plans cover various issues such as measures in the field of parking policy, infrastructure planning, and public transport.

The second institutional change is that firms become partly accountable for the total mobility they generate. Firms are, for example, stimulated to develop mobility reduction plans for commuting.

Goals Achievement in the Dutch Transport Plan

Is it possible to achieve the goals formulated for the Dutch transport plan with the policies proposed? There are several causes of uncertainty in this respect.

A first cause is general economic development. As already indicated in table 4, the differences between the scenarios are substantial. The policy measures have been proposed under the assumption that the middle scenario will occur. If the high growth scenario occurs, the proposed package is no longer sufficient. It is interesting to note that economic development since 1986 was nearer to the high scenario than to the middle one. It must be added that the scenarios distinguished pay little attention to possible qualitative changes in lifestyles, demography, the economy, and transport. A much broader formulation of possible developments in Europe until the year 2020 is given by Masser, Sviden and Wegener (1992).

Another cause of uncertainty concerns the models used. These have been tested for past and present data, but their adequacy for long-term projections is not always beyond doubt. Besides, there is often a gap between models and specific policy measures in the sense that proposed policy measures do not exactly correspond with the policy instruments in the models so that it is difficult to assess their impacts.

Part of the results of the policy analyses does not depend on models, but on assumptions about the long-term impacts of policies on variables such as fuel efficiency, emission levels of cars, etc. In several cases one may question the adequacy of the specific assumptions. For example, the expected reduction in pollution levels of trucks seems to be very optimistic.

Financial aspects are not always taken into account in a systematic way in the analyses. Therefore it cannot be guaranteed that there will be

TABLE 5. Growth indices of passenger kilometres on a workday in 2010 (indexed 1986=100).

	Unchanged Policy	Proposed Policy Package
Car (driven)	170	147
Car (passenger)	85	95
Train	109	139
Other public transport	94	117
Bicycle and walking	89	97
Total	131	127

Source: Bovy (1991).

sufficient funds for the investments needed to improve the quality and speed of public transport. This is particularly true for public transport within the main urban areas where substantial investments would be needed to achieve the targets.

Results of the policy analyses are shown in table 5. Implementation of the proposed policy package leads to a reduction in the growth of car kilometres from 70 to 47 per cent. It is striking that despite the measures to discourage car use, mobility by car remains the travel mode with the highest growth rate. Much stronger policy measures would be needed if one wants to achieve the target to reduce car mobility growth to 35 per cent. One would have to think in terms of a drastic increase in fuel prices, and toll tariffs.

It appears that the environmental targets cannot be achieved with the proposed standard package of measures, although in most cases the realization is not far removed from the targets presented in table 3. There is one target which remains far removed from the realization: traffic safety. In this area substantial additional measures are needed if one wants to achieve the targets.

Evaluation of Proposed Policies

The proposed standard package of policies has a considerable impact on the level of mobility by car. An increase of 70 per cent is reduced to an increase of 47 per cent. In 1988 some environmental groups advocated a 'trend-break' scenario which would lead to a substantial reduction in car mobility during the next decades (Peeters, 1988). The main reason that the proposed policies are so favourable for emissions of NOx and CxHy is that they rely strongly on technological improvements in car technology. The emission per car is expected to be reduced to about 20 per cent of the present level in the near future.

The proposed policies imply a clear shift of emphasis in infrastructure

TABLE 6. Intended infrastructure investments in the 1990s (ECU × 10⁶ per year).

	Netherlands	*Germany*	*France*
Highway	700	2 400	6 000
Rail	400	1 700	1 200
Waterways	200	400	300
Airports	200	100	300
Total	1 500	4 600	7 800

Source: Coopers and Lybrand (1990).

investments plans from road investments to rail investments. As indicated in table 6 the share of road investments will be lower in the Netherlands than in neighbouring countries such as Germany and France.

Freight transport by road receives a favourable treatment in the government proposals. For example, freight transport will not have to pay for toll roads. While for passenger transport the government uses both push and pull instruments to arrive at a shift in modal choice in the direction of rail, there is no such approach for freight transport. There are no clear push instruments proposed here. The reason is obviously that freight transport by road is considered as a vital sector in the Dutch economy, both from a national and international perspective. From an environmental viewpoint such a treatment is difficult to defend. The share of trucks in the total number of vehicles is only 10 per cent, but its share in the total pollution emitted is much higher (Van Gent and Rietveld, 1990).

The proposed policy package contains some interesting new ideas. In particular, the large-scale introduction of electronic road pricing in the Randstad would have been a major innovation, but this proposal has been dropped. There appeared to be a strong resistance to the idea from various interest groups and political parties. The plan has been criticized for several reasons, such as privacy problems, risk of technical failure of the system, risk of large-scale ignorance by the users, unintended relocation of economic activity and high implementation costs. Also adverse effects on traffic safety when car users try to avoid highways played a role in the discussion. But especially the negative impacts on low income households provided important arguments against electronic road pricing (In 't Veld, 1991). As an alternative a system of traditional toll roads has been proposed, but it is probable that this option also will disappear from the political agenda since it gives rise to the same kind of problems in terms of income distribution. This would imply that a major component of the plans would disappear, since the toll road system is expected to be a main determinant of the reduction in the growth of car use. The impact on congestion probabilities would even be more unfavourable since tariffs on the toll roads might be time dependent. The lesson must be that transportation planning needs to address the broad issues and to explore the direct and indirect effects of those issues including effects on the income distribution (see also figure 1). Political side conditions play an important role in transportation planning. One possible approach to the analysis of the political constraints would be through the public choice perspective (See Rietveld and Van Wissen, 1991).

Another issue which has received much attention in the political debates about the transport plans concerns the quality of infrastructure in the Netherlands compared with other countries in Europe. Several interest groups have expressed a concern that with the proposed policies the infrastructure quality (especially of highways) will become intolerably low. This may give rise to considerable economic damage since the transport sector is considered to be important for the Dutch economy. In particular the position of the major transport nodes (Schiphol airport and the port of Rotterdam) needs to be safeguarded.

The overall conclusion is that the Dutch transport policy plan contains several interesting proposals, but that it is improbable that the most far-reaching ones will be implemented. One must fear that there will be a considerable gap between words (policy plan) and deeds (actual implementation).

What Happened Next?

Some interesting developments have taken place since the formulation of the Dutch transport policy plan. But it is important to note that these developments are not part of this plan, neither are they entirely consistent with the plan. Since January 1991 public transport is free for all students at universities and other institutions of higher education in the Netherlands. The background of this free public transport is not in transport policy, but in budgetary problems with the Ministry of Education. The Ministry solved part of its budgetary problems by reducing the level of the scholarships for students. As a compensation the students would receive the free public transport. Of course the Ministry of Education has to pay public transport companies for the services they provide to students, but the amounts paid are smaller than the amounts saved by cutting the level of the scholarships.

The measures led to a rapid increase of public transport use: during the first half of 1991 the number of both bus and train passengers was about 15 per cent above the level in the preceding half year. At certain places during peak hours capacity problems occurred, but the problems were much smaller than anticipated. From the viewpoint of stimulating public transport this policy is obviously quite successful. Nevertheless it must be noted that the policy is inconsistent with the main philosophy of the Dutch long-run transport plan. According to the transport plan, the price of mobility must be increased, both for car use and for public transport. Free public transport for students does exactly the reverse: it makes mobility cheaper.

Another point which deserves attention is that an increase in the use of public transport does not necessarily mean a decrease in car use. First, making public transport free may just generate more trips or longer trips without reducing car use. Second, in the Netherlands the bicycle is a very important travel mode. About 28 per cent of all trips are made by bicycle. There are clear indications that good and cheap public transport is in the first place a competitor of bicycle use, rather than of car use.

It is worth noting that public transport use had started to grow before the introduction of free public transport for students. For example, the number of rail passengers in 1990 was 8 per cent higher than in the preceding year. For bus passengers a growth rate of 4 per cent can be observed. These figures are not as dramatic as the growth figures in 1991, but they are nevertheless remarkable, since in the preceding years the use of public transport was rather stagnant. Part of the sudden growth can be explained by the introduction of a new card type by the Dutch national railways. The card, which cost about US $60 per year gives a reduction of 40 per cent or more in the railway tariffs outside the morning peak period. Part of the growth remains unexplained, however. It is not impossible that the recent interest in public transport is related to a wave in environmental consciousness which can be observed in the Netherlands at the end of the 1980s, both in circles of policy-makers and parts of the general public. Changes in attitudes and lifestyles are no doubt very important factors in the solution of environmental problems. It is not yet clear how durable the present change in public opinion is regarding environmental problems. Implementation of the measures in the transport plan has been slow up to now. It is not impossible that the wave of environmental consciousness will soon come to an end. In that case one may expect that the policy intentions expressed in the long-run transport plan will not be realized.

REFERENCES

Bovy, P. H. L. (1991) *Verkeerskundige studies van infrastructuur: onderbouwing van het SVV–II*. Rotterdam: Rijkswaterstaat.
Coopers & Lybrand (1990) *Internationale vergelijking infrastructuur*. Rotterdam: Coopers & Lybrand.
In't Veld, R. J. (1991) Road pricing, a logical failure, in Kraan, D. J. and In t'Veld R. J. (eds.) *Environmental Protection, Public or Private Choice*. Dordrecht: Kluwer, pp. 111–122.

Masser, I., Sviden, O. and Wegener, M. (1992) *The Geography of Europe's Futures*. London: Belhaven Press.

Ministry of Housing (1989) *Nationaal Milieubeleidsplan*. The Hague: SDU.

Ministry of Housing (1990) *Nationaal Milieubeleidsplan – plus*. The Hague: SDU.

Ministry of Housing and Ministry of Transport (1988) *Tweede Structuurschema Verkeer en Vervoer*, (SVV–II), part a. The Hague: SDU.

Ministry of Housing and Ministry of Transport (1990) *Tweede Structuurschema Verkeer en Vervoer*, (SVV–II), part d, The Hague: SDU.

Peeters, P. M. (1988) *Schoon op weg, naar een trendbreuk in het personenverkeer*. Amsterdam: Milieudefensie.

Rietveld, P. and Van Wissen, L. (1991) Transport policies and the environment, regulation and taxation, in Kraan, D. J. and In t' Veld, R. J. (eds.). *Environmental Protection, Public or Private Choice*. Dordrecht: Kluwer, pp. 91–110.

Rijkswaterstaat (1990) *Het landelijk modelsysteem verkeer en vervoer*. Rotterdam.

Van Gent, H. and Rietveld, P. (1990) Road transport and the environment in Europe, Milieu. *Netherlands Journal of Environmental Sciences*, vol. 5, pp. 242–247.

Vleugel, J. M. and Van Gent, H. A. (1991) *Duurzame ontwikkeling, mobiliteit en bereikbaarheid, Infrastructuur*. Delft: Delftse Universitaire Pers.

PART II

The Role of the Institutions

6

The Role of Government

NEIL SCHOFIELD

Environmental issues have assumed a growing importance for transport policy-makers. The environment has moved to the forefront of the political agenda. Pollution, congestion, noise and the impact of new transport infrastructure on the countryside are all issues which arouse intense feelings. Although expert attention may focus on transport's contribution to the global warming problem, public concern tends to concentrate on localized problems such as transport noise.

While awareness of the impact on the environment is increasing, people also want to travel more and especially to make increasing use of the freedom offered by the car. Total passenger travel increased by 230 per cent between 1952 and 1989, from 197 billion passenger kilometres to 654 billion passenger kilometres. Car travel has increased even more dramatically – more than tenfold from 54 billion passenger kilometres in 1952 to 563 billion passenger kilometres in 1989.

Transport in Britain is dominated by road traffic. In 1989, 93 per cent of passenger journeys and 62 per cent of freight trips went by road. Yet Britain still has fewer cars for the size of its population than France, Germany or the United States. The National Road Traffic Forecast indicates that demand for road transport in Britain in 2025 will be between 83 per cent and 142 per cent higher than in 1988. As prosperity increases, the number of individuals wishing to use their cars increases, as does the number of cars.

One consequence of this is that the effects of technological improvements which benefit the environment – such as the introduction of more efficient engines which consume less fuel – are continually being offset by the growth in travel. The policy-maker is chasing a moving target. This is not a problem unique to environmental objectives; it applies equally to the question of infrastructure provision. Nevertheless for the environmental policy-maker it forms an important part of the backdrop.

Intervention in consumer choice is not to be undertaken lightly and the government looks for ways of responding to demand for road transport as efficiently as possible. However this can entail decisions not to provide extra capacity even where there is substantial congestion; radial routes into central London would be a good example.

The government's strategy on the environment was set out in *This Common Inheritance – Britain's Environmental Strategy*, the government's White Paper, published in September 1990. This places transport in its context as one of a range of activities leading to environmental difficulties. One of the central messages of the White Paper is that conserving the environment is a shared responsibility. Central and local government, transport operators and the travelling public are all expected to play their part.

Conflicts

We take mobility for granted; we assume that we can travel where we want, and we expect to be able to do so quickly and efficiently. The freedom and flexibility that the car in particular can bring are greatly prized, and are indeed welcomed by the government. We also rely on transport to provide the increasing quality and range of goods and services we consume. So against the background of increasing demand, there can be no easy solutions to transport's environmental impacts.

Sometimes the different aims of transport policy complement one another. For example, motorway speed limits can be justified for both safety and environmental reasons. But the policy-maker has to balance those objectives against the time saving available from greater operating speeds, the implications of different speeds for the capacity of the network and so on.

But at other times even measures to conserve the environment can conflict with each other – preserving the environment is not a single problem with a single solution. It involves a number of issues, often requiring different approaches, at different levels, in areas where there may be uncertainty and controversy among experts on the nature and extent of the problem.

For example, catalytic converters reduce certain vehicle emissions which are local and regional pollutants, but at the price of higher fuel consumption and hence emissions of CO_2, with implications of global warming.

Examples of conflict also occur at local level. For instance, the policy-maker may wish to consider banning lorries from a town centre at certain times of day. Banning lorries at night and weekends might reduce noise and inconvenience to residents. But to ease congestion, that might be the time they should be encouraged to run. Objectives may run counter to one another, and the distributional impact of a decision on different sectors of the community will vary significantly.

In practical terms, the policy-maker is involved in a constant balancing act, arriving at compromises by trading one objective off against another, and deciding on the priorities among the various aims.

Role of Government

It seems clear that, in Britain, public opinion looks to the government to take a lead on environmental issues. A survey conducted by MORI for the RAC in December 1990 showed that 80 per cent of motorists believed that the government should take an active role to protect the environment. This compares with 54 per cent for 'the man in the street', 53 per cent for manufacturing industry generally, 47 per cent for local authorities and only 39 per cent for motor manufacturers. But the wide distribution of decision making within the transport market means that government can take a lead only by influencing the decisions made by individuals and companies.

Governments can take action in a number of ways. They can impose regulation. Through fiscal policy, they can steer behaviour by market signals. They can also publish information and seek to change public attitudes over the longer term.

These approaches are, to some extent, linked – a government's ability to make effective regulations will, to some extent, depend on its ability to inform the public. In some areas it may be necessary to regulate to ensure that the information needed for the public to make informed decisions is available.

REGULATION

Regulatory measures can be introduced at various governmental levels. Some environmental problems, such as global warming, require an international response as they transcend national boundaries.

The movement towards a single European market means that measures involving, say, standards of vehicle design will tend to be taken at a European level. For example, the regulations on vehicle emissions standards which will, in effect, make the fitting of catalytic converters to cars compulsory were made by the EC – as will new standards for emissions for heavy diesel vehicles, due to be in force by 1996.

Some forms of transport such as shipping and aviation are by their nature international businesses and attempts to regulate their activities can best take place through international bodies, such as the International Civil Aviation Organisation and the International Maritime Organisation, enforced by national government agencies. Transport assets such as ships and aircraft are by definition mobile and it is difficult for one nation to influence the industry in complete isolation from its neighbours.

But international action does depend on there being a common view of the significance of the problem and agreement on the appropriate policy response. This will tend to make the policy-making process more protracted, especially where regulation may reduce the domestic economy's competitiveness.

Other environmental regulations are made at national government level. Examples include the introduction of an emissions check into the MOT test from November 1991 and the compulsory fitting of speed limiters to new heavy goods vehicles from August 1992 (a regulation which should bring both environmental and safety benefits).

Local government has a direct transport responsibility as local highway authorities are responsible for the large majority of Britain's road mileage. It also takes responsibility in areas such as planning, which can have a profound effect on transport provision. It can, for example, use traffic management measures to deal with congestion – often quite simple measures such as better signing in towns. Central government can offer advice and, by sponsoring research, can help inform local authorities' decisions. But the decisions on implementation rest with the local authorities, who will take transport decisions in the context of a wide range of priorities.

Local traffic management can have wider than local implications – a fact recognized, for example, by central government's provision of Transport Supplementary Grants to pay up to 50 per cent of the cost of local projects deemed to have a wider significance. The government has recently announced a bypass demonstration scheme involving six towns throughout England, in which the building of bypasses will be combined with local traffic management measures so that the benefits of removing through-traffic from towns can be maximized.

Another Government initiative which brings the various levels of decision-making together is a joint Department of Transport and Department of the Environment study into the ways in which planning policy can be used to steer new development to locations which entail less car travel – and hence less congestion and lower CO_2 emissions – either by reducing the length of car journeys or offering access to alternative, more energy-efficient modes. This also may produce conflicts of objectives: it raises such issues as people's aspirations to live in suburban areas away from their place of work.

It also raises questions about the instruments available to central government to affect the sum of local decisions which have a national impact – in particular in planning. Central government may issue guidance which local authorities are expected to take into account in making their individual planning decisions, but that guidance cannot be enforced. In the abstract there may be agreement at both central and local level that, for example, tight parking controls are desirable. But when individual decisions are taken there may be considerable pressure on a local authority not to apply those parking controls if they mean that a new development or existing source of local employment may go elsewhere.

Central government has to take a wide view of the national interest, including both wider economic benefits and the impact of new infrastructure on local environments through noise, visual intrusion and the severance of communities – all of which may be considerable, despite the measures taken to mitigate them. Local authorities are there, in part, to protect the local environment. The fora in which decisions are made, such as the public inquiry process in the case of new roads, help to trade local against national needs.

A different sort of conflict occurs when a new trunk road – possibly some distance outside a local authority's boundary – is opened, and a hitherto quiet local road is suddenly turned into a rat-run between the new road and an existing location or trunk road – which may, too, be outside the local authority's jurisdiction. The local authority is faced with a traffic management problem – arising from, say, a sudden increase in traffic through a village centre – which is not of its own making.

Conflicts may also arise between local authorities. For example, one local authority may be seeking to use traffic management measures – including tighter parking controls – to ease congestion. But a neighbouring authority may be attempting to attract businesses to its areas, possibly drawing traffic through the first authority's jurisdiction, and actively encouraging the provision of extra parking space to enhance its attractiveness as a commercial location.

MARKET MEASURES

The use of pricing or other fiscal signals to internalize environmental externalities is attractive because it involves minimal bureaucracy and still leaves freedom of choice.

Pricing can have a considerable effect on transport-users' behaviour. For example, changes in the real price of fuel affect motorists' choice of vehicle; in the late 1970s and early 1980s, the rise in the real price of fuel was reflected by an improvement in the average fuel consumption of new vehicles, as manufacturers marketed and their customers chose more fuel-efficient models. More recently, as the cash price of petrol has remained steady and has therefore fallen in real terms, the average fuel consumption of new vehicles has increased.

During this time, improved technology has meant that the scope for improving fuel-efficiency has increased, through engine improvements and the use of lighter materials. But there is a trade-off between fuel economy and performance; and as the real price of fuel has fallen, consumers have tended to favour cars with rapid acceleration and high top speeds – often very much higher than the legal limit.

The government has given pricing signals to encourage fuel efficiency by shifting the balance of motoring taxation from the annual Vehicle Excise Duty – which remained unchanged at £100 from 1985 to 1992 – to fuel duties, which have risen by more than the level of inflation. Between January 1984 and January 1990, the proportion of the price of petrol at the pump accounted for by taxation increased from under 40 per cent to more than 50 per cent. Increased taxation on the private use of company cars has also proved a market signal.

One success story has been the increasing use of unleaded petrol. In 1987, the government introduced a lower level of fuel duty for unleaded. It now accounts for more than 40 per cent of petrol sales. Since 1990, all new cars have been capable of running on unleaded and any car fitted with a catalytic converter must use unleaded petrol. But it is clear that the price differential has acted as an incentive.

One area in which the government is currently planning to conduct research – in the context of a major project on urban congestion – is road pricing. This can involve a range of issues including the effects on development – whether, for example, it might alter employment patterns by encouraging firms to move out of areas where road pricing is in force, with implications for local authority policies on planning and traffic management.

If development is encouraged to shift to the margins of towns, the options may be to release green belt land for development – depleting what many people regard as an important environmental resource – or to preserve it, encouraging commuting from beyond the green belt, thus increasing the length of car or rail journeys. Another issue is whether local shops and businesses would suffer as customers might decide to drive to another, neighbouring town where road pricing is not in force – or where the price is lower – thus increasing journey lengths and causing CO_2 emissions to rise.

Not charging for the use of congested road space may provide a case for subsidizing railways to encourage car users on to the train. But this may encourage those who already commute to live further from the urban centres where they work, adopting a more rural lifestyle with its greater dependence on the car – and thus perhaps increasing the level of car use for some households.

It is also necessary to identify some of the longer-term impacts of such price changes, such as how individuals trade off fuel economy against performance; if prices are increased, how will consumers and manufacturers react – will they buy slower cars? smaller cars? fewer cars? more efficient cars? drive fewer miles? Or what combination of all of these? Uncertainty is no excuse for inactivity, but it does present difficulties for the policy-maker faced with controversial decisions to take. It suggests a gradualist approach towards pricing decisions.

It is also important to examine how the burden of an increase in the cost of motoring would be distributed, especially in an environment where the growth of car ownership has meant that facilities have been relocated to accommodate the car – such as out-of-town shopping centres with large car parks.

PROVIDING INFORMATION

The government can play an important role in ensuring that transport users have access to the information they need to make informed decisions about the way they travel, and to recognize the effects on the environment that those decisions may have. The government publishes data on the relative fuel consumption of new cars – the performance of cars of a similar engine size can vary dramatically. It obliges manufacturers to display fuel consumption figures for their models in the showroom. It also publishes advice on driving techniques that can save fuel.

The government, of course, is only one source of information. Pressure groups and other bodies such as the motoring organizations can also help to raise awareness, not only enabling transport users to take decisions that are better-informed but also to produce a climate of opinion within which other, more direct measures – such as regulations or price-rises – can be implemented. Because transport does have such an impact on our lives, measures to change travel behaviour may encounter considerable resistance. Information is one way of countering it.

The government has recently taken action to encourage manufacturers to stress economy and safety in advertising, rather than maximum speed and acceleration – for safety as well as environmental reasons. This raises issues concerning the way people perceive their cars, and how they are likely to react to the need to change their habits.

Public Attitudes

Some environmental problems are obvious and immediate, such as smog and congestion. Others – which may be just as pressing – are much less obvious. Global warming takes place over a long period and is invisible, so it is not immediately perceived. Its existence is accepted by the general public, up to a point, as an act of faith, perhaps reinforced by largely unrelated effects such as an unusually warm summer.

A survey by the Lex Group of motor retailers, published in 1991 found that more than 40 per cent of motorists interviewed believed that cars were responsible for half or more of the CO_2 emissions leading to global warming. In fact, transport as a whole is responsible for about 20 per cent of United Kingdom CO_2 output – although the bulk of that comes from road transport. The largest source of CO_2 is electricity generation at power stations, accounting for about 37 per cent of total emissions. Yet the impression persists that electricity is a 'clean' fuel. A recent Department of the Environment report on Energy Conservation in the Home – the Hedges Report – suggests that most householders do not perceive any link between domestic energy consumption and global warming.

The MORI/RAC survey mentioned earlier showed that 65 per cent of motorists believed they acted responsibly towards the environment – while only 17 per cent believed that their own behaviour was irresponsible. But the same sample, when questioned about the attitudes of other motorists, said that only 37 per cent of their fellow drivers were behaving responsibly, while 31 per cent were behaving irresponsibly. This sort of inconsistency showed up in almost every aspect of the survey – whether the issue at stake is safety, environment or economy. Motorists tend to regard themselves as paragons of righteousness in a world tainted by the sins of others.

The Lex survey showed that 21 per cent of respondents supported the banning of cars from city centres – against 15 per cent who opposed it – while only 4 per cent supported a charge of £3 per day to drive in a city, with 38 per cent opposed. One message from this may be that price increases evoke a greater resistance than regulation – the same survey suggested that the £3 charge would induce 43 per cent of motorists to reduce visits to town centres, and 41 per cent to use public transport. 12 per cent said they would stop visits altogether. Only 16 per cent said they would simply pay up.

One problem arises from the way issues are discussed. Debate may take place about an entity such as 'congestion' in a way which overlooks the fact that it is caused by individual decisions. The driver stuck in a traffic-jam arguing that somebody – usually the government – ought to 'do something' about traffic congestion may be unwilling to accept that he is a part of the problem – or that his contribution towards solving the problem by changing his behaviour can be anything other than infinitesimal. Persuading him that he *is* part of the problem – and that his actions as an individual can be significant because general changes in behaviour are made up of individual decisions – is an important part of tackling the problem.

Public opinion can be complex and contradictory. This can have import-ant consequences for policy-makers considering the effectiveness of both regulation and fiscal measures; public understanding is an essential part of environmental policy.

REFERENCES

Department of the Environment (1990) *This Common Inheritance – Britain's Environmental Strategy*, Cmnd 1200. London: HMSO.

Department of the Environment (1991) *Attitudes to Energy Conservation in the Home – Report on a Qualitative Study*. London: HMSO

Department of Transport (1991) *Transport and the Environment*. London: HMSO

Lex Services plc (1991) *Lex Report on Motoring 1991*. London.

MORI (1990) *Green Drivers – Research Study for RAC Motoring Services*. London.

7

Statement on the Role
of Energy Research Agencies

DAVID MARTIN

This commentary is aimed mainly at the energy supply and utilization aspects of transport and its effects on the environment, since this is the main thrust of our transport work at The Energy and Technology Support Unit (ETSU).

I would like to discuss two areas in outline, and these are:

- current work being carried out at ETSU, which is mainly concerned with the technology opportunities for reducing environmental problems caused by transport, including energy efficiency measures which reduce fossil fuel demand and hence reduce the emissions of greenhouse gases;
- policy orientations regarding transport and the environment, which are currently centred on developments taking place in the European Community.

Current Work at ETSU – the Technological Dimension

ETSU is responsible for initiating, managing and promoting the results of research, development and demonstration projects funded by the Department of Energy in the topics of renewable energy, energy efficiency and coal technology. ETSU also carries out work in the energy sector for other customers in the public sector, both in the UK and abroad.

Transport has featured in some of this work, most notably in a recent analysis of energy use and energy efficiency changes in transport over the next twenty years or so, and in some of the projects which we manage for the Department of Energy. For example, we are currently promoting the use of aerodynamic designs of heavy goods vehicles based on projects which have demonstrated the attractive energy savings which can be achieved as a result of carefully designed vehicle bodies. We are also involved in promoting the use of monitoring and targeting fuel consumption in commercial road transport, as an extension of energy management techniques which in recent years have been successfully developed for industrial applications.

Also in the transport sector ETSU is participating in a study for Environment Directorate (DGXI) of the European Commission to develop a research and technology strategy to help overcome environmental problems caused by transport. The study is aimed at providing the Commission with a series of recommendations on the main priorities for Community funding in research and development in transport technology and is structured around five main environmental issues, namely:

- local pollution;
- global pollution;
- resource utilization;
- quality of life impacts;
- technological developments outside the transport sector.

ETSU is one of six international contractors involved in this work, and it has just been completed (1992). ETSU is responsible for the analysis of global pollution issues, comprising global warming and ozone depletion caused by air pollution emissions from transport operations, fuel processing and supply and vehicle manufacture and disposal.

The three key areas of research and technological development emerging from this analysis are:

- alternative fuels to petroleum derived products, including the possible use of electricity, natural gas and biofuels;
- engine technology aimed at improving combustion processes so as to reduce air pollution and capable of utilizing new and alternative fuels:
- vehicle design technology aimed at improving the energy efficiency of transport equipment by novel design approaches and new materials of construction.

We hope that the Commission will use the results to plan its research activities for the mid-1990s in these areas.

ETSU is also carrying out the transportation analysis for the Scottish Regional Energy Study, being funded by the European Commission and Scottish Enterprise. The main output from this work is a set of recommendations for projects aimed at improving transport energy efficiency in Scotland and reducing the environmental impact of transport operations. We expect that the most cost-effective projects will be attractive enough to command financial support from both the public and private sectors in Scotland so that they can act as worthwhile demonstration and field trials of new techniques and technologies.

Our work at ETSU in these various transport and energy related studies and projects has led us to believe that there is much to be done in this field. There is a significant number of technological solutions which can be brought forward into the transport supply market by suitable research, development and demonstration activities. What is needed is a partnership of public and private sector interests to come together in joint efforts to exploit these opportunities.

Policy Orientations

Although there appear to be good prospects for technological solutions to some of the environmental issues surrounding transport, there still needs to be sufficient political momentum to bring about the necessary developments and changes. The formulation of policy, within both the UK and the European Community, will increasingly need to reflect the growing public concerns about the impact of road, rail, sea and air transport on the environment.

In our work for the Commission, we have examined the research and technology implications of the current policy orientations within the European Community regarding the environmental problems caused by transport. All twelve Member States of the European Community are in the process of developing or devising new policies which take account of environmental pollution caused by transport. Reducing greenhouse gas emissions by encouraging energy efficiency, while maintaining per capita GDP is a key policy direction. Transport is universally acknowledged as a highly significant sector because of its rapid growth in energy consumption and the resultant greenhouse gas emissions and because it is highly dependent on petroleum fuels.

Measures which are proposed fall into two classes, namely those which are designed to improve vehicle efficiency and those which improve traffic management. Vehicle efficiency measures usually comprise some or all of:

– public awareness and education on environmental issues;
– improved standards for vehicle fuel consumption etc;
– fiscal measures aimed largely at reducing fuel consumption.

The European Commission itself is also developing policies on similar lines. By developing these policy measures, Member States will hope to stimulate the necessary improvements in environmental pollution, at local, regional and global levels. Nevertheless, there still remain many questions to be answered, such as the effectiveness of these measures, the responses of the public to them and the timescales over which the measures are likely to have an effect.

Conclusions

I hope that in this short commentary on the energy aspects of the issues surrounding transport and the environment, I have managed to identify some key issues which will be important over the next few years.

I would like to draw three main conclusions:

- Technological developments in areas such as energy efficiency on their own are not going to solve the environmental problems caused by transport. Interactions with national and international policy areas such as the social, fiscal and land-use planning policies will be important.
- As the process of economic and political integration accelerates within the European Community, the European Commission will have an increasingly important role in helping to frame transport policy and in funding projects of interest to the transport sector.
- Analysis and assessment of the energy and environmental issues involved will require collaborative work between technologists, such as ourselves at ETSU, social and economic scientists and the transport industries themselves.

8

Statement on the Role
of the Euro Agencies

JACK SHORT

This statement reviews how transport policies are changing in Europe
in response to environmental concern. The international background to
environmental problems is first set out. Next some information on traffic
and on transport emissions is presented. Actions taken at international
and national level are then described. Finally the approaches being taken
in different countries are examined and compared.

International Framework

The last five years have seen unprecedented concern and activity at international level on environmental problems. The publication of *Our
Common Future* (the Bründtland Commission Report)(World Commission on Environment and Development, 1987) and the international
acceptance of the idea of sustainable development provided an important
impetus.

Numerous international meetings and conferences have taken place,
and at ever higher levels. Several international conventions have been
agreed, including the 1985 Vienna Convention on the protection of the
ozone layer and the 1987 Montreal Protocol. The Convention on Long
Range Transboundary Air Pollution, agreed within the framework of the
United Nations Economic Commission for Europe (UNECE), has led to
the signature of protocols on SO_x in 1985 and NO_x in 1988. Under the
aegis of the United Nations Environmental Programme (UNEP) and the
World Meteorological Office (WMO), negotiations on a framework convention on climate are underway and some agreements may emerge during
1992.

The individual sectors of the economy have also been active and for
example, Transport, Energy and Agricultural Ministers have all held meetings on the topic.

In particular, European Transport Ministers in an all-day session in November 1989 dedicated to the environment, made a declaration and adopted a resolution (ECMT and OECD, 1989) that went further than any previous international agreement.

The Transport Sector and the Environment

Traffic Growth and its Consequences

In the twenty years since 1970, traffic by private car and truck in Western Europe has practically doubled. The number of cars has more than doubled to over 130 million. Railways' share of the market has reduced from a third to less than a fifth for freight and halved from 13 per cent to 7 per cent for passengers. In recent years the increases in road traffic have been particularly striking; road freight transport (in t/km) increased by about 20 per cent between 1985 and 1988. Reflecting the downturn in economic activity, there was a much lower growth in 1989 and none at all in 1990. In most cases international traffic is growing faster than national traffic. Citing just one example, in Germany international transit truck traffic was 10 million tonnes in 1980, in 1988 this was 140 million tonnes.

Published forecasts of growth in vehicle numbers or miles travelled are uniformly high. For example, in the UK, growth of up to 142 per cent is forecast by 2025. The Netherlands see increases of 76 per cent in vehicle kilometres by 2010 under unchanged policies. France envisages 40 to 60 per cent growth by 2010. Estimates for the United States are for more than 100 million extra cars by 2010. The size of these forecast increases is provoking intense debate in many countries on mobility.

A consequence of the traffic growth is that congestion is acute on many major international routes and in almost all cities. Recently a 300 kilometre traffic jam was reported in Germany. For the UK, the traffic flows in the South East are heavier than anywhere else in Europe. Existing infrastructure cannot handle the traffic at all times. This applies most to roads but also to rail. Intense calls for infrastructure investment (for example, from the European Round Table of Industrialists (1989)) are encountering strong opposition from environmentalists. Even in combined transport, the repository of so many political hopes, the needed terminals cannot be built because of local opposition. The growing hostility to traffic, especially by truck, is best illustrated by the Austrian ban from 1st December 1989 on night traffic of trucks over 7.5 tonnes unladen weight with noise levels in excess of 80 dB(A).

ENVIRONMENTAL EFFECTS

While transport reacts on the environment in numerous ways, this section focuses only on the air pollution emissions. Estimates of the share of total emissions due to transport show wide variation between countries; for example, transport sector NO_x emissions in different countries vary from 20 per cent to 80 per cent of total NO_x emissions. More relevant is the evidence that transport sector emissions have become relatively more significant. Between 1970 and 1987 transport's share of SO_x, NO_x and particulate emissions increased almost everywhere. For CO relative increases were seen, for example in the UK and Germany, but due to earlier legislation, relative falls were recorded in the US and elsewhere.

There were also significant increases in absolute levels of transport emissions from most countries in the 1970s and 1980s. NO_x transport emissions have increased particularly sharply in Germany and France. For C_xH_y, emissions in the United Kingdom increased rapidly, while those in the US halved in the same period, a reflection of the tougher legislation there.

For CO_2, transport related emissions have increased both absolutely and relatively since 1973, showing the enormous challenge for the sector to meet the kinds of targets being discussed in the context of climate change agreements.

Actions in the Transport Sector to Reduce Environmental Damage

EMISSION STANDARDS

The regulatory bodies in Europe are the UN Economic Commission for Europe (UN/ECE) and the EC. UN/ECE has set minimum norms and standards for all European Countries and the US and Canada. Until recently EC adopted ECE standards but has now begun to take a lead by introducing, independently, its own norms.

Roughly speaking, three groups of developed countries for air pollution regulations should be distinguished. First the United States and Japan, then the Stockholm Group (Austria, Canada, Denmark, Finland, Norway, Sweden and Switzerland) and finally the other EC countries.

The United States and Japan were first to introduce emission standards in the 1970s for CO, C_xH_y and NO_x. Catalytic converters were required on all new cars in the United States from about 1976, more than fifteen years earlier than in the EC. A new Clean Air Act in the United States is expected to provide a further impetus to improving air quality through tightening existing standards but also through requirements on alternative fuels. Another driving force is the legislative requirements being drawn up in California. Unlike Europe, the principle of norms being 'technology forcing' is applied in the US. For example, the 1994 Standards for emissions from trucks were set at levels that had not been achieved in practice.

The Stockholm Group agreed in 1985 to adopt US 1983 standards and most of the countries have now implemented the proposals.

After lengthy wrangling the EC has now accepted norms that are similar to US 1983 standards. This means that from 1st January 1993 all new cars will be required to be fitted with a regulated three-way catalyst. New regulations on emissions from trucks are being introduced and these will be as strict as the new standards coming into force in the US in 1991 and 1994.

INVESTMENT APPRAISAL

Another area where progress has been made is in environmental investment assessments or appraisals (EIA). An EEC Directive from 1985 (EEC/85/337) requires that all major infrastructure projects are subject to an appraisal of their environmental consequences. Most countries now carry out EIAs and do so at an earlier stage and with more public consultation than in the past.

LEADED AND UNLEADED PETROL

Lead had always been added to petrol to better the performance of the fuel. The amount of lead added has gradually been reduced and leaded petrol nowadays contains much less lead than formerly.

Petrol deemed to be 'unleaded' can contain no more than 0.013 g/l. An EC Directive (85/210/EEC) required that a network of unleaded petrol stations be in place by October 1989. This has been largely done in the northern EC Countries but the network is not yet dense in the Mediterranean countries.

Almost all countries now give a price incentive (generally unleaded is about 5 per cent cheaper), and the market take-up has been rapid. Over half the petrol sold in Germany, Finland, Sweden, Denmark, Switzerland, Austria and the Netherlands is unleaded.

CATALYSERS

All new cars sold in the 'Stockholm' countries are fitted with a catalyser. EC countries like Germany and Netherlands have encouraged the purchase of such cars. In Switzerland 45 per cent of the fleet is now catalyser equipped, while the figure for the UK is less than 1 per cent. Many countries have given tax reductions to buy catalyser equipped cars. Among these are Austria, Switzerland, Germany, Finland, Norway, Sweden, Japan and the Netherlands.

The UK and US notably have been against such incentives believing that legislation is the most effective method to introduce clean fuels or technology and that financial incentives could cause market distortions. However, the experience from other countries shows that fiscal incentives are a powerful instrument. If there is a serious interest to introduce best available technology, supplementing legislative provisions with their long lead times, then fiscal incentives are an effective policy instrument. Moreover, these schemes can be constructed to be revenue neutral.

ENCOURAGING OTHER MODES

Several countries put a heavy accent in their transport policies on switching traffic from road to rail both for passengers and goods. Switzerland and Austria are two of the main advocates. In several countries investment in combined transport facilities is also central. Several countries, including Germany and the Netherlands, have stepped up on rail investment at the expense of road spending.

Policies to improve the environment by switching traffic away from roads are almost bound to fail in many countries. Simple arithmetic shows why. For Europe the 5 per cent growth in road traffic in 1988 was equivalent to 50 per cent of rail traffic. Obviously such increases cannot be handled by the railways in the short term.

General Policy Approach

No country has a transport policy that is completely consistent with environmental improvement. Very few have a comprehensive idea of what 'taking account of the environment' means for transport policy. Some emphasize emission standards, others concentrate on providing good urban public transport services, others on switching traffic to less polluting modes. Some focus on reducing or on distributing effects but not on attacking the causes. Some do not particularly care since economic development is their priority.

In general, the approach is piecemeal and *ad hoc*. A few countries, including Sweden, Austria and the Netherlands, have comprehensive plans and targets to reduce transport's effect. For Sweden and the Netherlands these plans have been jointly prepared by Transport and Environment Ministries and are 'environmental' in that they set out specific emission targets for transport to achieve.

The pricing and taxation system provides many examples where transport or fiscal objectives run counter to environmental objectives. Fixed taxes on vehicle purchase, and low marginal charges for operation are widespread and encourage the use of vehicles once purchased. Charges per period of time for using infrastructure, as is the case for the vignette in Switzerland, again encourage maximum use to get value for the charge. Many countries give travel incentives, usually for public transport, but sometimes also for car travel. The tax treatment of company cars is a prime example in many countries of where users pay no marginal costs. In the Netherlands the dispersion of the population was encouraged through commuting incentives, both for private cars and for public transport. The proposal to remove these incentives in 1989 was the proximate cause of the fall of the Dutch government. Subsidies, to many an essential element of an environmental transport policy, result in no users paying their full costs.

The lack of consistency between transport actions and environmental objectives is not surprising given the pervasiveness of transport, the range of objectives assigned to it and, until recently, the lack of concern about the environment.

Transport ministers have an increasingly unenviable role. They are pressured on the one side by industry interests (vehicle manufacturers, road builders, trade and commercial interests) to expand capacity, to improve links, in general to meet all demands, and now, on the other, by a growing hostility to traffic and its effects. Politically this is a new position for transport ministers, since their role has been mainly to facilitate traffic. Now popularity may be more readily found in showing a concerned face to the adverse effects of mobility.

This dilemma between more mobility and a better environment is bringing about a change in the attitudes of transport ministers in many countries. First some are beginning to argue strongly for the introduction of best available technology. This seems entirely logical since if emission reductions can be achieved technically, less needs to be done in the political minefield of demand management. There are signs of a more sceptical attitude towards the claims of the strong supply side interest groups. In many cases too, investment priorities are being reconsidered. Though transport ministers are not usually responsible directly there are numerous initiatives at regional or local level. On the other hand, ministers have not made progress in reforming the pricing system to take account of the environment. Another area where transport ministers have so far taken a passive role concerns land-use planning. It seems logical that they should insist on being involved in decisions which may generate mobility.

Conclusions

Transport's effects on the environment are numerous and complex and efforts to reduce or limit these require actions in many domains. Comparing the actions in these domains by countries needs to take account of the widely differing extent of the problems, the existing transport system and the resources available. Certainly most European countries have begun to accept that transport is a major and growing cause of environmental harm. Some have reacted more vigorously in trying to improve the situation but most have a relatively narrow view of what the challenge is. The threat of global warming has added a new dimension to the challenge of reducing transport's environmental effects. An international agreement to limit CO_2 emissions is likely to emerge during 1992 to consolidate the commitments made within the EC and in some other countries. At present few countries have sector specific targets or plans to achieve CO_2 reductions. One thing is certain; with the continuation of present trends in vehicle use and purchase patterns, stabilizing and reducing CO_2 emissions will not be possible. New actions and policy measures will be required. These must include a strong push to take advantage of technical possibilities to step up the fuel efficiency of vehicles as well as other measures including carbon taxes, road pricing, land-use measures and encouraging other modes. So far there is very little evidence of countries having come to grips with the complexities and difficulties in introducing such a package of policies. There is no convincing strategy to deal with the substantial traffic growth forecast for the next twenty years. Even countries with a relatively comprehensive approach are finding that practical politics are forcing a more cautious approach. Though there are some promising pupils, for the entire class, the assessment must be 'could do better'.

REFERENCES

ECMT with OECD (1989) *Transport Policy and the Environment*, Background and political papers together with the Resolution agreed by ECMT Ministers at a Special Session dedicated to Transport and the Environment, 23rd November 1989.

European Round Table of Industrialists (1989) *Need for renewing Transport Infrastructure in Europe – Proposals for Improving the Decision Making Process*. Brussels: ERTI.

World Commission on Environment and Development (1987) *Our Common Future* (the Bründtland Commission Report). Oxford: Oxford University Press.

9

The Role of NGOs

DAVID COPE

Humanity has always had an ambivalent attitude to mobility. On the one hand, there is the 'Grand Tour' syndrome – perhaps best summarized by the aphorism 'travel broadens the mind'. From this perspective, to be able to be mobile is one of the most fundamental of human freedoms, set against the tyrannical fixation of slavery or feudalism. Under such systems, people might live their entire lives never venturing more than a few kilometres from where they were born.

On the other hand, there is the 'Flying Dutchman' syndrome – perhaps best summarized by the aphorism 'east-west, home's best'. There is no more pathetic individual than the one condemned to be perpetually on the move, forever denied a place of rest.

Given this ambivalence, we might expect it to be reflected in voluntary associations of men and women, aimed at advancing perceived common interests.

Non-Governmental Organizations – A Definition

What are 'non-governmental organizations' (NGOs)? It is perhaps slightly strange to define a category in terms of what it is *not* rather than what it is. In its most inclusive interpretation the term would embrace all organizations, outside of government, from Royal Dutch Shell to the Oaks-in-Charnwood Women's Institute (if such exists) – hardly a useful category.

The United Nations uses the term in a way which most closely matches the logical definition given above. It groups together confederations of enterprises, professions, sectors and individual interests to define its NGO category. Such an approach, which accords, for example, the International Chamber of Commerce, the same status as Friends of the Earth International, while perhaps institutionally faultless, does not find favour with the latter organization.

If one questioned the man or woman on the Clapham omnibus (if they recognized the term at all), they would probably equate 'NGO' with 'pressure group'. In the environmental field, some organizations are more overtly involved in 'pressure' than others. Greenpeace might lie at one end of such a continuum, organizations such as the Royal Society for Nature Conservation or the National Trust at the other.

If humanity has an ambivalence towards mobility, it also has an ambivalence towards categorization. On the one hand, there is the taxonomic rigour of Linnaeus, on the other, the 'Humpty-Dumpty approach' ('when I use a word, it means exactly what I choose it to mean – nothing more, nothing less').

For the purposes of this chapter, therefore, I will take 'non-governmental organization' to mean public membership organizations, often (but not always) in the UK context constituted as registered charities. The term does not include professional institutions, the academic and independent research institutions, trade associations, and so on. Looking at issues of interest to readers of this book, it *would* include the motoring organizations and other 'modally-focused' organizations such as the Railway Development Society, the Pedestrians' Association, etc.

Means Whereby NGOs Influence Policy Formation

A considerable range of different approaches to achieving their goals is open to NGOs:

(a) DIRECT INTERFACE WITH CENTRAL GOVERNMENT AND LEGISLATORS

The main aim of NGOs is usually to effect developments in legislation – to initiate or influence new legislation or to repeal or modify existing statutes and regulations.

Central government in democracies undertakes various forms of consultation on proposed legislation and more general policy. In the UK, the publication of Green Papers is an invitation to submit comments. An increasingly common feature in the UK is for NGOs to issue 'alternative' White Papers, when such official documents are published, outlining their counter proposals. A recent example was the cooperation of nine NGOs to issue their response *Roads to Ruin* to the Department of Transport's 1989 White Paper *Roads to Prosperity* (Transport 2000 *et al.*, 1990).

For more general overview of government policy, legislators have the select committee procedure (including, in the Lords, formal overview of the impact of European Community legislation on the UK). NGOs have become skilled at using the select committee procedures to advance their goals, by submitting evidence and appearing as witnesses.

There is also, of course, the traditional direct method of lobbying individual legislators. Either by direct approaches to individual Members of Parliament and peers, or by convening meetings in the Palace of Westminster, NGOs attempt to convey their messages. On some issues, some NGOs have gone further than such information dissemination by publishing voting records of, or Parliamentary utterances made by, individual MPs.

The aim is to provoke press coverage of MPs with unfavourable profiles and thereby to encourage the MPs' constituents to persuade them to change their position by writing letters. Of course, NGOs often 'lubricate' such expressions of democratic dissent by local action in appropriate places. Most NGOs, however, recognize that form letters and other types of standardized approaches are far less effective in conveying the strength of constituency opinion than individual letters.

Many NGOs have MPs and peers who are members, or sympathetic to their aims. These can be encouraged to raise issues in adjournment debates and, in particular, through Parliamentary questions. Parliamentary questions can be an effective way of obtaining information on, or pointing out inconsistencies in, government policy.

Specialized commissions and committees, reporting either directly to Parliament or to individual ministries are also a means whereby NGOs can attempt to influence policy. Of the bodies reporting to Parliament, the Royal Commission on Environmental Pollution is the most important, at least for the pollution aspects of transport and the environment. It is significant that the Royal Commission chose to focus on emissions from diesel engines for the first of a proposed series of 'mini-studies' aimed at responding to rapid policy development more effectively.

There are many departmental advisory committees of one form or another relevant to aspects of the transport/environment issue, such as the Standing Advisory Committee on Trunk Road Assessment. For NGOs, a preferred aim is to have a member or sympathizer as a member of the committee, rather than simply to submit evidence to such bodies.

Finally, under this heading, there are various informal links between NGOs and policy-makers. Increasingly, over the past few years, NGOs have found themselves invited to various ministerial and departmental staff briefings and discussions.

(b) DIRECT INTERFACE WITH LOCAL GOVERNMENT

Many overall manifestations of environment policy are essentially the summation of many decisions taken at the individual local authority level. Most NGOs concerned with environmental policy in the UK therefore try to establish local organizations of one form or another. Indeed, it is a general feature of most environmental NGOs that they are often an

amalgamation of many locally-based groups, with a small central service
and policy collation agency. The Council for the Protection of Rural
England is a good example of such a structure.

The local organizations are the obvious location for action on issues
which are local in nature, such as individual road proposals. Sometimes
NGOs, rather like manufacturers testing new products, may choose individual locales to try out policies which they hope may subsequently be
adopted more widely. An example is the campaign by the London Region
of Friends of the Earth over reporting diesel vehicles emitting dark smoke.

Local activities inevitably bring NGOs into contact with local government. Local town and country planning decisions, in particular, are a
target for NGO activity. However, somewhat akin to the official procedures for determining development proposals, NGOs may sometimes 'call
in'[1] major development proposals – they allocate them to central policy
staff. This requires careful liaison with local supporters: differences of
interpretation have, in the past, led to strained relationships between local
branches and the national secretariat of NGOs.

(c) PROVISION OF ADVICE AND INFORMATION TO MEMBERS AND THE PUBLIC

The better known NGOs have increasingly found themselves almost inun-
dated with requests for information on environmental topics. In response,
they have drawn up various forms of information sheets, briefing notes,
etc. In the field of transport and the environment, Friends of the Earth,
in particular, have compiled a comprehensive series of such documents.
These are, of course, also good recruitment material.

Some NGOs see the provision of such information, either to the general
public or to schools, as their primary function rather than the other means
of influence discussed in this section.

A specialized form of such information provision has been increasingly
in demand with the growth of 'green consumerism'. This is information
on specific products or on general purchasing guidance. For example,
Friends of the Earth have produced a briefing on cars with catalytic
converters while the National Society for Clean Air, in a guide to 'Clean
Cars', has attempted to consider the complex issue of the relative merits
of petrol versus diesel vehicles. To my knowledge, only one NGO has
gone in for a broad ranging strategy of product endorsement. This is the
World Wide Fund for Nature, through the use of its panda logo. Other
NGOs have linked up with individual enterprises in fund-raising pro-
motions of one form or another.

Another specialized form of advice has been information on how to
prosecute local campaigns of one form or another. The Council for the
Protection of Rural England, for example, provides advice on how to

monitor local development control proposals and to object to individual proposals.

(*d*) PROVISION OF SERVICES

This is a comparatively recent development for NGOs, although some of those dedicated to the interests of particular sectors (ramblers, pedestrians, cyclists etc) have for some time negotiated special deals on services such as insurance or on products required by their members.

The creation of the Environmental Transport Association has been an attempt to go beyond this. It is, to my knowledge, the only example of such an initiative, with the aim of providing for 'travellers', as an overall collectivity, a range of services which were formerly essentially available only to those using a specific mode, especially road transport.

(*e*) OWNERSHIP AND MANAGEMENT OF ASSETS

For some NGOs, especially those concerned with management of land for aims such as nature conservation or amenity promotion, direct ownership of land is an important part of their operations. Given the levels of expense usually involved, such activities are usually open only to the better endowed, more 'established' NGOs and then often only as a result of special appeals. The attraction of this direct activity is that assets can be used for a variety of 'test-bed' purposes. Voluntary labour and specialist skill provision often means that the NGOs can operate successfully at lower costs than market economic operations.

In the transport field, this is not an option which has, to my knowledge, been taken up by NGOs, for fairly obvious reasons. Transport infrastructure is expensive to provide or purchase. New structures may require rights of compulsory land purchase, which are not open to non-statutory agencies. There are, it is true, various railway preservation associations. In most cases, the aims of these have been to preserve the infrastructure for historical reasons, although the provision of a form of service for, usually rural, areas has sometimes been a secondary consideration in their operation.

Nevertheless, this is a potentially interesting option and is discussed further below.

(*f*) INTERACTIONS WITH THE PRESS AND BROADCAST MEDIA

Such interactions are, of course, a means to an end rather than an end in themselves for NGOs. Publicity puts their case before the general public and decision-makers. It also helps to recruit new members and to satisfy existing members of their organization's virility.

For the larger NGOs, it is difficult to overemphasize the importance of press and broadcast coverage. It would not be unfair to say that for at least some of their staff, success is measured in terms of column centimetres and minutes of air time rather than by, for example, hectares of land saved from development or tonnes of sulphur dioxide emissions reduced.

The relationship between NGOs and the media is, however, as with most organizations, delicate. NGOs are frequently favoured by media journalists as the source of pithy and controversial statements. There is, however, an exposure tolerance threshold and, at least in the recent period of rise in environmental concern, some journalists have sought to turn away from NGO gurus to find new faces, such as academic 'experts'.

(g) 'DIRECT ACTION'

This is the form of activity which is probably most closely associated by the general public with NGOs, although by no means all NGOs favour it as a tactic to advance their goals. In its most extreme form it can involve civil disobedience (such as 'sit-ins' at public inquiries), or other activities which hover at the margins of legality. Many forms of direct action are essentially publicity stunts, designed to obtain the media coverage discussed in the section above. In this way, pressure can be put on individual enterprises, and sometimes government departments, to modify their practices to conform to the NGO's goals. It is probably generally true to say that direct action activities are more successful with individual enterprises than government departments. These can be highly resilient and can muster opposing evidence of the legitimacy of their operations more readily than an individual enterprise.

(h) MOBILIZING THE POWERS OF THE EUROPEAN COMMUNITY

To end this discussion on the means open to NGOs to achieve their goals with a section on direct action would tend to lead to exaggeration of its significance. NGOs are quite adept at identifying new means to advance their interests.

Recently, there has been increasing resort to using the provisions of European legislation to influence policy in the UK. NGOs have, as with national legislation, sought to influence the form of EC directives and regulations and have, in some cases, questioned the way in which national governments have implemented EC legislation. The most notable example in the UK to date relates to a transport case and is the approach made by the Council for the Protection of Rural England over the alleged non-application by the Department of Transport of the provisions of the 1988 EC directive on the environmental assessment of large projects in the case of the proposed completion section of the M3 motorway and certain other road building schemes.[2]

With the growth in the 'competence' of the European Community in the environmental field, this is likely to be an increasing area of NGO activity.

The Effectiveness of NGO Action

It is difficult to provide an objective measure of the effectiveness of NGO operation in the environmental field generally or the transport field in particular. One surrogate measure which is widely quoted is the membership numbers of NGOs. Although recent economic conditions have seen a downturn in the rate of growth experienced in the 1980s, there is no doubt that many of the NGOs have displayed rates of growth which have led their staff whimsically to question whether they were themselves following a path of 'sustainable development'!

It would be interesting to know whether NGOs which have specialized in the transport field have experienced mean, below mean or above mean rates of growth in their membership, compared with NGOs focused on other environmental issues, or the wider, multi-issue NGOs. In particular, an impression I have is that the transport and the environment issue arose to prominence somewhat later during the 1980s than some other issues ('acid rain', 'global warming', some of the rural management issues, etc). Does this mean that the transport focused NGOs are enjoying a late peak in their membership growth? Such analyses could be fairly readily provided.

Membership levels are, however, really only a surrogate. Defining a measure of success for NGOs is something of a challenge and I am not privy to the internal management meetings of NGOs to know how, if at all, they attempt to measure success. One would imagine that one dilemma is how to separate out their *own* influence from the myriad of other forces which may be working towards the fulfilment of their policy goals.

As a first impression, historical experience shows some stunning successes for NGO activity – the creation of the National Parks and other designated areas, linked to the activities of long-standing organizations such as CPRE and CPRW, the Ramblers' Association and the Open Space Society; the 1956 Clean Air Act, as a result of the lobbying of the NSCA and, most closely related to the subject of this book, the halting of many of the 1960s and early 1970s (plus a few in the late 1980s) urban roads schemes as a result, primarily, of locally-based NGO activities. Taking the last as a specific example, however, to what extent were the NGOs, unknowingly, pushing at an open door because of the unpredicted occurrence of central government financial constraints? There are obviously some rich areas for political science research contained within such questions.

Research and the NGOs

It is my impression that the weakest link between environmental NGOs and other constituencies in the environmental debate is the link to the research, especially the scientific and technological research, communities.

This is, at least in part, because *some* members of NGOs, often the more vociferous, see scientific and technological research and development as part of the problem, rather than the solution. In particular, they are hostile to technological research because they fear it could provide a 'fix' to perceived problems which they would prefer to be addressed by their purported 'social' solutions.

A more sophisticated presentation of a similar train of thought argues that the environment extends beyond a positivistic, scientific interpretation to more fundamental concerns about the nature of human relationships, the forms of social organization, 'consent' and so on. While there are some elements in this argument which resonate even with me, I would respond by asking 'where is the "feeling" in stratospheric ozone depletion, or the occurrence of radiative forcing atmospheric trace gas effects?'

These are both issues on which (perhaps disproportionately) much NGO activity has recently focused, yet both depend for awareness of their existence on the findings of orthodox scientific research.

A welcome trend in NGO activity over the past five years has been an increasing recognition of the role of well-researched supportive evidence in advancing the causes on which NGOs are campaigning. Research, of course, costs money, and this is something which has traditionally been in short supply for NGOs. They have sometimes been able to rely on volunteer scientific effort.

More recently, however, research funding has become more abundant and NGOs have increasingly resorted to commissioning studies from the 'orthodox' research community. We all know that initial approaches have sometimes generated a *frisson* of concern in research institutions, fearful of being tainted in the eyes of their more 'conventional' clients.

What is also encouraging is that NGOs have increasingly been willing to accept that the findings of such research may deflate some of their more extreme expectations.

Conclusions: Challenges for the NGOs

One of the few general analyses of the role of NGOs in the environmental field is the perceptive paper presented by Chris Patten, the former Secretary of State for the Environment (an individual not adversely predisposed to the activities of the NGOs) to the Charities Aid Foundation in June 1990.

Having identified the positive features of NGO activity, which he linked to the virtues of voluntary activity with which his political philosophy harmonized, he identified some areas where he hoped that NGOs would evolve to make their contribution even more effective. These were:

(*a*) A need for commitment *and* perspective, recognizing that pursuit of single issues may be legitimate for an NGO but is impossible for government, which must balance conflicting aims and claims, even within the policy field of an individual department. No great perception is required to see that the transport field is full of such conflicts.

NGOs, by their very nature, tend to latch onto emotive, blatant (in the non-prejorative sense) issues. In such areas, constituencies are easy to mobilize. Conflicting interests, no less valid, may coagulate less easily. There is a Council for the Protection of Rural England but no 'Council for Homes for those Prevented from Achieving Home Ownership because of High Land Prices due to Restrictive Planning Policies'.

Above all, there is often a failure on the part of NGOs to recognize the constraints of resource scarcity. This could be generalized to say that there is a weakness on the part of NGOs to understand the operation of economic principles and the production function in particular.

(*b*) NGOs sometimes fail to recognize that they are institutionalized and may subscribe to perspectives which are dated and which do not accord with the aspirations of the bulk of the population. In the transport field, there is a cloying consensus among NGOs to extol the virtues of public transport as a solution to environmental problems and an unwillingness to consider possible private transport technical developments which could harmonize the overwhelmingly recognized advantages of personal mobility with the needs of environmental protection.

(*c*) NGOs are sometimes inclined to criticize government whatever it does. Patten linked this to the oft-quoted criticism of the role of the press in criticism without responsibility. There is a body of thought among some NGOs which sees such 'permanent criticism' as the essence of NGO activity. Theirs is to point to the problems, not to attempt to identify, let alone help to bring about, the solutions. This perspective does, however, increasingly seem to be in decline, and the future of NGOs as research agencies and pressure groups seems to be assured.

NOTES

1. 'Call in' is a planning procedure which allows the Secretary of State to make a decision on any planning application which would over-rule the local decision-making process (Cullingworth, 1988).
2. However, despite the threat of action from the European courts, the Department of Transport has decided that all the statutory procedures have been followed with respect to the M3 at Twyford Down, and construction has now started.

REFERENCES

Cullingworth, J. B. (1988) *Town and Country Planning in Britain*. London: Unwin Hyman, pp. 39–41.
Transport 2000 *et al.* (1990) *Roads to Ruin: A Response to 'Roads to Prosperity'*. London.

10

The Car User's Perspective

BERT MORRIS

This chapter puts forward the case for the continued development of motoring through the rest of the decade and into the next century. It reflects the views and the policies of a major representative body concerned with promoting and defending the interests of car users.

The Automobile Association (AA) is the world's leading motoring organization, with more than 7½ million members. Its policies and views reflect the needs, expectations and aspirations of these members, based on regular market research.

As an organization representing the interests of car owners and users, the AA seeks to maximize the benefits and advantages of car ownership and use at minimum cost to the consumer.

The chapter looks at the growth in ownership and use of cars, and examines the need for an improved and better-managed road network. It sets out the need for greater investment in public transport and outlines some of the fundamental objections to road pricing.

The contribution of the transport industry to air pollution and the greenhouse effect is considered, relating this to the lifestyle benefits that car ownership provides. The chapter concludes with a summary for use as debating points.

Car Ownership Now and in the Future

Over the last thirty years there has been a three-fold increase in the UK car stock – from 5.7 million cars in 1960 to more than 19 million in 1990 (table 1).

Over the next thirty years or so, car ownership will continue to grow. The rate of growth very much depends on the growth of the economy. In 1989 the Department of Transport produced revised forecasts that incorporated new assumptions specifically to reflect more optimistic views about future economic growth and lower rates of increase in fuel prices.

TABLE 1. Cars in use (millions).

Year	Private cars
1960	5.7
1965	8.9
1970	11.3
1975	13.6
1980	14.8
1985	16.4
1988	18.4
1989	19.3
1990	19.7

Source: British Road Federation (1991).

TABLE 2. Forecast of cars in use (millions).

Year	Economic growth	Cars
1988		18.4
1989		19.3
1990		19.7
1995	Low	21.6
	High	22.9
2000	Low	23.6
	High	25.8
2005	Low	25.2
	High	28.2
2010	Low	26.7
	High	30.4
2015	Low	28.2
	High	32.3

Note: Low = low economic growth;
       High = high economic growth.

Source: Department of Transport (1989a).

It has been assumed that GDP will grow from its 1988 level by 24–46 per cent by the year 2000, and by 101–215 per cent by 2025 (DTp, 1989a).

The 1989 forecast of car-traffic growth – which combines the forecasts of car ownership, car use and population growth – projects that by the year 2000 car-traffic will increase between 29 and 49 per cent, and by the year 2025 will increase between 82 and 134 per cent (table 2) (DTp, 1989a).

Many factors influence the growth in car ownership and use. These include income, the cost of buying and running cars, journey requirements (work and non-work), quality of public transport and the way people's expectations and preferences about car ownership change over time.

In the absence of government intervention, car ownership could even-

TABLE 3. Vehicles per 1000 population (1988).

Country	Cars per 1000 population
Belgium	324
France	402
West Germany	477
Italy	423
Netherlands	403
Great Britain	333
Japan	250
USA	561

Source: Department of Transport (1989*a*).

tually reach a limit or 'saturation level' as a larger proportion of the population acquires cars. In the UK the saturation level of car ownership is believed by the Department of Transport to be 650 cars per 1000 inhabitants.

Table 3 shows the vehicle ownership level of the UK and other major industrialized countries, expressed as vehicles per 1000 inhabitants. It shows that for Great Britain the simple act of catching up with the rest of Europe will result in an enormous increase in car traffic. Past experience suggests that the growth in car ownership will continue. The present economic difficulties are temporarily suppressing increased growth. When the recession bottoms out, car ownership is likely to grow at the forecast level.

The statistics for cars in respect of individual English counties are worth examining (table 4). Car ownership and use is very much determined by the economic activity and the rural nature of a county. In dense urban areas well over half of the households now own a car, even in those areas with relatively good public transport such as London.

Table 4 clearly shows that the forecast increase in car ownership and use will not be uniform around the country. The Department of Transport's estimate of a maximum level of car ownership of 650 cars per 1000 population means that car ownership could nearly triple in Merseyside but increase by less than half in Surrey. And so the much feared '142 per cent increase in all motor traffic by the year 2025' is not going to happen in the most prosperous regions, and particularly not in the south of the country.

The continuing increase in the ownership and use of cars will coincide with distinct demographic changes in the driving population. By the year 2001 there will be more than 15 million people in the UK over 55 years of age; there will be 6.7 million over 70 years of age. By 2031 there will be 19.4 million people aged over 55, and 8.3 million of them will be more than 70 years old (AA, 1990*b*). This growing population of older people

TABLE 4. Cars per 1000 population.

County	Cars per 1000 population
Greater London	350
Greater Manchester	320
Merseyside	260
South Yorkshire	310
Tyne and Wear	246
West Midlands	382
West Yorkshire	308
Avon	391
Bedfordshire	419
Cleveland	307
Derbyshire	284
Devon	377
Dorset	418
Durham	279
Gloucestershire	421
Humberside	307
Kent	389
Northumberland	288
Surrey	474
West Sussex	416
Wiltshire	453

Source: Department of Transport (1989*a*).

will be accustomed to a highly mobile lifestyle based principally on the use of a private car. It is estimated that there are 10 million driving licence holders in the UK over the age of 55; by the year 2001 this may rise to 12 million, and by the year 2031 there could be 17 million. The proportion of these older licence holders who are women will steadily increase over this period.

A major study of older drivers was carried out in 1988 (Automobile Association Foundation for Road Safety Research, 1988) which confirmed that as people grow older their dependence on a car increases. Many older drivers will continue to drive well into old age, and over the next thirty years many older drivers will be of very advanced years. The road environment must be adapted, improved and managed to provide a better level of service and safety for this growing number of older drivers. And if this is to be achieved, work needs to start now on reviewing highway design, traffic management and road maintenance standards to take account of the particular needs and reduced abilities of the growing proportion of older drivers.

The Road Network

The increase in car ownership will add to the pressures on the road system and will require investment in new roads, improved roads, traffic management and traffic calming, as well as investment in public transport.

The UK network of roads may conveniently be divided into three groups:

- inter-urban roads (mainly motorways and all-purpose trunk roads);
- main roads in urban areas feeding residential and commercial areas, and giving access to the inter-urban network;
- local roads in housing and industrial/commercial estates.

(a) INTER-URBAN ROADS

Trunk roads are the backbone of Britain's road system. They represent only 4.4. per cent of the total road mileage, but carry 31 per cent of all traffic, including 54 per cent of heavy goods vehicle traffic.

The purpose of the trunk road network is to cater for through-traffic, and the government's objectives underlying the trunk road building and improvement programme are:

- to assist economic growth;
- to improve the environment by removing through traffic from unsuitable towns and villages;
- to enhance road safety.

The need to improve the UK's road transport infrastructure, and particularly the inter-urban road network, is dictated by the forecast growth in traffic. This is why the government has recognized that the trunk road network needs to be upgraded and improved. The programme, with a value of £15 billion (at 1988 prices), includes new bypasses, widening of existing motorways and assessment studies for new routes.

The importance of the trunk road network, and particularly motorways, to the UK's future economic success cannot be overstated. And yet the UK has the most congested motorway system in Europe, as table 5 shows.

The motorway improvement programme will add extra capacity to the network while the provision of traffic management and driver information systems will also help improve flow and safety. It is essential to the UK's medium- and longer-term economic prospects, and to the lifestyle of its people, that the trunk road programme is completed as soon as possible.

The bypass programme (currently 500 schemes planned) is an essential part of the government's road programme, either directly funded as trunk

TABLE 5. Vehicles per kilometre of motorway.

Country	Vehicles per kilometre
Belgium	2 017
Denmark	3 163
France	3 971
Germany	3 622
Italy	4 406
Netherlands	2 842
Great Britain	8 361

Source: Department of Transport (1989*b*).

road schemes, or half funded through the Transport Supplementary Grant to local highway authorities (DTp, 1990).

A recent study by Townroe (1991) found clear evidence that bypasses improve the quality of life for people in the bypassed communities, as well as improving the overall environment, providing opportunities for business, and reducing accidents. There is growing evidence that bypasses are a good investment in financial and environmental terms and this points to the need for the programme to be speeded up (Crow and Younes, 1990).

(*b*) MAIN ROADS IN URBAN AREAS

The urban main road network gives access to residential and commercial areas, and feeds the inter-urban network. During the morning and evening peak commuter periods, these roads are often very congested. The development of sophisticated traffic management and control systems such as SCOOT (Split Cycle and Offset Optimization Technique for traffic signals) has helped to improve the capacity of the network. But there is little scope or desire to widen urban roads, beyond some improvements to critical junctions. The problem with the urban main road network is that it is susceptible to relatively slight obstructions that have very serious repercussions for traffic flow.

Illegally parked vehicles and badly planned roadworks seriously disrupt traffic flow, particularly on the approach and exit to signal controlled junctions. Part of the problem relates to the public's perception of parking enforcement: where enforcement is not apparent, contravention is very apparent. The government is addressing this problem in two ways:

– 'Red Routes' – main traffic routes on which stopping is prohibited unless signed otherwise and where enforcement effort is concentrated and highly visible; the penalty for contravention is severe (£40 and a high likelihood of vehicle removal);

- local authorities are to be allowed to enforce parking restrictions and waiting prohibitions in controlled parking zones.

The government's initial proposal was only to allow the London boroughs powers to enforce parking meters and resident parking bays. However, during the passage of the Road Traffic Bill it became apparent that virtually all of London's traffic wardens would be required for the enforcement of the 'Red Route' network. As a consequence the government did a 'U' turn and local authorities in London will in the future be allowed to enforce all restrictions (yellow line, meters and resident bays) in controlled parking zones. The Road Traffic Act 1991 also allows for local authorities outside London to apply for these enforcement powers.

If the enforcement effort is targeted on people who persistently offend, it will also act as a restraint mechanism by reducing substantially the number of illegally parked vehicles in central areas.

The other major disruption to traffic flow, particularly on main urban roads, is badly planned, uncoordinated and poorly operated roadworks. The New Roads and Street Works Act 1991 addresses this problem. Local authorities are required to coordinate all roadworks in their area, a certification system is to be introduced for roadworkers and their supervisors in respect of training and operations; new requirements will be introduced with regard to reinstatements; and a network of designated traffic-sensitive priority routes will be defined.

A reserve power in the Act gives the local highway authorities powers to impose charges on utilities for working on designated traffic-sensitive routes. The idea is to require utility companies to give greater account to the needs and expectations of road users, and not to cause unnecessary delay to traffic. This is a reserve power that the government will introduce if roadworks standards do not improve, and greater coordination of roadworks between agencies does not take place.

The need for improved standards is shown by AA surveys of roadworks over the last ten years. These show that probably a third are badly planned and poorly operated (Morris, 1988).

(c) LOCAL ROADS

Local roads provide access to houses and links into the urban main road network. In the UK, housing development roads are subject to design standards. The earliest standards in the UK were those defined by local authority bylaws and first introduced under the Public Health Act 1875. That legislation required local authorities to make bylaws in respect of such matters as layout, width, levels, falls, kerb heights, construction, surface water drainage and footways.

The bylaws were inflexible because no provision was made to allow any relaxation of standards. Over the last twenty years much greater flexibility has been allowed and developments have been designed to minimize traffic speeds and create layouts dominated more by the needs of pedestrians than of cars. However, the majority of residential roads in the UK were built to 'bylaw' standards. As a result there are often high pedestrian casualty rates, particularly among children, because of excessive vehicle speeds.

Traffic calming techniques have been developed over the past few years. These physically slow traffic down and create a sense and feeling of pedestrian domination. In Holland *woonerven* – residential areas where traffic speeds are reduced by changing the character and environment of the road network – have become the basis for Europe-wide traffic calming techniques. But traffic calming in Holland is not anti-car. The requirements to create a *woonerf* are very strict: one is that parking provision of 1.5 car parking spaces per household unit must be created (Guens, 1981).

In the future traffic calming in residential areas must be developed as an aid to road safety and to create a people-dominated lifestyle area, while at the same time catering for the desire and aspirations for car ownership. This will require investment on a large scale, but it is an investment that will bring good rates of return in terms of accident savings and environmental improvements.

Public Transport

For many people public transport is the only means of travel they have. For many car-owning households it is the only alternative mode, and for some in the household it may be the only mode available for most journeys.

As car ownership in the United Kingdom has increased, public transport patronage and availability has declined. If increasing dependence on the car as the primary means of mobility is to be slowed down, there needs to be a substantial and continual investment in public transport. Nowhere is this more important than in urban areas. Car owners must be persuaded, gently, to use their vehicles less. But it is inconsistent to talk about restricting car use when often the only alternative transport available is an unreliable and dirty bus or train (for many people, of course, there is no public transport at all).

People have a growing expectation of quality and comfort. Our public transport systems have to be improved to provide a higher level of customer care and satisfaction. Public transport must take people where they want to go, and it must take them when they need to go. They should travel in comfort and in safety and at a price that they can afford to pay.

The provision of park-and-ride facilities will also encourage greater public transport patronage. The government does not like the word 'integration', but park-and-ride is nothing else than the integration of the private car into the public transport system. The car provides the vital link between the home and the bus stop or the railway station – a link that public transport cannot easily offer. If it can, there will be an attractive alternative to the private car.

Some towns and cities have developed park-and-ride systems as an essential part of their transport and land-use planning strategies. They include Oxford, Chester, York and Exeter. These are ancient cities with modern shopping centres. To be viable and vibrant, they need to attract car users – and the evidence is that their park-and-ride systems work very well. Park-and-ride is not the solution to urban congestion in every town and city, but where it is well operated, it contributes to a significant switch from the car to public transport.

Road Pricing – Is It the Solution to Urban Congestion?

The continual growth in car ownership and use has led to calls for restraint measures to be implemented. The major political parties believe that car ownership should be allowed to increase, but that the use of cars should be discouraged, particularly at peak traffic periods and in environmentally sensitive areas. How this restraint is to be achieved is part of a wide-ranging study into urban congestion recently announced by the government. The most popular proposed 'solution' to urban congestion is road pricing, and the government study will look at this sensitive issue.

The economic and philosophical arguments in support of road pricing are well known. What are not so readily discussed are the social, political and consumer economic aspects.

(*a*) THE SOCIAL ASPECTS OF ROAD PRICING

Road pricing is proposed as *the* demand management solution to traffic congestion. But will it *manage* demand – or is it no more than a crude technique, using sophisticated and expensive equipment, designed to price off the road those who cannot pay the charge?

The theory of road pricing does not take account of the ability to pay, the need to make the journey, or the alternative transport mode available. It could be argued, therefore, that the concept of road pricing is socially divisive and designed to give an advantage to the better off at the expense of the less well off. But for many lower-income people use of a car is essential. For them the choice will be stark: either not to travel and be disadvantaged in respect of job opportunities, or bear the road pricing cost at the expense of other necessities, and of their social, recreational or cultural lifestyles.

In explaining this, social scientists may categorize social groups and disguise the real effect. This is an alternative definition:

> Road pricing will reserve the use of public roads for the better off, who can afford to pay, and business users who will pass on the cost to their consumers. The less well off will be forced to use public transport, assuming a satisfactory service is available.

This definition is put forward as the basis for further discussion on the social issues that supporters of road pricing often choose to ignore (NEDO, 1991).

(b)   THE POLITICAL ASPECT OF ROAD PRICING

Support for road pricing is based primarily on academic and transport economic arguments. For example, 'The user must pay for the cost of the congestion he causes'. But how much will the user pay? Current evidence is that once an individual has a car, he or she will make financial sacrifices to continue to own and use it. If the road price is set to low, most people will pay, albeit reluctantly. If a significant reduction in car use is to be achieved, therefore, the charge will have to be punitive – and as such probably unacceptable, both socially and politically.

The academic and economic arguments in favour of the Community Charge were also sound – but what was projected in its support, in terms of cost and equity, did not come about. The Community Charge was probably the most politically damaging 'tax' this century. Politicians, and particularly future governments, will look at road pricing very warily – one new and unpopular tax may be quite sufficient in the decade of the 1990s!

(c)   THE ECONOMIC ASPECT OF ROAD PRICING

If road pricing is to be effective in lowering demand for road space, it will have to be a charge that is additional to existing taxation, and be set at a level that achieves the desired result, a reduction in vehicle use. To achieve this, however, the charge will have to be significantly greater than existing vehicle user costs. This will be inflationary.

Many vehicle users will pay the price, particularly business users who will pass on the cost to the consumer. Middle and senior management, and key workers, will then seek higher wages to compensate for the increased cost of living. Again the cost will be passed on to the customer.

Those employers who choose not to bear all or part of the cost will be disadvantaged when they try to retain or recruit staff.

The net effect will be that the lower wage earners will be prevented from using their cars but will still have to bear the cost of road pricing through the increased cost of goods and services.

It must also be borne in mind that road pricing equipment will be expensive to install, and the necessary administration to operate the system will account for a significant proportion of the income generated.

Road pricing may be a solution of last resort. But it does not address the fundamental issue – that development and redevelopment continue to take place with little or no regard to the demand to travel that they generate.

Town and city centres need people. Because of the planning system people are often forced to travel long distances to work or to shop and to enjoy recreational and cultural facilities. That cannot be changed overnight. Travel patterns need to be changed in the way that they evolved: slowly.

The priority, therefore, is to change the town planning system so that urban areas evolve through development and redevelopment in a manner that will reduce the need to travel in the future. Road pricing may have the effect of forcing that change, but at great cost to towns and cities, and to individuals. It is a cost that is unacceptable.

The Motor Industry and the Environment

The motor industry's objective is to satisfy the demand for the growing level of car ownership. The industry is well aware of the impact of motor vehicles on the natural environment. It seeks to provide improved products that will minimize this impact through self-initiated research and development and by changing the product to meet legislative requirements (SMMT, 1991).

The motor vehicle, and particularly the private car, impacts on the environment in several ways:

- air pollution;
- the greenhouse effect;
- lifestyle.

These elements interact with each other. On the one hand, increasing vehicle ownership and use contributes to air pollution and the greenhouse effect. On the other hand, vehicle ownership enhances the lifestyle of those families fortunate enough to possess a car (DOE, 1990).

It must also be borne in mind that motor vehicles, through their manu-

TABLE 6. Reduction in exhaust emission by catalytic converters (grammes per kilometre).

	CO	C_xH_y	NO_x
1989	35	4	2.5
2002	4	0.25	0.25

Source: Automobile Association (1990a).

facture and use, are probably the most important single influence on the UK economy.

(a) AIR POLLUTION

The problem of gaseous emissions from petrol engines is being addressed by the introduction of catalytic converters, which can reduce between 75 and 95 per cent of carbon monoxide, unburned hydrocarbons and oxides of nitrogen. Their use on all models of cars will be mandatory in 1993 to meet European Community legislation.

By the year 2002, even allowing for the forecast increase in the car stock, less than half the 1989 emissions of these three gases will be produced (table 6).

Further reductions of the remaining gaseous emissions will require new technology which so far is not available.

(b) THE GREENHOUSE EFFECT

The main man-made greenhouse gas is carbon dioxide (49 per cent); others are methane (18 per cent), CFCs (14 per cent), nitrous oxide (6 per cent) and other gases (13 per cent).

It is estimated that road transport worldwide contributes less than 5 per cent of total man-made gases, mainly through the production of the carbon dioxide produced when petrol and diesel fuels are burnt.

Road transport in the UK contributes less than 0.25 per cent of the

TABLE 7. UK carbon dioxide emissions.

Source	Percentage
Power stations	33
Other industries	23
Road transport	18
Domestic	14
Commercial	6
Other	6

Source: Automobile Association (1990a).

world total, although it accounts for some 9 per cent of UK greenhouse gases or 18 per cent of UK man-made carbon dioxide (table 7).

Measures to curb carbon dioxide emissions from vehicles will have far reaching economic and lifestyle implications and will make only a small contribution to the global problem. Unilateral action by the UK at a national level will seriously distort the framework of international competition, and will be against European Community law.

(c) LIFESTYLE

The term 'environment' is seen by many to be the natural environment and the amenity enjoyed by individuals, families and groups. But 'lifestyle' is also part of an individual's environment. Car ownership and use has improved the enjoyment of life of many millions of people. Action to curtail the ownership of cars will bear most heavily on those individuals and families who are marginal owners and users: ordinary working people.

Measures to reduce the impact of cars on the natural environment have to be achieved by lessening dependence on the car for some vital journeys, and by the development of new technology designed to reduce emissions.

Petrol and diesel fuels will predominate for many years to come. During this period the amount of carbon dioxide produced will be directly proportional to the amount of fuel consumed.

In the longer term, new fuels may be developed that minimize the effect of traffic on the natural environment. In the meantime, motor cars must be developed that will lower fuel consumption by reducing power and acceleration, and by improved aerodynamics and weight saving.

Marketing of vehicles also has a role to play. The power and performance of a car are no longer acceptable as a primary marketing feature. Over the longer term car owners should develop an attitude to their cars that emphasizes the environment and road safety. Car advertising should focus on these features and not on power, acceleration or performance.

Changes in vehicle design to lessen the environmental impact of vehicles may be implemented by the industry itself because of its awareness of the growing concern for the environment. But legislation will also be required. Experience in the past has shown that the lead time between identifying a need for technical change and its implementation takes many years. The change to unleaded petrol, for example, took more than a decade to achieve.

If technical changes to vehicles are required early in the next century, *legislation is necessary now*.

REFERENCES

Automobile Association (1990*a*) *Transport and the Environment – A Policy Paper*. London AA.

Automobile Association (1990*b*) *Helping the Older Driver*, A Report produced by the Automobile Association and the Medical Commission on Accident Prevention, London.

Automobile Association Foundation for Road Safety Research (1988) *Motoring and the Older Driver*, London: AA Foundation.

British Road Federation (1988) *Basic Road Statistics*, London: BRF.

Crow, G. and Younes, B. (1990) Rochester Way Relief Road: An Appraisal of the Operational, Environmental and Economic Impact, Report for the British Road Federation.

Department of the Environment (1990) *This Common Inheritance: Britain's Environmental Strategy*, Cmnd 1200, London: HMSO.

Department of Transport (1989*a*) *National Road Traffic Forecasts (Great Britain)*, London: HMSO.

Department of Transport (1989*b*) *Roads for Prosperity*, Cmnd 693. London: HMSO.

Department of Transport (1990) *Trunk Roads – England into the 1990s*. London: HMSO.

Guens, L. A. van (1981) Pedestrian barriers and benefits: experiences in the Netherlands. *Journal of Urban and Environmental Affairs*, Vol. 13, no. 2, pp. 121–134.

Morris, H. T. (1988) Road Works – A Consumer View, Paper prepared for the Annual Conference of the Institution of Works and Highways Management, London.

National Economic Development Office (1991) *A Road Users Charge? Londoners' Views*, A Report prepared for NEDO, the London Planning Advisory Committee and the Automobile Association by the Harris Research Centre, London.

Society of Motor Manufacturers and Traders (1991) *The Motor Vehicle and the Environment*. London.

Townroe, P. M. (1991) *Bypasses for Communities*, Report prepared for the British Road Federation by Sheffield Polytechnic, Sheffield.

11

The Airline Industry's Perspective

HUGH SOMERVILLE

Commercial aviation is an essential part of world economic and communication infrastructure. A fleet of some 8800 subsonic jet aircraft (>9 tonnes take-off mass/40 seats) flew over 1.7 million million passenger kilometres in 1990, excluding the contributions of the USSR domestic fleet and the many turbo-prop and piston-engined commercial aircraft. As one component of this industry, British Airways in 1990–91 carried over 25 million passengers on a fleet of 230 aircraft. The turnover of British Airways for the same period was some $8 billion and the company has some 46,000 direct employees.

A recent study of the industry in Western Europe (SRI International, 1990) found that economic activity attributable to the provision or use of commercial aviation approaches $75 billion annually, while providing 2.5 million jobs. The average annual growth in the number of passengers has been about 6 per cent with a European total of some 500 million passengers in 1990. There was a significant step increase in the rate of growth over the preceding two to three years when passenger growth increased by more than 10 per cent per year. All sectors of air travel shared this growth, including UK domestic, intra-European and intercontinental. It is our expectation that this pattern of growth has only been interrupted by recent events, and this is confirmed by current trends.

It is self-evident that an activity of this magnitude will have some impact on the environment. In this chapter the major areas of impact are identified, and those most pertinent to this book are discussed in greater depth. Thereafter, the response of the airline industry to these impacts is discussed.

Noise

Historically, in terms of environmental impact, commercial aviation has been almost exclusively associated with noise. Unlike other modes of transport the impact of noise from modern aircraft is minimal along the journey 'corridor' and is confined to the areas around the points of departure and arrival. Consideration, largely of noise levels close to airports, has led to international conventions which have progressively led to more stringent requirements for the control of noise generated by subsonic jet aircraft. Advances in engine technology and aircraft design have led to significant reductions in the noise generated. In some locations at least, this has led to significant benefits to the communities living close to airports. For example, the area included within the 35 NNI noise contour around Heathrow Airport has decreased significantly over the last twenty years and the number of people affected within this area has dropped by nearly 75 per cent over that period. (35 NNI [noise index number] is the measure of aircraft noise that is accepted as the threshold of nuisance in the UK, recently replaced by the similar L_{eq} measurement; neither is, however, a measure of the nuisance from any one particular aircraft movement [see also table 4, Chapter 2]).

These improvements have largely resulted from the development of the high by-pass turbofan engine. Advances in such engine technology are, however, approaching the point where there is little more to be gained. Indeed, in some of the most modern aircraft a significant proportion, which can be close to 50 per cent, of the noise on approach to landing is generated by the airframe, independent of the engines.

It has been generally predicted that the noise climate around most airports would continue to improve until at least the late 1990s, (Smith, 1989), until the number of aircraft movements and the size of aircraft overtakes the reductions in noise from the overall modernization of the commercial fleet. This still seems a reasonable prediction although the timing and shape of the predicted pattern will be affected by the current state of the industry.

One factor that will contribute to this improving trend is the increasing proportion of twin-engined aircraft which, with their more rapid climbout, reduce the noise impact of takeoff. However, the main impact will come from the phasing out of Chapter 2 aircraft in response to recent regulatory developments arising from a resolution of the International Civil Aviation Organisation (ICAO) whose recommendations have been implemented by subscribing countries. The consequences in Europe can be briefly summarized as:

– no further addition of Chapter 2 aircraft to the fleets of EC-based airlines.
– from 1st April 1995 a requirement for Chapter 2 aircraft to have an age of less than twenty-five years.
– from 1st April 2002, all aircraft comply with Chapter 3 requirements.

There are, of course, a number of qualifications to the EC requirements.

Following developments within Europe, similar proposals have been made within the United States, with an earlier planned date (1999) for implementation.

The effect of these moves will be to reduce and then virtually to eliminate Chapter 2 aircraft from the world fleet. The present composition of individual airline fleets varies with respect to the proportion of Chapter 3 aircraft. British Airways intends its Chapter 2 aircraft to be taken out of service well ahead of these requirements.

One of the most significant factors to emerge from the ICAO deliberations is the omission of mention of further major developments in noise categorization of aircraft. This reflects the general realization that most of the potential technological improvements have already been made (for example, Smith, 1989) and that remaining improvements will be small relative to those already achieved. There is genuine concern in the aviation industry over the consequences of further noise regulations. Further improvements in the noise environment for local communities need to come from:

- better land-use planning with particular respect to housing;
- possibly, from changes in operating procedures, for example, curved approaches, i.e. 'spreading the load', where there could be as many losers as gainers in terms of impact on the community.

Brief mention should be made of hushkitting and re-engining. Re-engining is a route that could lead to net environmental benefit both in terms of fuel efficiency and noise; no doubt this option will be taken up for some younger Chapter 2 aircraft where the economics are attractive. Hushkitting, however, presents a dilemma in that it is of debatable net benefit to the environment as the additional weight of add-on equipment can lead to significant penalties in fuel efficiency, of the order of 3–5 per cent. Also, in some cases, the noise benefit can be reduced by the necessity to use cut-back procedures after take-off in order to comply with Chapter 3 requirements.

At the end of 1989 some 58 per cent of the world fleet of 8,800 aircraft did not meet Chapter 3 requirements. Obviously phasing-out, which is supported by British Airways, will have a major economic impact.

From the airlines' point of view it would seem reasonable to assume that some of the noise benefit resulting from this massive investment is translated into increased freedom of movement – for example through fuller use of runway capacity – in turn contributing to the reduction of congestion in the air. Before this can be achieved, the industry will have to communicate effectively with the public on the massive investment which has taken place in noise amelioration, and on the considerable benefits that have resulted in reductions in the level of noise impact. These need to be placed in the context of local economic benefits arising from the aviation industry.

Congestion

Perhaps the most obvious immediate potential benefit to the environment associated with our industry would be the elimination of traffic congestion both on the ground and in the air.

In Europe, moves already in hand to improve air traffic control will have favourable effects but these are likely to be minimal and transient. Assuming that the pre-Gulf crisis pattern of growth is resumed within the next two years or so, the strangling effect of congestion could increasingly damage the air transport industry and the quality of life of those that use it.

The crippling effect of congestion does not only arise from limitations in the means of transport, i.e. aircraft, automobiles and other modes. It also arises from limitations in the supporting infrastructure – in terminal capacity, security, customs clearance, roads etc.

Congestion is a serious environmental problem because almost every resulting effect that it has leads to a decrease in energy efficiency, as well as using materials unnecessarily and creating needless waste. For example, British Airways internal estimate of additional fuel consumed by British Airways because of holding over airports in the UK, almost entirely Heathrow and Gatwick, is some 43,000 tonnes per year. This arises almost equally from:

– fuel burned while in holding patterns; and
– fuel burned because of the additional weight of fuel carried because of uncertainty at departures as to whether or not there will be delays at the arrival end.

Including engineering wear and tear, we estimate the direct costs of delays in the air to be some £42.5 million per year to the industry in the UK.

Specific problems that arise in this area and that are related to noise are illustrated by the example of intercontinental flights, limited in departure time because of constraints at the point of departure, which can, as a result for example of favourable tail winds, arrive in the early hours before noise regulations allow landing. Is it really environmentally desirable that we should force such aircraft to circle and, in some cases, exacerbate the impending morning congestion at and around our airports?

Thus there is a strong environmental argument to be added to the economic incentives for concerted action by governments, and their relevant bodies such as air traffic control, to address the long-term aspects of congestion. As indicated below, the airlines have taken a lead through IATA – the other sectors of the commercial aviation industry must participate in developing solutions.

The general call for deregulation and increased competition could well represent one of the major dilemmas faced by the industry with respect to the environment. Although the future cannot be foretold with accuracy, it is commonly held that the consequence will be more, smaller aircraft flying the same routes leading not only to lower fuel efficiency and higher emissions, but also contributing directly to the pressure on airport capacity.

Emissions and Fuel Consumption

This is an area on which increasing interest is being focused (Snape, 1990). Quantitatively, the overall consumption of hydrocarbons by commercial aviation is likely to remain small, for the foreseeable future, compared to other major areas such as ground transport and power generation.

The advances in engine technology that have made aircraft quieter have been paralleled by reductions in hydrocarbon and carbon monoxide emissions and, of course, by greater fuel efficiency. A UK government report has shown that over a period of fifteen years or so the fuel efficiency of commercial aircraft has doubled, in terms of fuel consumed per passenger kilometre flown (Department of Energy, 1990). British Airways' own figures confirm this trend, although in the last few months a downturn in one of the significant contributing elements – load factor – will no doubt cause a decrease which we hope is transient.

Comparison of fuel consumption in aviation with other transport modes should take into consideration the different factors involved. Apart from speed of arrival and being the only option for many journeys, fuel consumption by aircraft is a complex product of a number of factors including:

– air traffic control;
– weather;
– seat occupancy;
– flight altitude and altitude profile;
– take-off weight.

Consequently simple comparisons can be misleading. The overall fuel efficiency of British Airways fleet is approximately 2 megajoules per passenger kilometre. Of more interest, perhaps, is the comparison between the different aircraft types in the Boeing 747 fleet, all of which fly long-

TABLE 1. Fuel consumption figures for Boeing 747s.

Aircraft Type	Average Age (years)*	Relative Fuel Consumption (per passenger km)
747–100	17.9	1.2
747–200	10.6	1.0
747–400	0.7	0.8

* as at 31st March 1990.

TABLE 2. Emissions from British Airways aircraft worldwide.

	1000 tonnes per year
carbon dioxide	11 700
carbon monoxide	18
hydrocarbons	8
sulphur dioxide	22
water	4 600

haul. Some approximate relative values for these are shown in table 1; these are not corrected for the various factors indicated above.

Nonetheless, air transportation does have the potential to input significantly to local and global atmospheric problems. It is known that the contribution of aircraft to ground level atmospheric contaminants close to airports is relatively small alongside other sources, such as automobiles (see, for example, Williams *et al.*, 1980; Raper, 1989; Longhurst and Raper, 1990). However, as increasing controls are applied to ground transport the relative contribution of aircraft to contaminant levels within, and in the neighbourhood of, airports is likely to increase and already this is being monitored by a number of individual airports.

Quantitatively, current estimates of emissions, worldwide, from the British Airways aircraft are as shown in table 2.

It has not yet been possible for the airline to estimate the emissions of nitrogen oxides with any confidence (see below.) The contribution of civil aircraft in the UK has been estimated at a total of 14,000 tonnes, or 1 per cent of the total NO_x (Department of Environment statistics for 1989).

Commercial aviation emissions of carbon dioxide in the UK 'sector' are probably less than 12 million tonnes (Department of Environment estimate 4 million tonnes) and from commercial aviation worldwide, about 500 million tonnes.

This compares with estimates of total carbon dioxide emissions of more than 600 million tonnes in the UK and of more than 20,000 million tonnes worldwide from fossil fuels.

Some interest has centred on the water vapour emissions from aircraft and the potential of condensation trails, when formed, to contribute to global warming. This is a question that should be carefully evaluated. Of more immediate interest is the contribution of aircraft to global problems related to nitrogen oxides. The very technology that has led to improvements in fuel efficiency and in fuel-derived emissions leads to increased generation of nitrogen oxides.

Various airlines and other bodies have published estimates of emission quantities. Within British Airways, we have developed a data base of our fleet which allows us to estimate emissions of contaminants from engine certification and fuel consumption data. However, because of the complex relationship between temperature and pressure of combustion and nitrogen oxide generation, we have not yet felt confident in estimating NO_x generation at cruise altitudes – the area of most current interest. Although new engine designs have been proposed which would lead to step reductions in NO_x generation, the potential for NO_x reductions within present technology is limited to some 20 per cent. British Airways is investigating this area with engine manufacturers and atmospheric experts to try to reach an understanding of the nature and scale of the problem. This is preferable to any precipitate rush into new regulatory standards.

Perhaps the most important question facing commercial aviation, and indeed society, is the extent to which the use of hydrocarbon fuels will continue to be acceptable, because of the direct relationship with the generation of carbon dioxide, the principal greenhouse gas. With respect to transportation, we believe that this should be less of a problem for air transport than for other modes, on the following grounds:

- Human aspirations for leisure travel continue to increase.
- As long as the world continues the trend to a single community, the increasing demand for business travel is likely to be resumed.
- Unlike other modes of travel, there do not appear to be foreseeable alternatives.
- Subject to the qualifications expressed above, the contribution of air transport to local and global atmospheric problems is small relative to some other sectors.

Where there may well be room for some substitution of air transport is in fuller use of rail links for short-haul traffic as illustrated by the example of Lufthansa in Germany. This approach could exploit the potential of the high speed rail system being developed in Europe. Such rail links might be more effective in meeting environmental requirements if they were to be designed on a 'travel-centre' network centred on airports. Thus, fast single city centre links such as the Paddington to Heathrow line, soon to be implemented, would serve as the prime public transport access to city centres. The end result for airports could be to turn them into focal points for public transport and to free slot capacity for long-haul traffic. The end result for the public could be a transport system more suited to general requirements.

Waste

The minimization of waste and its proper disposal are tasks facing all sectors of society. The obvious dilemma for airlines in this area is the conflict between the provision of the high quality of service that the customer expects and the creation of apparently unnecessary waste. The 'average' traveller is not yet prepared to do without in order to conserve materials. There is a specific challenge to those who develop brands and other services to build in waste minimization and disposal at the conceptual stage. Although we feel that British Airways is showing the way, there is still a long way to go.

We have recently carried out a review of our waste disposal and, as a result, have established a series of working groups to generate initiatives in areas such as recycling and overall waste management. Not least among the problems is the lack of stable markets for recyclable items. Where governments identify the desirability to recycle materials for which there is no market they should take appropriate measures to provide incentives, such as initial subsidies.

Tourism

While there is always a tendency to regard the impact of tourism on the environment as a problem of some other group, all elements of the travel industry share the responsibility. This industry, 'the world's largest', can claim to employ more than 100 million people, or one in fourteen workers world-wide, and estimates for 1992 show a gross output of $2,450 trillion.

There are already instances where the adverse management of airbourne tourism has adversely affected the development of tourism, for example in the Adriatic, and the 'Stonehenge Syndrome' of fencing-off tourist attractions to protect them from potential damage by tourists. Tourism is a major or dominant factor in many countries and the development of policies to try to manage environmental impact is increasingly evident. In discussing tourism, it should be remembered that almost all airlines have a national base and that, consequently, close to 50 per cent of the passengers carried are entering a single country.

Acting alone, airlines, airports, tourist authorities, or travel agencies may make some small contribution. Together, there is a possibility that they can make a genuine contribution to conservation without adverse environmental and economic effects on the industry. An obvious area to

start is the education of the traveller on the general and location-spec
dos and don'ts with respect to the environment; this area is current
under research in British Airways. British Airways is also taking the lea.
in supporting initiatives such as the World Travel and Tourism Council,
through which we hope to develop a sound and well researched information base to guide the different groups of the industry to the implementation of environmentally responsible management.

Airlines' Response

BRITISH AIRWAYS

Within British Airways there is an established record of environmental
involvement especially in the engineering operations and in the recycling
of various items, as well as supporting the conservation of threatened
species through our 'Assisting Nature Conservation' programme. The
growing importance of the environment as a focus for responsible management was recognized by the appointment of David Hyde as Director of
Safety, Security and Environment in April 1989, followed by the appointment of myself as Head of Environment in December of that year.

From this a formal environmental programme has developed with two
main arms of technical and 'light green' activities linked to the central
body of management, interfaces and communication. The initiatives within
the airline include the following:

- commitment 'To be a good neighbour, concerned for the community
  and the environment' – one of seven corporate goals;
- carrying out a review, or audit, of our activities at Heathrow and the
  world-wide flying operations (British Airways, 1991). This has led to
  a number of recommendations, many of which are now being
  implemented;
- separate, more detailed reviews of waste, atmospheric emissions and
  aqueous effluents;
- continuing our 'Assisting Nature Conservation' programme, which has
  already aided the survival of more than fifty species worldwide;
- establishing at Director level an Environmental Council;
- establishing an environmental suggestion scheme, 'Greenwaves' and a
  'Greenseal' award for excellence for employees;
- initiating a number of additional 'pilot' schemes in recycling, some of
  which are already established as a robust part of our business.

Other airlines have also recognized the growing importance of environmental issues. A number have established environmental focal points at
senior level. Examples of actions taken by European airlines include

statements on atmospheric emissions by Lufthansa and Swissair and publication of environmental policy statements by SAS.

INTERNATIONAL AIR TRANSPORT ASSOCIATION (IATA)

IATA has responded to the growing importance of environmental issues by establishing two new groups within the last two years to supplement the established, technical, Aircraft Noise and Emissions Task Force. (ANETAF).

– Recognizing the economic and environmental significance of congestion, IATA has set up a specific action group (IAG, Infrastructure Action Group) to demonstrate to governments, the media, business and travel interests the negative impacts that arise from constraints on air transport. In turn this group has taken the initiative in setting up ATAG (Air Transport Action Group) to act as an 'umbrella' for all organizations which have similar interests in congestion problems, and with a wider base of membership drawn from all the sectors with major interests in commercial aviation.

– The Environmental Task Force (ETAF) has been set up with objectives including consideration of a wide range of environmental issues.

There is close liaison and limited cross attendance between all three IATA groups. In addition to these IATA initiatives, AEA (Association of European Airlines) has also established an environmental task force to complement internal groups already working on technical issues.

New Technology

New technology, i.e. radically different concepts to those in use, has the potential to impact all of the above areas. Perhaps the area of most relevance to aviation is that of engine technology and its impact on noise, fuel efficiency and emissions. While reference should be made to the relevant experts (see, for example, Blazowski, 1975; Snape, 1990) some of the key points are summarized below.

– Airworthiness considerations are paramount and will require lengthy development periods for new engine configurations.

– For noise and emissions, future supersonic transport aircraft will have to operate in a legislative framework closely similar to that for subsonic aircraft. There are engine concepts which could come close to meeting these requirements.

– For subsonic aircraft, concepts such as the unducted prop-fan appear to have little net benefit in terms of community noise. Ultra high bypass ducted rotor configurations, because of the large diameter of fan cowls, would appear to lead to a conflict between noise benefit and loss of fuel efficiency.

– The main routes to major reductions in NO_x emissions would appear to be through staged combustion based on alternative lean- or rich-burn approaches. Both have major drawbacks, principally and respectively the safety of ignition and the potential for smoke and hydrocarbon emissions.

– It is in areas such as these that there is a clear need for interaction with those concerned with total global impacts and in identifying possible targets for the future.

Capacity of Airports

Success on the part of airlines in tackling environmental problems will be of little use if the ability to operate is restricted because of congestion or other constraints at airports. Particularly in Europe, capacity will be a major problem over the next two decades, given a return to overall growth in demand. Success in accommodating this demand will depend on resolving an even wider range of environmental issues and accommodating the opinions of a wider range of interests than those problems more directly related to aircraft.

One approach is to develop an idea first put forward for airports, not by airlines or airports, but by a federation of airport community interest groups (Department of Energy, 1990). This approach has now been developed in consultation with British Airways, the IATA Infrastructure Action Group and the IATA Environmental Task Force. The proposal recognizes the environmental implications of aviation but also points to the wide range of benefits to society. The factors covered include:

– requirements and impacts of other transport modes;
– planning and land use, including land take, local and regional planning policies;
– infrastructure including housing, centres of employment, skill bases, surface transport education and other services;
– the disruption arising at other locations from a development in one particular place;
– noise, vibration and vortices;
– emissions and effluents;
– conservation issues;
– economic factors.

The proposal envisages a grid based georeferenced system (GIS) into which the range of environmental factors can be integrated with appropriate weightings to give an overall 'environmental impact'. The system would be flexible, allowing different weightings to be selected to assess the effect of different points of view on the overall impact. It is emphasized that the proposal envisaged is only a 'management tool' – a method by which different viewpoints can be considered. At this stage it is doubtful whether this approach could include consideration of major economic factors such as the value placed on additional capacity at different locations and, indeed, 'national interest'. For this reason it is seen as only one input into decision making.

Such an approach would provide a logical background to decisions on land use, one of the key areas in determining the capacity of airports. How many airports have experienced 'housing creep' – the gradual intrusion of houses closer to airports whose residents are future objectors – against a background of decreasing noise impact as described earlier.

Conclusions

1. Commercial aviation has a range of environmental impacts. There are few simple or outright solutions. There are many conflicts and dilemmas. These require careful scientific and technical examination before regulatory action. The accepted environmental adages 'Think Global, Act Local', 'Good Environmental Management is Good for Business' apply here as elsewhere.

2. Advances in engine and aircraft technology have resulted in considerable improvements in the environmental performance of aircraft. However, relatively little remains to be extracted from further modifications of present technology. New concepts are being investigated, but these are largely unproven particularly in terms of airworthiness.

3. Public aspirations for access to air travel are likely to continue to rise. While there are foreseeable methods to ameliorate the present environmental impact there are few, if any, realistic options for the basic technologies of mass air travel.

Should access to travel and transport be regulated through taxes, direct regulation, or other measures, all modes should be considered together. There is a strong case for less unfavourable treatment of air travel.

4. There is a need for a cohesive approach to informing the public about the actions taken to protect the environment and the benefits that aviation brings, with particular respect to communities near airports.

The industry must become more proactive in informing the public about the measures taken to protect the environment and about the benefits arising from the industry.

5. Determination of airport locations to accommodate increases in air traffic requires careful consideration of a very wide range of environmental factors, in particular land use. The industry and the relevant public interest groups should cooperate to develop a method of evaluating the acceptable capacity of airports, with particular attention to environmental factors.

The most logical approach to airport capacity is to develop a computer-based system, as proposed by AEF/IATA and endorsed by other air transport groups, that will allow different viewpoints to be reflected through appropriate weightings attributed to specific factors. This would be a management tool and not a decision-making mechanism.

6. While environmental factors are important today they are likely to become dominant in future. There is a high probability of considerations such as global warming and local air – and water – discharge quality being of overriding importance in the future.

A range of alliances including groups outside the industry will be necessary to agree acceptable environmental inputs. These will include:

– airports;
– 'competent' planning authorities;
– pressure groups;
– tour operators;
– national government departments;
– tourist organizations.

Airlines such as British Airways are taking the lead – it is up to other sectors of the industry to extend the initiative.

REFERENCES

Blazowski, W. S. (1975) Aircraft Altitude Requirements: Fundamental Concepts and Future R & D Requirements. American Institute of Aeronautics and Aeroengineering paper 75–1017.

British Airways (1991) *British Airways Environmental Review. Summary*. London: British Airways.

Department of Energy (1990) *Energy Use and Energy Efficiency in UK Transport up to the Year 2010*, Energy Efficiency Office, Energy Efficiency Series. London: HMSO.

Logan, M. (1990) *Environmental Protection and Airport Capacity*. Airfields Environment Federation.

Longhurst, J. and Raper, D. (1990) The Impact of Aircraft and Vehicle Emissions on Airport Air Quality. Paper presented at the International Civil Airports Association Conference, Brussels.

Raper, D. W. (1989) Nitrogen Dioxide Concentration at Styal, Manchester: the Influence of Airport Emissions. Acid Rain Information Centre, Manchester Polytechnic.

Smith, M. J. T. (1989) *Aircraft Noise*. Cambridge: Cambridge University Press.

Snape, D. M. (1990) Aircraft Exhaust Emissions – A Future Constraint on Airport Capacity? Paper presented at the International Civil Airports Association Conference, Brussels.

SRI International (1990) *A European Planning Strategy for Air Traffic to the Year 2010*. London: SRI International.

Williams, M. L., Perry, R., McInnes, G., Spanton, A. M. and Tsani-Bazaca, E. (1980) Air Pollution at Gatwick Airport – A Monitoring/Modelling Study in Connection with Airport Developments proposed by the BAA. Warren Springs Laboratory Report LR 343 (AP).

12

Assessments of Institutional Responses

TERENCE BENDIXSON and JOHN WHITELEGG

In considering the institutional responses to issues of environmental policy and transport, Terence Bendixson and John Whitelegg raise a number of key questions and criticisms, and highlight areas where research is needed to clarify the way forward.

COMMENTS FROM TERENCE BENDIXSON

Transport Futures

(a) Is there an Alternative to Responding to Market Forces?

All the authors assume the existence of powerful popular desires to drive and fly and that these consumer demands provide the context for any debate about transport research. With state dictatorships crashing on all sides perhaps this is not surprising. But if it is millenarian to suggest a future in which personal mobility is not based on cars, is a drive-in Europe indeed the aspiration of all? Are there no minorities with different aspirations? And if there are, how do they live? How do they get about? If they can be found, the study of their living patterns promises to provide insights that could help policy-makers to perceive alternatives to increasing car-dependence and to pursue a plurality of transport futures.

(b) Assessing the Likely Effects of Current and Proposed Best Practice

Transport gets a bad press. It is portrayed as voraciously hungry for resources ranging from steel and water to land; a polluter of urban air; a prime source of urban noise; and a destroyer of the upper atmosphere.

How far can this depressing picture be expected to change over twenty years? Cars designed to be recycled have been developed by VW, BMW and other makers. A second generation of low-polluting, post-catalyst cars is under development as a result of California clean air legislation. There are grounds for expecting these 'zero-pollution' cars to be as influential as the catalyst generation of cars which California pioneered twenty-five years ago. There is also a wide range between the most and least environmentally friendly vehicles. For instance, Friends of the Earth (FoE, 1990) say that the fuel efficiency of 1300cc cars varies by as much as 45 per cent. Economic instruments could be used to signal to the market the benefits of the cleaner models.

What is likely to be the potential over twenty years of these and other environmentally friendly passenger transport changes to reduce emissions in European countries? What technology and policy gaps does such a scenario reveal? How could the pace and the benefits of such an evolution be maximized? And how long will it be before such trends begin to occur in developing countries?

(c) London's Future Airport Needs

Somerville emphasizes the economic and environmental costs of congested airports. He hints that trans-Atlantic flights arriving early in London on jetstreams be allowed to land before curfew ends to save fuel and spread the load of morning arrivals. But what about the residents whose morning sleep would be lost? People living within the 35 NNI (the zone of nuisance) at Heathrow in 1988 numbered over 500,000. This number is falling as Chapter 3 replace Chapter 2 aircraft but is likely to rise again as air transport movements increase and aircraft increase in size (Bendixson, 1991).

London Heathrow is Europe's number one airport and an asset as valuable to Britain as Rotterdam's Europoort is to the Dutch. What developments in air transport (passenger and cargo), air traffic control, and airport management are likely over the next twenty-five years? (They could include 24-hour operation, the interaction of sea and airborne cargo movements, high-speed railway collection and distribution of air passengers, 600 passenger subsonic jets, a son of Concorde and so on.) Given such futures will London's existing airports be able to compete successfully in the longer term with Paris, Amsterdam and Frankfurt? How should the London airport system be developed to maximize its economic benefits while minimizing its environmental costs?

What, in particular, will be the economic and environmental consequences of expanding Heathrow or Stansted to provide for the longer term future? Should a site be sought instead in the Thames estuary for a new airport serving north-west Europe?

Reducing Car Use

(*a*) LAND-USE PLANNING AND CAR USE

The White Paper *This Common Inheritance* (Department of Environment, 1990) concluded that it was worth examining the hypothesis that cities can be planned to minimize car use and carbon dioxide emissions. Already some supporting studies have been commissioned by the DoE/DTp.

One approach would be to consider the effects of controlling the location only of major travel generators – hospitals, shopping centres, large employers, colleges, town and county halls and so on. But into what pattern should they be pushed – one based on centrality or dispersal?

Centralization should lead to increased use of public transport (particularly if associated with park-and-ride, bus-and-lorry lanes and central pedestrian streets) but might it not also be associated with slow moving inner-city traffic and high pollutant emission levels as well? Maybe the centralization of major travel generators would be practical only if combined with innovations in traffic management such as red routes or road pricing? This underscores the need to look at land-use changes in conjunction with traffic management measures.

Milton Keynes is probably Britain's best model of planned decentralization. It has car use levels only marginally above the UK urban average and, seemingly, much lower levels of fuel consumption and emissions. According to consultants, Milton Keynes, 'the city of the car' is more energy efficient than UK urban averages because of higher driving speeds made possible by fewer stops and less congestion (Perdue, 1991).

More light needs to be thrown on this counter-intuitive finding. Comparing Milton Keynes with UK urban averages (which include conurbations), as Perdue was obliged to do, may have biased the results. It is necessary to compare the transport and energy efficiency characteristics of Milton Keynes with those of other towns in the population range 150,000 to 200,000.

(*b*) TELECOMMUNICATIONS AND TRAVEL

If you ring British Telecom's Directory Inquiries in London you are likely to be assisted by a girl in Kirkcaldy in Fife. Associated Rediffusion of Crawley have an office in Glenrothes in Fifeshire where systems engineers work on line with their colleagues in Sussex. They are operationally-speaking in the next room and Xerox, Cambridge are designing systems that will enhance the illusion of such proximity. Xerox see it as an important market. Customers of the Midland's First Direct Bank, wherever they are, do their banking with tellers in Leeds. The bank has no branches whatsoever.

As traffic congestion gets worse in the busiest places, and as telecom costs fall relative to travel costs, telecom alternatives to transport are likely to become more attractive. Are telecoms part of the solution to traffic congestion? And if so what uses of telecoms are likely to grow fastest and bring the biggest benefits in reducing travel and the environmental costs of transport?

What, more precisely, are the transport and telecom implications of the full or partial decentralization of large firms, home-office working by employees and home-office working by those who are self-employed? If travel is reduced and emissions are reduced, what is the relative scale of the reduced travel benefits of the different forms of working?

Public Transport

(a) IS PUBLIC TRANSPORT CAPABLE OF ATTRACTING CAR USERS?

Over the past forty years car travel has grown by about 3 per cent per year while bus travel has declined by about 2 per cent. Rail travel has remained stable. Such figures suggest that cars have brought about trips and travel that did not exist in pre-car days. It therefore seems reasonable to argue that, were car use to be limited, only those journeys previously made by public transport would be capable of returning to it. The 'new' journeys made since cars became available would not do so since public transport services suited to them do not exist (Wootton, 1991).

Nothwithstanding such arguments, many transport NGOs cherish the idea of a renaissance of public transport. Is this, as the Secretary of State for the Environment ruefully implied, the triumph of political ideology over common sense? Or given, say, an increase in the perceived costs of car-use, might not new public transport services spring up to serve the new, car-generated, patterns of demand? And if so, what might be the pattern of such services?

Transit in centralized British cities tends to be based on radial routes but in the low-density, suburban city of Edmonton, Alberta, where only 22.5 per cent of the workers are located in the central area, buses and trams provide for cross-city travel between suburban centres (Richards, 1990). A weaker version of such a non-central transit grid may be observed at Milton Keynes.

The hypothesis about the limited scope for a switch in travel from car to public transport therefore needs to be tested against a criss-cross as well as a radial system of transit services. Trips never before travelled on public transport might begin to take place if transit's routes were designed for inter-suburban journeys.

(b) PAYING FOR PUBLIC TRANSPORT

Morris urges the provision of public transport saying people 'should travel in comfort and safety and at a price they can afford to pay'. But different people can afford to pay different amounts and providing safety and comfort are expensive. What steps would be involved in shifting from the subsidy of bus operations to the subsidy (with vouchers?) of those travellers who need it? And in what ways could traffic management be used to increase the productivity (and quality of service) of bus operations and thus off-set the loss of direct subsidy?

(c) IMPROVING THE EFFECTIVENESS OF PARK-AND-RIDE

Oxford, Chester, York and Bath are all towns where park-and-ride services enable city centre accessibility to be maintained while minimizing the need to provide city centre roads and parking places.

How could the use of such interchanges be made more convenient and the use of such services be increased? Would improved driver information help? What would be the effect of installing variable message signs on the approaches to the car parks? And what information do drivers most want to know? Would it be useful for instance, to know the departure time of the next bus, its time of arrival in the city centre and the overall cost of the service?

And how do town-wide and city centre emissions compare in towns of a similar size with and without park-and-ride? If park-and-ride does reduce emissions, can further reductions be contrived? How? By bus lanes, improved engine technology, marketing or other measures?

Highways and Traffic Management

(a) HOW DOES THE UK ROAD INFRASTRUCTURE COMPARE WITH THAT IN OTHER EUROPEAN COUNTRIES?

Morris uses figures of vehicles per kilometre to sustain an argument that Britain has 'the most congested' motorways in Europe. He would have us believe that Britain, with three-quarters of the cars per person of France and Germany, has motorways carrying more than twice the traffic (see table 1).

This looks fishy. A cursory look at a copy of the AA *Big Road Atlas*

TABLE 1. Vehicles per kilometre of motorway and per 1000 inhabitants in three European countries 1988.

	Vehicles per km of motorway	Vehicles per 1 000 inhabitants
Great Britain	8 361	333
France	3 971	402
West Germany	3 622	477

of Europe suggests that the main road network in Britain – particularly England – is much denser than in France and Germany. But many English main roads are dual-carriageways not motorways. Britain may therefore have much hidden road capacity. It may even have a more extensive network of high quality (but non-motorway) routes than neighbouring countries. It is time to review the ways in which the principal road systems of the UK and other countries are compared. It may be that false claims are being made about Britain being under-roaded and needing massive investment in new infrastructure.

(b) ROAD CAPACITY

The White Paper *Trunk Roads, England into the 1990s* announced a £12.4 billion (November 1987 prices including VAT) investment programme (Department of the Environment, 1990). The length of schemes in the programme on 1 January 1990 was over 2500 miles. It included:

170 miles of new motorway;
600 miles of widened motorway;
43 miles of motorway converted form all-purpose trunk road;
1,600 miles of trunk roads to be widened from single to dual carriageway.

Since then the DTp has announced the upgrading of the A1 to motorway for almost all its length in England.
  What will be the capacity of this expanded system? How will it relate to the forecasts made in *Roads for Prosperity* (Department of Transport, 1989)? If demand should exceed capacity what will be the effect on the distribution of traffic? What will be the extent of congestion costs? Are there likely to be land-use implications?

(c) THE CONCEPT OF SATURATION: DOES IT STILL HOLD GOOD?

Morris refers to the DTp's belief that with 650 cars per 1000 inhabitants the country will reach a state of 'saturation'. It may be that this hypothesis needs re-examining. Just as some people have more than one house so some *individuals* own more than one car. Since it is impossible to drive more than one car at a time this is not likely to make much difference to traffic but it could influence choices about residential location and reinforce preferences for suburban spaciousness. Maybe saturation will lie at 800 cars per 1000 or even higher?

(*d*) ROAD PRICING

Road pricing makes many people uneasy yet is widely accepted to be about the only instrument with power to defeat the monster of congestion. Do we want to use it at all? Road congestion as we know it is the great leveller, probably the greatest revelation that rich and poor can be forced into equality. When congestion descends, the millionaire in his Rolls is no better off than the student in his banger. The car/highway system has been justly described as 'democracy on wheels'. Maybe the costs of congestion are a cheap price to pay for such an ideal?

But there are problems. Congestion damages the local transport of the car-less even more than it damages car travel itself. Further more the CBI says (on questionable grounds) that it costs Britain £15 bn a year. Congestion also compounds the environmental damage caused by road transport. Quinet (this volume) estimates that all the social costs of transport in the OECD countries average 0.5 per cent of GDP (Barde and Button, 1990). Could some of those wasted resources be redeployed?

Schofield (this volume) observes that drivers appear to view paying for the roads less favourably than bans. French opinion polls tend to confirm this view. In 1988 39 per cent of a sample of Parisians favoured banning drivers, except residents, from the city while only 13 per cent favoured tolls (CETUR, 1990).

The effects of road pricing are likely to be so complex that opinion polls may be a poor guide to public acceptance of them. Of course no one wants to pay for something that is free. But how would people react after being given a full briefing on road pricing and an opportunity to discuss it? What would be the effect of discovering that with road pricing traffic would run smoothly, buses would be more numerous and come on time, the air would be cleaner, and that drivers might have to forego, say, only one in ten trips? Would this put paying to drive in a different light? Road pricing, because if its nature, requires a more extensive and intensive kind of attitude research than opinion polling.

Morris talks of road pricing causing 'a significant reduction in car use'. But what reduction would be needed to have a useful effect on air quality, noise and delay? Would it be 1, 3, 5 or 10 per cent? And how significant would such reductions be? How would they impinge on individuals with different incomes?

Morris also assumes that road pricing would increase total transport costs and push up prices. But if all goods movements and the majority of car travellers were able to move more speedily, and if all the buses became more productive, would total costs go up? What would it cost in road user charges and additional transit services to eliminate the CBI's £15bn?

What about the politics of road pricing? The poll tax fiasco is a warning that popular revolt can kill a new impost. What methods of introducing road pricing might be used to help gain its acceptance? Transport costs are a sizable chunk of household expenditure. Governments meddle in such budgets at their peril. But what about phasing out the existing system of motoring taxation and phasing in road pricing over ten years? What annual increments of change would be needed? And over what area should road pricing be tested and then, if shown practical, implemented. Is it practical to test it in a free-standing town such as Cambridge? Beyond that should it be introduced just in congested places or should it be introduced nationally to influence trip distances and carbon emissons?

(*e*) TRAFFIC CALMING

Traffic calming is widely held to be necessary to reduce road casualties and to improve the setting of home life. What are the network consequences for noise, air pollution and fuel consumption of different calming techniques?

Elderly Drivers

There is no disagreement that the years ahead will see more elderly drivers. But what effect will this have on traffic and what should be done about it? The DTp reports that older people drive less and this is reflected in their lower overall risk as car occupants. 'However the risk per mile of being involved in a fatal accident is as high for the older drivers as for young inexperienced drivers' (DTp, 1991). This looks serious.

Morris urges adapting and improving the road environment. Other possibilities are modifying the architecture of vehicles to make them more comfortable for elderly drivers; limiting the performance of all vehicles; introducing an elderly driver 'L' plate or some other (stigmatizing?) sign; requiring cars driven by elderly drivers to carry special safety equipment. (Would air-bags be of special benefit for elderly drivers? They might lessen the likelihood of rib fractures in collisions). It would be helpful to find out what elderly drivers themselves think should be done. And what are motor manufacturers doing? How can increases in casualties amongst elderly drivers be prevented?

TABLE 2 Differential impact of road and rail freight transport on a number environmental variables.

	Unit, per tonne-km		Lorry	Rail
Primary energy	g	coal equivalent units	98.4	23.7
End energy	g	coal equivalent units	85	11
CO_2	kg	CO_2	0.22	0.05
NO_x	g	NO_x	3.60	0.22
NO_x 1993	g	NO_x	3.18	0.16
CO	g	CO	1.58	0.07
C_xH_y	g	C_xH_y	0.81	0.05
Particles	g	particles	0.27	0.03
SO_2	g	SO_2	0.23	0.33
SO_2 1993	g	SO_2	0.17	0.12
Accidents	injuries per tonne-km $\times 10^9$		248	10
Land take	m^2 per year per tonne-km		0.007	0.0025

Source: Teufel, D. (1989) Gesellschahftliche Kosten des Straßen-Güterverkehrs. Kosten-Deckungsgrad in Jahr 1987 und Vorschläge zur Realisierung des Verursacherprinzips (Societal costs of road freight. Cost coverage in 1987 and suggestions for implementing the 'polluter pays' principle). UPI-Bericht Nr 14, Umwelt and Prognose Institut, Heidelberg.

COMMENTS FROM JOHN WHITELEGG

All the contributors to this part of the book underplay the hard information which is available on the environmental performance parameters of each mode. This information, based on German data (tables 2 and 3) shows why organizations in the transport and environment field do place a lot of emphasis on public transport. It is hard to understand why Cope (this volume), for example, should be so dismissive of public transport when it can deliver so much for such a low environmental price. Similarly, the accounts presented by Morris, Somerville and Schofield (this volume) all fail to grasp the nettle, which is that we can organize transport and land-use systems to deliver economic and quality of life gains whilst minimizing environmental disbenefits, but we cannot satisfy the demands of the air and car industries for growth and we cannot accept the crude dictum that this growth is simply the result of the exercise of preference in a market where many options are available. Our options are surprisingly few and in a society where much of the initiative for infrastructure provision comes from government (not a free market) this is not acceptable.

Environmental matters now command attention at the highest levels of public and private policy-making though none of the papers conveys the seriousness of the environmental problems that face the planet nor the culpability of transport in this situation. These issues are, however, taken up elsewhere in this book.

All the chapters make it quite clear that strategic planning demands an

TABLE 3 Differential impact of road and rail passenger transport on a number of environmental variables.

	Car	Car with 3-Way Cat	Air	Unit
Land use	120	120	1.5	m²/person
Primary energy use	90	90	365	g coal equivalent units/pkm
CO₂ emissions	200	200	839.5	g/pkm
NOₓ emissions	2.2	0.34	6.4	g/pkm
Hydrocarbons	1	0.15	1.4	g/pkm
CO emissions	8.7	1.3	8.1	g/pkm
Air pollution	38 000	5 900	95 000	polluted air m³/pkm
Accident risks	11.5	11.5	1.4	hours of life lost/ 1000 pkm

	Rail	Bus	Bicycle	Pedestrian	Unit
Land use	7	12	9	2	m²/person
Primary energy use	31	27	0	0	g coal equivalent units/pkm
CO₂ emissions	60	59	0	0	g/pkm
NOₓ emissions	0.08	0.2	0	0	g/pkm
Hydrocarbons	0.02	0.08	0	0	g/pkm
CO emissions	0.05	0.15	0	0	g/pkm
Air pollution	1 200	3 300	0	0	polluted air m³/pkr
Accident risks	0.4	1	0.2	0.01	hours of life lost/ 1000 pkm

Source: Teufel, D. (1989) Die Zukunft des Autoverkehrs (The future of motorized transport). UPI-Bericht Nr 17, Umwelt- und Prognose Institut, Heidelberg.

understanding of environmental concerns and a keen perception of future trends in environmental policy and regulation. For the suppliers of transport services this is essential for their future corporate viability and it may also be true that governments can only build credibility and electoral support with a strong package of environmental policy measures. In this sense actors from both sides of the regulating/regulated divide are united by common needs to understand complex scientific arguments, complex political issues related to consumer and pressure group influences, and a wish to be seen to be concerned and take action without threatening basic organizational cultures and the long-term objectives of those organizations.

The problem with environmental concerns is that they are often incompatible with the organizational goal of selling more cars or more seats on aircraft and this central paradox is not really addressed in any of the chapters. Those written from an industry perspective display a belief in the ability of technology to allow all of us to carry on with the same kinds of behaviour and at the same time solve environmental problems. This is at best a high risk (for the environment) strategy and at worst just plain wrong.

At a seminar convened in 1990 by Lancashire County Council, James Lentz of the South Coast Air Quality Management District and responsible for air quality in Los Angeles described how stringent air quality regulations and the widespread introduction of catalytic converters had not solved air quality problems. What we might term the 'California Effect' – the inability of technology and regulation to expand the capacity of the environment to absorb ever increasing amounts of pollution and transportation demands – is not compatible with the remit of the private sector to sell its products and the remit of government to make that selling possible. This point has been made very clearly by Paul Ekins (1991) in his discussion of the formula $I = PCT$. Environmental impact *(I)* is a function of population *(P)*, consumption *(C)* and technology *(T)*. Globally, any of the available estimates of the size of *P*, even assuming a very modest growth in *C* would require results from *T* which are not attainable. Ekins works through the sums of show that *T* would have to deliver an 80 per cent plus reduction in environmental impacts just to cope with low levels of population increase and 2–3 per cent annual increases in GDP. If India's 100 million middle-class population begin to approach European car ownership levels or air travel propensities then global production of greenhouse gases or consumption of non-renewable resources is at a level which is not sustainable.

Even at the level of Northern Europe with stable or declining populations, rates of increase in C (essentially the California effect) present enormous climatic and environmental problems which cannot be resolved by technological progress. The issues are not well described in any of the chapters. Travel is very expensive in its use of energy, materials and space and has health effects on third parties that are only barely understood. A vehicle which is virtually emission free carries with it an energy penalty from its manufacture and the manufacture of all its components. The environmental impact of this energy use is rarely documented just as the implications of storing, discarding and 'neutralizing' the waste products is a topic rarely addressed. A vehicle in motion or when accelerating and braking produces particulate products from braking systems and tyre/road wear. A vehicle makes demands on space which in an urban context dictate the form of cities and the quality of life of millions who walk and cycle or simply socialize in a car-dominated environment. The space occupied by car parks, roads and garages is not available for other uses, restricts non-vehicular movement and itself represents a large energy use through the manufacture of concrete, asphalt etc.

Helmut Holzapfel who directs the transport section of the research arm of the Ministry of Urban Development and Traffic in Dortmund has described how vehicles are used for only 5 per cent of the time available, rarely occupied by more than one person, need more space than that required for a German household's living purposes, consume one-sixth of their lifetime's energy consumption in manufacture and across the world kill 250,000 people per year whilst injuring 10 million. It is not an impressive record.

Both chapters from the industry refer (quite rightly) to the massive consumer demand for their products and to the likelihood that this will continue to grow. In the case of air transport this growth seems assured as European integration gathers momentum and tourism seeks out even more exotic places to incorporate into the global leisure industry. The demand for travel is therefore an integral part of bigger structures which are economic, social and cultural and that demand cannot be turned down like a volume control without some major rethinking of the wider context. This is being done in a serious way at different levels and one can point to the work at the European Institute for Environmental Policy in Bonn and the Worldwatch Institute in Washington. At the urban level the EC has taken a welcome initiative in its environment directorate and several cities in Germany are actively considering car-free city concepts. Interestingly, a similar concept was introduced by the Chairman of Volvo. The motor industry at the strategic level is well aware of the way things are going.

All the chapters duck the issues raised by the sustainability debate and display a very narrow view of the future. This is particularly surprising from the government representatives as the UK government has made some effort to incorporate the ideas discussed by Pearce (1991) and 'green economics' into their discussion of environmental policy. It may be that these worthy ideas are more useful for PR than policy. The dominant idea from all presentations is basically the business as usual scenario which cannot even deliver the results required by international agreements on greenhouse gas reductions. There is no discussion of what alternative futures might reveal – something the Dutch have cleverly termed a 'trend breach scenario' – and no discussion about how to manage change at a time of environmental uncertainty and rapidly changing views about what citizens actually want from their polluted and stressed environments. Germans in particular are confused with a strong vehicle industry underpinned with very strong ideological appeals to freedoms at the same time as environmental quality and basic quality of life are threatened by these other kinds of freedoms. Hillman, Adams and Whitelegg (1991) addressed an important freedom in a study of children's independent mobility which they showed to have been dramatically reduced in the period 1970–1990.

The transport debate is a debate about freedoms and also a debate about quality of life. We are not very good at these complex questions which cut across traditional disciplinary boundaries but we will get better and these chapters are a good start.

REFERENCES

Barde, J.-P. and Button, K. (1990) *Transport Policy and the Environment* London: Earthscan Publications for OECD.

Bendixson, T. (1991) *Europe One: London's Long Term Airport Needs*, Report for Airports Policy Consortium. Surrey County Council (c/o J. M. Bailey).

CETUR (1990) *10 ans de mobilité urbaine; les années 80*. Paris: Centre à la Recherche d'Urbanisme.

Department of Environment (1990) *This Common Inheritance – Britain's Environmental Strategy*, Cmnd 1200. London: HMSO.

Department of Transport (1989) *Roads for Prosperity* Cmnd 693. London: HMSO.

Department of Transport (1990) *Trunk Roads – England into the 1990s* London: HMSO.

Department of Transport (1991) *The Older Road User: Measures for Reducing the Number of Casulties among Older People on Our Roads* London: HMSO.

Ekins, P. (1991) The Sustainable Consumer Society. A Contradiction in Terms? Third Allen Lane Lecture, February.

Friends of the Earth (1990) *Stealing Our Future: FoE's Critique of 'This Common Inheritance', the Government White Paper on the Environment*. London: FoE.

Hillman, M., Adams, J. and Whitelegg, J. (1991) *One False Move* London: Policy Studies Institute.

Pearce, D. *et al* (1991) *Blueprint 2: Greening the World Economy*. London: Earthscan Publications.

Perdue, J. W. (1991) *A Comparison between Milton Keynes and other UK Urban Areas from a Transport Energy Consumption and Pollution Viewpoint*. Milton Keynes: Milton Transport Management Ltd.

Richards, B. (1990) *Transport in Cities*. London: Architecture Design and Technology Press.

Wooton, J. (1991) Road Transport Solutions with 2020 Vision. Paper for the Fellowship of Engineering given at the Institution of Mechanical Engineers, London, January.

PART III

Analyses: Problems and Prognoses

13

Can We Value the Environment?

EMILE QUINET

Transport economists of the previous decades have been very bold in assessing values of non-marketable impacts of transport, such as time or safety. But, nowadays, we are very timid about valuating environmental impacts, although these are of growing importance to the public.

Why such a change of attitude? Is it only a question of temperament, or has it more profound reasons?

Is it really necessary to valuate environmental impacts? Why not limit ourselves to physical predictions?

And, if it is necessary, how should we valuate them?

These questions will be addressed in this chapter, while the conclusion will be devoted to assessing the main research fields.

Why such a Timidity in Valuating Environmental Impact?

The first reason that comes to mind is a chronological one: between the moment when one recognizes a type of effect and the moment when this type of effect occurs, several years could elapse. But, in fact, the time span between acknowledging the importance of time and finding a means of valuing time was very brief. In contrast, the importance of the environment has been recognized since the early 1970s. However, this importance has not hitherto been valued.

Thus, we cannot deny the phenomenon and we must turn to real explanations. Those explanations can be classified in two categories: first, valuation of the environment incorporates all the difficulties of cost calculation; second, the shift towards multicriteria analysis seems to make valuation less necessary.

In economics textbooks, examples are given of a plant where only one good is made, with a well-determined amount of capital and labour, and which is used as soon as it has been bought. Environment goods are quite different from that situation.

To start with, they are in general produced through a process of joint production. For instance, air pollution caused by cars is a by-product of transport, with its numerous quantitative and qualitative attributes. From another point of view, devices included in the motors of cars to reduce air pollution cannot be separated from the whole conception of motors, and the cost of those devices does not clearly appear.

Furthermore, many environmental goods (or 'bads') are produced through processes with large fixed costs. It is the case for car plants and also, for instance, the use of transport infrastructures, which is often recognized to include a large proportion of fixed costs. And it is well known that there is no undisputable method for distributing the total fixed cost among the different products.

When costs are difficult to calculate, economists often rely upon market prices, the idea being that in a competitive market, prices stick to costs. Unfortunately, environmental effects are, in general, non-marketable goods, i.e. there is no natural market where they can be bought and sold. For instance, there is no natural market for air cleaning or air pollution, nor for noise, nor for aesthetic improvements or deterioration of the landscape.

This situation is often expressed in more technical terms by saying that environmental effects are external effects, i.e. effects where the profit or usefulness of somebody is affected by the actions of somebody else without any payment being received by the person who suffers damage from the person who causes it.

Furthermore, environmental transport effects encompass a very large span of time. For instance, infrastructures stay in the landscape for decades, even centuries, and their environmental effects, especially in terms of their consequences on the landscape, last as long as those infrastructures.

From another point of view, carbon dioxide emissions produce a greenhouse effect, a warming of the atmosphere, the consequences of which will last for several generations.

One can easily conceive that it is especially difficult to valuate such consequences, because it is necessary both to estimate what will be their impact in the far future, and to guess what will be the changes in tastes and technologies.

Thus, there is another feature of environmental effects, and that is the uncertainty attached to them. Economic theory gives us tools to deal with uncertainty: the optimal decision is the one which maximizes mean expectation, given the value of the outcome, and the probabilities of the events. But this rule is especially difficult to apply when one knows neither the value of the outcomes nor the probabilities of the event!

THE SHIFT TOWARDS MULTICRITERIA ANALYSIS DIMINISHES THE IMPORTANCE OF VALUATION

Because of the difficulties in calculating costs, the need for valuating seems to decrease. In France, for instance, the influence of cost-benefit analysis has decreased since the 1960s, and decisions are more and more often taken on the basis of multicriteria analysis.

This trend appeared when it seemed necessary to take into account the consequences of transport infrastructure on regional development. It turned out that those consequences could not be introduced into traditional cost-benefit analysis, and merged with other direct consequences such as time and cost saving, so as to produce at the end a single index, such as rate of return, or net present value.

This tendency was strengthened after the oil crisis: it appeared that petrol had a value larger than its price from a collective viewpoint, and that the effect of each project on trade balance had to be taken into account. The effect of each project on unemployment had to be taken into consideration as well, for instance by reckoning the number of active people generated by it; but it was deemed impossible to reduce this effect to a common denominator with time or cost.

This tendency was reinforced by the growing concern towards environmental issues. And now, in France, all those effects (effects on regional development, employment, energy, environment) are taken into consideration through separate indexes which are not reduced to a single indicator.

This tendency has been supported by the stream of political changes towards decentralization, which have become stronger in France since 1960 and gave more and more power to local political leaders concerning technocracy and bureaucracy. To convince those political leaders and their electors, it was necessary to use simpler and more convincing methods which would be understood by everybody. However, sophisticated procedures of cost-benefit analysis do not fulfil those kinds of requirement.

Furthermore, decision-making is more collective, and the numerous decision-makers do not put exactly the same weight on objectives and have not exactly the same constraints. It makes a single index more difficult to operate.

Is it really Necessary to Valuate Environmental Impacts?

We face now two facts: it is difficult to valuate environment, and it does not seem to be useful, given the tendencies of decision-making procedures. Then, is it really necessary to valuate environmental impacts?

This question is debatable. Many people feel that such valuation is not necessary, but I believe that the answer is 'yes'. Why?

First, it is a question of economic analysis. This science aims to value costs and goods, in order to achieve the best possible utilization of scarce resources. In this respect, it is necessary to compare decisions and outcomes on a single scale, which by nature is a monetary one. Of course, different people may value the same item differently and the discrepancies arising must be taken into account.

If we try to look more closely into those general considerations, we realize that valuation is necessary in order to take proper decisions, and more precisely to achieve good trade-offs between multiple, and often contradictory, goals such as quality of service, safety, environment, regional development, etc.

We can find a first point of application in national accounting. National accounting is already a well-established branch of economics; it aims at putting in the same framework all the operations of an economic nature, and it allows comparisons between sectors or between nations. For that purpose, it has taken into consideration marketable goods and services and some non-marketable (or non-marketed) services such as education, justice, defence, evaluated at their cost of production.

The next step would be to introduce into national accounting external effects such as environmental effects and in fact, in many countries, there is a growing concern about patrimonial accounting, in which environment takes an important place. In the field of transport, for example, many authors have reckoned the importance of the environmental effect of transport activity as compared to the GNP.

Valuation of environment is also necessary for proper decisions regarding behaviour orientation. It is well known that in the presence of external effects, the natural equilibrium of economy does not lead to an optimum, because some goods (or 'bads') are not priced at their marginal cost. In general, they are free and this leads to an over consumption. For instance, car users do not pay for the noise they cause to the people living in the houses by the roadside. Therefore, they use the road more than they would if they had to pay for the noise they produced.

The same applies to air pollution, to damages to the landscape, to the greenhouse effect. This over-consumption of road transport leads to a misallocation of resources, the manifestation of which is a too large amount of traffic, a too great share of road transport *vis-à-vis* the other modes.

There are different ways to cope with this situation. One is regulation, and it is widely used. For instance, there is a very extensive regulatory body for car building (carbon dioxide emission limits, or noise), and for car use (speed limits in order to improve safety, etc.). But this way to restore the optimum is somehow blind, in that it could lead to local misallocations. For example, a single upper limit of noise transmission for new infrastructures, regardless of the local situation, can lead to a very costly project in one situation while, in another situation, it would have been very easy and uncostly to achieve a better goal. Besides, regulations lead to well known perverse effects.

Another way to restore the optimum and avoid these kinds of local misallocation is to price the environment, for instance to set up a tax based upon the emission level of noise: each user would pay for the cost caused to other people, i.e. to the collectivity as a whole.

Economic theory teaches that the cost to take into consideration is the marginal cost, that is the extra cost generated by an extra user to all other people from this collectivity. Of course, such a calculation is not an easy task, for the reasons already described in the first part of this chapter. But, in fact, these difficulties underlie any method for correcting the negative effects of non-marketable goods. In particular, there are underlying regulations, even if they are not visible. But, as we have already seen, regulation has some more drawbacks, especially in that it does not permit specific situations to be taken into account.

Valuation is also necessary for public decision-making pertaining to regulations – for instance how to determine the best threshold for pollution emission – or to investment choices. This point needs some more clarification: is it necessary to distinguish between choices inside a well-defined sector, and choices for investments belonging to different sectors?

In the first case – choices inside a well-defined sector, for instance choice for an anti-noise programme among different investments the essential characteristic of which is to abate noise – it is not necessary to have a valuation of noise in order to rank the projects. Cost-efficiency analysis is sufficient: it is possible to define, for each project, an index which is the ratio of the noise abatement allowed by the project to the cost of this project. The projects are then ranked according to this index, and the total budget is allocated by considering each in turn.

The situation is different when it is necessary to combine projects aimed at abating noise and projects aimed at saving time in the same budget. In that case, a comparison will be made between noise-abating and time-saving projects. This can be correctly done only through a valuation of time versus noise. And if the projects also have the property of saving money, which is quite frequent, it is necessary to convert time, noise, and money into the same unit, which will often be money (but it is not compulsory). Otherwise, errors in logic will certainly appear.

Of course, it is difficult to fix those values. It is quite possible that they are different from one decision-maker to another, but this point leads to making an important distinction between behavioural and normative values. When you ask somebody what he is ready to pay for noise abatement, you obtain a behavioural value, provided that the answer is sincere. But it is not certain that this value should be used in project appraisal. It is quite possible that political decision-makers may have another view of the collective will and may, therefore, choose a value different from the behavioural one, which will be called the normative value.

This discrepancy seems quite natural in matters such as alcohol or drugs where the health of people is at stake. The same situation may apply to environmental goods, for several reasons. First, decision-makers may wish to take into account distributional effects and, for instance, to favour the people living by the roads to the detriment of the car users, or to value differently the advantages brought to some groups of people in comparison with others.

Of course, those normative values can be different according to the kind of public power involved. Valuation by the mayor of a city, by the council of a county or a region, and by a minister of the state may be quite different from one another.

Nevertheless, this does not exclude valuation. It only makes it more difficult.

How to Valuate the Environmental Effects of Transport

In fact, this question has already been addressed earlier in this chapter. Specifically when the difference between cost and price was mentioned, and also when various definitions of cost were quoted. We wish now to try to answer the following questions:

- What are the different concepts to be measured?
- How can they be measured?

THE DIFFERENT CONCEPTS OF VALUE OF THE ENVIRONMENT

We shall first consider a fictive world, without uncertainty or problems of duration. In that world there are, nevertheless, some difficulties due to the fact that there are both prices and costs, and that there are different definitions of costs, mainly marginal and average costs. In addition, we should consider the total cost to the nation, i.e. what should be taken into consideration in a national accounting systems enlarged to encompass the environment. How do these concepts relate to each other?

Economic theory produces simple and precise results when the economic goods in question have the following characteristics:

- they are marketable, i.e. can be bought and sold on a market;
- they are for individual use, i.e. the use of goods by one person excludes their use by others;
- they do not generate external effects, i.e. the impact of their use concerns only those in possession of them;
- their production costs are constant (i.e. producing twice as much costs twice as much), or decreasing;
- lastly, they do not involve the State as an economic agent.

Under these conditions, economic theory yields remarkable results which can be expressed in ordinary terms[1] as follows: the marginal cost (cost of one additional unit produced) is equal to the average cost (total production cost divided by the number of units produced) and also to the opportunity cost (optimum alternative use of the resources used to manufacture the article in question); this cost is also a measure of consumers' marginal propensity to consume (the willingness to pay is greater for the first units consumed and the consumer's need gradually diminishes), and thus also a measure of the value of the article for the consumer and the value for the community (the collective well-being and collective utility are increased by the cost of the article if one additional unit is made available).

Furthermore, with these conditions market forces lead to equilibrium at the optimum point (the satisfaction of one individual cannot be increased without diminishing that of another individual) at which market prices are equal to costs.

Under these conditions, total expenditure (or more precisely value added) incurred by individuals performing a given activity, and which represents the GDP share of that sector, can be called the 'social cost' of the activity in question. This is also the sum of the marginal values of the activity for consumers. The social cost of the activity is the sum of those private costs, and gives a measure of the share of the sector in the national accounts.

But, as far as the environmental effects on transport are concerned, these appealing results no longer hold. The values to be taken into account for national accounting, for pricing, and for investment choice may not be the same, and many difficulties appear in trying to define them.

Let us take a look at this field and firstly, in the case of the national accounting problem, we can try to mark the effects of environment on present national accounts. To that end, we must draw the consequences of transport activities which can be summarized by looking at them from the standpoints of the main groups involved, having regard to the nature of the goods in question:

(*a*)   *Government* is in general concerned with infrastructure management, an activity for which costs tend to fall. It is similar to the provision of a public good, use of which cannot, or can only indirectly be tied to payment of some fee (for example, ordinary roads). It is also concerned with the taxes it levies or the subsidies it provides for transport.[2] Lastly, it is concerned with safety in seeking to preserve the lives and health of its citizens.

(*b*)   Private or public *transport producers* provide the transport service (operation of public transport), incur production expenditure, generally at constant costs, and receive user payments and subsidies from the government, to which they pay taxes.

(*c*)   *Users* spend money (fuel, public transport tickets, private vehicle maintenance) and consume the non-market goods of time and safety. They impose external effects on each other (inconvenience and extra expenditure in terms of time, fuel, anxiety, etc.) and on non-users (noise, air pollution, etc.). They derive profit (in the case of business) or satisfaction (in the case of private users) from the use of transport.

(*d*)   *Non-users* suffer from air pollution, noise and the visual consequences (usually negative, though they may be positive) of transport (effects which can be felt by users, too). Both the level and the nature of general economic activity is affected by transport. All these consequences (some of which, such as air pollution, affect public goods) are external effects.

All this shows that the impact of transport as a whole goes well beyond the users themselves, and that in this sector marginal costs, average costs, prices (where they exist) and marginal willingness to pay can become disconnected.

Thus, as regards noise, account must be taken not only of expenditure by government to reduce infrastructure noise (under (*a*) above) and by operating firms and private motorists to make vehicles less noisy (under (*b*) and (*c*) above), but also of local inhabitants' expenditure to soundproof their dwellings and remedy the effects of noise on their health, as well as the productivity losses which they may suffer (under (*d*)). Even if all these costs are included in national accounts, they will not be identified for what they are (medical care due to noise is not identified in hospital accounts).

Another direction would be to try to quantify the notion of social cost on a nation wide basis. It has been studied in Quinet (1990), who gives two possible definitions of it:

- a narrow definition representing the actual remedial expenditure recorded in the national accounts;
- a broad definition, which adds to the narrow one the value of unsatisfied demand for abatement of damage, in other words the sum of the willingness to pay to be rid of damages by those who suffer from those damages.

But those notions relate to flow effects. Another definition must be used for stock accounting of natural resources, in order to include it in a national patrimonial accounting system. We must then turn to the total economic value (see Pearce and Markandya, 1989 or Lichfield, 1988) which includes:

- option value: the probability that the non-user, direct or indirect, will wish to make use of the environment at a later date;
- bequest value: willingness to pay to preserve the environment for the benefit of descendants;
- existence value: willingness to pay to ensure that the value will exist, even if no actual, intended future use is in mind.

If we now turn to the pricing, there is a special difficulty because marginal willingness to pay is not equal to marginal social cost. Firstly, marginal social cost must include consequences which are not perceived by the user, either because they occur to him but he does not realize (he is not aware of the illness which will be caused by air pollution), or because they occur to somebody else.

A second reason for discrepancy between marginal willingness to pay and marginal social cost, which is of special importance in the choice of investments, is due to the limits to and the indivisibility of certain kinds of production, and of the intermediary character of transport. Thus if a new and more rapid means of collective transport is introduced, for which a higher price has to be paid, this price increase will in general be less than the value of the time saved by each user, who would have been prepared to pay more for the time saving offered.[3] The price paid and the propensity to pay are not equal, as they would be in the base model. The user would be prepared to pay for a greater time saving (up to a point at which the price paid and the marginal willingness to pay for the time saved are equal), but he cannot because no faster means of transport exists, and he will not make additional journeys (which would be another means of making price paid equal to the marginal value of time) if the travel in question is, for example, the journey from home to work.

The prices charged do not therefore give direct information on users' marginal willingness to pay; to find this out, assumptions must be made about user behaviour and preferences; this is the purpose of traffic models to place a value on time, which then becomes a parameter in a model, the estimation of which is subject to the usual statistical inaccuracies.

One more comment about these subjects, related to the willingness to pay: in fact, this notion is not as easy to deal with as it may appear. Economic theory makes a distinction between two definitions: the willingness to pay and the willingness to accept. Willingness to pay is the amount of money users are ready to pay in order to be as well off with the environmental goods, the valuation of which is in question, as they are now without them. Conversely, willingness to accept is the amount users wish to receive in order to be as well off without the environmental goods as they would be with them.

Economic theory shows that those two measures are different and that they are the more different the larger the valuation is. It can also be shown that the difference is not very large in usual situations.

We shall now look at two complications: uncertainty and introduction of duration. Uncertainty is all around us, but from an economic point of view, it appears either in the attitudes and utility functions of users, or in the production processes. Of course, it is more important for goods for which consumption is of longer duration, a situation which happens principally in capital goods and, as far as environment is concerned, in natural capital.

It can be shown (see Pearce and Markandya, 1989) that the introduction of uncertainty leads to a valuation of the goods which is different from the willingness to pay of the consumer. The difference is the option value, and is for the most part positive. That means that, in general, uncertainty increases the value of goods (that is always true for technological uncertainty; in presence of uncertainty upon utility functions, the sign of option value can be either positive or negative).

Another difficulty for the valuation of capital goods related to environment is the fact they last through a long span of time. We should think, for instance, about the duration of a landscape, or about the fact that the warming of the atmosphere through the greenhouse effect cannot be erased until many decades have elapsed. Thus, to valuate natural goods, it is necessary to use discount rates, and it is well known that their determination is controversial.

PROBLEMS OF MEASUREMENT

This section will be rather brief because a remarkable survey has been done on the subject by Pearce and Markandya (1989).

Roughly speaking, there are four categories of methods used for setting up the value of environmental goods: hedonist price, cost of trip, stated performance, and dose-response method.

(*a*) *Hedonic prices*. This method is applicable for non-marketable goods when it is possible to find a substitute market. If we take, for instance, the case of noise, it is clear that the degree of exposure to noise is an important component in the price of houses or flats. Between two houses equivalent in all respects, except for their exposure to noise, the cheaper one will be the house which receives the larger amount of noise, and from the price difference, it is possible to get a valuation of noise. For instance, if the difference in their rent is £1,000 a year, and if the cheaper house receives 10dB more than the other, it can be deduced that 1 dB per year is worth £100. Of course, things are much more complicated. The price of a flat depends on many parameters, such as noise, air pollution, etc. It depends also on the characteristics of the household, for instance size, income, and attitude about noise.

Difficulties of estimation are large. Bias can come from the omission of variables, or from a mis-specification of function. The sensibility to such errors is high, especially because the value in question is the partial derivative of the price relative to noise quantification. Nevertheless, this method is widely used and has been very useful especially to calculate the value of noise.

(*b*) *Cost of trip*. This method, akin to hedonist prices, has been used for the value of leisure resorts. The idea is the following: people going to a leisure resort, such as a forest, a beauty spot, or a swimming pool, achieve a trade-off between the satisfaction they get from using the leisure resort and the cost of the travel (this cost includes monetary and time costs). Of course, this trade-off depends on many variables such as attitudes, family size, income, etc. Besides, this trade-off has two components: the number of visits and the length of each one.

So, the determination by this method is even harder than the determination through hedonist prices. Nevertheless, as Pearce and Markandya quote, it has been used in many situations, and leads to values not too far from those given by other methods.

(*c*) *Stated preferences*. This method consists of asking people what they should be willing to pay in order to get the environmental goods in question. It encompasses several difficulties. A first one is technical; how to ask questions in order to get sincere answers. Another one comes from the fact that the question can be asked in two ways: 'How much would you pay in order to get the goods?' or 'How much would you be willing to accept in order to get rid of the goods?' These two ways correspond to the willingness to pay and the willingness to accept.

These two methods should, in general, lead to very close figures, except for very large items. But, in fact, figures given by inquiries conducted through these two methods are quite different, often in proportions of 1 to 3. Scholars say that this discrepancy is due to a psychological bias in that people give a higher value to a loss than to a gain. But this point makes the method very uncertain.

(*d*)   *Dose-response method.* The three previous methods lead to a willingness to pay, i.e. the personal valuation of users. But, very often, users do not perceive all the consequences of environmental goods (or 'bads'). For instance, air-pollution is often viewed by the users as leading to a bad smell. Yet, it may be dangerous to the health and lead to health-related expenses, loss of income and so on.

The dose-response method tries to encompass all those consequences. Its principle is to take into account all consequences of a certain amount of the environmental goods. The first step is to quantify them in physical units – for instance, the number of dead or injured people. The second step is to put a value on each of the items surveyed. This second step causes no problem for marketable goods: the value is the market price. But there is a problem for non-marketable goods (or 'bads'), such as illness or death.

As for the results, this method leads to collective and not behavioural valuations. Furthermore, its results may make no sense if the amount of environmental goods is too high and does not correspond to a current achievement. It would be like valuing a type of car by calculating the cost for an amount of production very different from the actual amount; the value found by this method would be too high or too low, due to the non-constant return-to-scale of this industry.

Conclusion

In conclusion, it is possible to set up the landscape of issues for research, while stressing the most important unresolved problems.

1.   The fundamental problem is to identify where valuation is possible and where alternatives must be used. For the economist, valuation is the ultimate goal. But, realistically, it is not yet possible to value all the items. Some will probably never be valuable, and others give way to a very uncertain valuation. So, it is important to know in what fields valuation is overcome by other ways, in order to achieve the same goals. For instance, valuation is in balance with multi-criteria analysis for project appraisal and, furthermore, it is in balance with regulation for consumer's orientation.

2. In the fields where valuation is thought to be the best way, it is necessary to determine what kind of valuation is necessary. For instance, in price fixing, what kind of price is to be applied and, in particular, how are fixed costs, which are often very important in environment matters to be covered? Or how may a market of rights be set up; what kind of organization is required to achieve that objective?

3. If we come now to the valuation methods, the most striking fact is the gap between the willingness to pay and the willingness to accept. There is an urgent need for analysis of this gap. The reasons why this is so important, and how to deal with it are: what is the best valuation, the willingness to pay, the willingness to accept, or some other value?

4. As for dose-response methods, one important fact is that they are not linked with behavioural values such as the willingness to pay, another one is that they are in some cases unrealistic. Research is urged on these two points.

For the first one, studies should determine the part of consequences taken into account by behavioural enquiries, and more generally they should explain the relationship between the two types of results. What are people aware of? What kind of information could increase this awareness?

5. The methods of hedonic-price type are well used and give good results. Nevertheless, it would be interesting to explore the bias incurred by these methods when variables are omitted, or the function is mis-specified, or when the substitute market is at risk, for instance for evaluation of real values through the price people are ready to be paid for risky activities.

6. As for applications, the best known are noise and safety. But there is still a large uncertainty on the values of landscapes, beauty resorts, for which the unique valuation methods are of the stated-preference type, and also for air pollution, as is shown by the very different estimates from one country to another. Research would be very useful in these fields.

7. The difficulty of valuation of air pollution is akin to our sparse knowledge of non-local and long-lasting effects, such as acid rain, or greenhouse effects.

These problems constitute a compendium of almost all difficulties of valuation: duration, uncertainty, imperfect knowledge of technical processes, international – or even global – aspects. Yet, they seem to be very important and presumably represent a major part of environmental costs. It makes research in their field both important and difficult.

NOTES

1. The strict mathematical expression of these properties and the assumptions they imply can be found in works on microeconomic theory such as that by Laffont (1985).
2. This analysis does not take macroeconomic effects into account (for example, effects on employment or the balance of payments), which might induce governments to treat certain activities differently from users' marginal willingness to pay.
3. This is due to the fact that tariffs cannot – or only roughly – be adapted to each individual. Hence, they do not match the total users' surplus.

REFERENCES

Ahmad, Y. J., El Serafy, S. and Lutz, E. (eds.) (1989) *Environmental Accounting for Sustainable Development*. Washington DC: The World Bank.

Barde, J. P. and Button, K. (eds.) (1990) *Transport Policy and the Environment*. London: Earthscan Publications.

Kanafani, A. (1983) *The Social Cost of Road Transport*. Paris: OECD.

Laffont, J. J. (1985) *Théorie micro-économique*. Paris: Economica.

Lichfield, N., (1988) *Economics in Urban Conservation*. Cambridge: Cambridge University Press.

Pearce, D. W. (1971) *Cost Benefit Analysis*, London: Macmillan.

Pearce, D. W. and Markandya, A. (1989) *Environmental Policy Benefits: Monetary Valuation*, Paris: OECD.

Quinet, E. (1990) *The Social Cost of Land Transport*, Paris: OECD.

14

Problems of Valuation Discussed

NATHANIEL LICHFIELD

Emile Quinet has structured his chapter most usefully for discussion, since it raises and answers a succession of interrelated questions, to which I can respond.

He first asks: compared with the boldness of previous decades, transport economists are now very timid in valuing environmental impacts although these are of growing importance to the public. Why is this so?'

Any such timidity is certainly strange in one respect. It comes at a time when the methods and techniques of environmental valuation have exploded with the increasing attention to necessities of coping with environmental problems (Pearce, *et al.*, 1989). The timidity is necessarily linked with the difficulty of estimation, which is Quinet's first reason (see p. 192). But there are also doubts as to both desirability or necessity.

As to desirability, there are two main kinds of obstacle (Barde and Pearce, 1991):

1. Ethical and philosophical, proceeding from a conventional criticism of the welfare foundations of cost benefit analysis: natural resources, human life and health are not economic assets and cannot be valued in economic terms, particularly one which fails to take distributive implications into consideration;

2. Political: cost benefit with its valuations introduces specifics into the political debate, where the decision-making structures may be ill-adapted to the process.

In Quinet's view (p. 193) the difficulties in applying calculation to contemporary problems (ramifications of the oil crisis, the environment, regional development, employment, energy) have, in France for example, led to a withdrawal since the 1960s from cost-benefit analysis (CBA). These problems cannot be illuminated by the single index (such as rate of return or net present value) but need the introduction of a wider range of criteria. The alternative method has been found in multicriteria analysis

(MCA) which provides, in the decentralization of decision making since 1960, 'simpler and more convincing methods which would be understood by everybody'.

While it is true that there has been disenchantment with cost-benefit analysis in Britain since the 1970s, we have not seen the same growth in reliance on multicriteria analysis, as has also been experienced in, for example, the Netherlands and Italy. While MCA is a powerful tool for many problems, and can supplement CBA, I myself think that we should not pursue that path as a substitute for cost-benefit analysis, as also does Quinet. Following are some reasons based upon my amiable disputation over recent years with protagonists of multicriteria analysis in the field of urban and regional planning (Lichfield, 1988a; Nijkamp, et al., 1990).

Advocates of multicriteria analysis often seem to start with a simplistic rejection of cost-benefit analysis because of its tendency, noted by Quinet, to aim at a single index expressing the conclusion from calculations in monetary terms. In my view the criticism is valid; indeed, while urging the cost-benefit approach in urban and regional planning as far back as the early 1960s, I showed that it needed to be adapted for the purpose, because of its shortcomings in this regard, as well as others (Lichfield, 1960; 1964). But what seems to have been ignored by MCA protagonists is the fact that adaptations of CBA have been sought over the years, so that continuing to attack the 'traditional cost-benefit analysis' is creating something of an Aunt Sally. For example, in my own work I have adapted the traditional approach into 'planning balance sheet'/'community impact analysis' (Lichfield, 1988b), which I have applied to the widening issues just noted, to such effect that it has been honoured by my disputants into its elevation to a *form* of 'multicriteria analysis'.

My objection, however, is not that 'what you can do we can do better' (which I believe), but rather on the weaknesses of MCA itself in what it purports to provide. Following are some reasons, necessarily simplified within the scope of these comments.

1. MCA seems to ignore the reality that any good or service can be analysed from both the supply and demand side. It concentrates on the supply side where each good or service comprises a complex bundle of attributes which can be objectively analysed and measured by scaling, etc. (Nijkamp, 1987).

2. Within the price that is paid for the bundle, any of the bidders would value each of the attributes differently.

3. Accordingly on the demand side it is necessary to know how the individual bidders who make up the market would value each of the attributes, within the market price and any consumer surplus.

4.   When, however, there is no market price (a common situation in the issues with which we are here concerned) there needs to be introduced surrogate valuation methods (see pp. 196–202).

But while the cost-benefit approach recognizes this necessity for valuation of demand, for all the reasons given on p. 194–196, MCA does not. Rather, it concentrates on the supply side, with considerable virtuosity in mathematical analysis, enriching the quantification and ranking of the attributes. This then somehow becomes the *value*. Furthermore, since the underlying mathematical analysis is far from simple, MCA tends to reduce it to a mathematically drawn 'single index'. But whereas the 'single index' in cost-benefit analysis can be interpreted as having some meaning in relation to the chosen use of scarce resources, the index of the multicriteria analysis only explains what the method of analysis puts into the model. Its meaning is typically far from clear (Lichfield, 1990). And it is probably this simplicity of the mathematically derived index, based on a welter of complex attributes, that leads Quinet to suggest that MCA offers 'more convincing methods which would be understood by everybody' (p. 193).

If this perhaps outrageous simplification of the literature on MCA be accepted (and I am offering it for discussion) then clearly while MCA has a powerful contribution to make to the analysis of our problems, it is not 'substitute for wool', where wool is the necessity for introducing the demand and value side into the question.

Necessity for valuation is raised in Quinet's next question: 'Is it really necessary to value environmental impacts? (p. 194). But while I accept the first premise of his opening paragraph, that 'it is difficult to valuate the environment', it is apparent that I do not accept the second, 'it does not seem to be useful given the tendencies of decision-making procedures'. Quinet argues for necessity in general terms but rightly points out that there can be exceptions. He gives an example. Where the decision has already been made to invest, the worthwhileness of the investment is not in question. Then valuation is not needed to lead to choice. With a given cost, cost efficiency/effectiveness requires that the benefits from the project only be *measured* (using for example MCA techniques) in order to provide a ranking. And even where the costs are variable, the rankings can be achieved by using points as surrogate for benefit.

Quinet then presents reasons for pricing externalities to reduce pollution in a form which is acceptable to those in economics who favour the cost benefit approach. But while agreeing, I would like to add some comment to open up the controversy.

Regulation or Pricing

1. Regulation as a means of coping with environmental pollution: he must be right in saying that regulations which are designed to apply generally cannot discriminate between all situations and are therefore 'somehow blind'. But to suggest that the aim of the regulation is to 'restore the optimum' is asking too much. It clearly takes a broad brush to ensure by dictat that certain levels of pollution are internalized on the polluter. But such regulation raises the need to compare the costs it imposes upon the industrialist, motor-car user, etc., with the benefits to the community. In this regard more use might be made of the approach introduced in the halcyon days of deregulation in Britain in the early 1980s, where every new regulation affecting *business* was to be well tested beforehand by means of exploration of its impacts, and an assessment of their costs and benefits following the regulation compared with before (Department of Trade and Industry, 1985).

2. Taxation to make the polluter pay: this must be just as blind as regulation, because of the very difficulties of setting the level of tax to achieve the desired result (Pearce, *et al.*, 1989). But it has a weakness compared with regulation in possibly not avoiding the pollution. If the affected industry/activity is inelastic in its capacity to bear the tax, then there could be an increase in price (which would eventually find its way to the consumer) without achieving the benefit of diminishing the pollution.

Of the two, regulation seemed to be the more attractive in that while costs would also be passed on to the consumer the benefit could be clearly identified.

Behavioural or Normative Values

This distinction between the behavioural value to the individual in terms of willingness to pay, and the normative value of the political decision-maker who 'might have another view of the collective will', is certainly a useful one; any individual could make the same distinction. But I do not see the normative value being used within project appraisal as a substitute for the behavioural, for the following reasons.

The methods of valuation which are referred to by Quinet (p. 196–202) are largely based on estimating the behavioural value, which is then aggregated (in the theory of welfare economics) to represent the collective value. That is the starting point. But an individual is unlikely to take account of externalities. In Quinet's alcohol or drugs example, consumer sovereignty and ultra-liberalism would argue in favour of the individual being allowed to indulge should he so wish. The objection arises in terms of the implications for society (driving when drunk adds to accidents and all the losses that flow: disruption of the individual's life and productivity, public costs of hospitalization, etc); the drug habit leads to the waste of lives, premature deaths, criminal tendencies to secure the money for purchases, etc. There therefore arises *following* aggregation in the project appraisal, the need for the decision-makers to make a 'social choice'. It is here that decision-makers, in my view, are justified in departing from the assumptions of welfare economics, that the aggregation of individual value equals collective value, and impose their own normative value in the social choice, on behalf of the society which they have been elected to govern.

Then there is the other situation referred to: 'Decision-makers may wish to take into account distributional effects'. But if the decision-makers wish to do so they are at a disadvantage with the traditional cost-benefit analysis which does not aim to show how the impacts are distributed among sectors. If so, how can they 'favour the people living by the roads to the detriment of the car users' unless they are provided with the kind of breakdown into sectors which is a feature of the Department of Transport Framework Appraisal for the environmental impact of roads.

Indeed, so important is this in the desired adaptation of cost-benefit analysis that it is an essential feature of community impact analysis, which has as its *central focus* the exploration of the impacts and their costs and benefits on *all* sectors of the community who are impacted. This then makes possible decisions on equity and social justice as well as efficiency. In this process to be sure one man's benefit is another man's cost (the costs to airline operators by a prohibition on night flights over built-up areas against the benefits to residents who can have a peaceful night). This very distribution raises problems for traditional cost-benefit analysis since, on the principle of welfare economics, the losses and gains should be aggregated to arrive at net benefit to the economy as a whole. Otherwise there could be double-counting. In community impact analysis this double-counting is accepted and referred to as 'double-entry' in the book-keeping sense (the cost to a customer of purchasing is the benefit to the shopkeeper in turnover) for the purpose of exploring conclusions on equity as opposed to efficiency.

Having made the case for valuation Quinet closes with theory on the concepts of value of the environment (pp. 196–199) and then a brief survey relying on the literature on measurement methods (p. 199–202). Except for his own theories (Quinet, 1990) the ground is well-trodden in Britain and is of less interest for discussion than the philosophical questions in the early part of the chapter. But one comment is called for in conclusion.

Whereas in economics generally it is the 'use value' of different kinds which is the focus of the valuation, in the valuation of irreplaceable environment other concepts have arisen. In development which destroys the environment not only are the values relating to these uses displaced but also three other dimensions which comprise the total economic value (TEV) of the environment which is threatened, namely willingness to pay for (Pearce *et al.*, 1990):

– option value: the probability that the non-user, direct or indirect, will wish to make use of the environment at a later date;
– bequest value: to preserve the environment for the benefit of descendants;
– existence value: to ensure that the value will exist, even if no actual, intended future use is in mind.

In all these, willingness to pay (and willingness to receive) are the criteria. It is here that the limits of credibility in valuation would appear to be reached. The questions posed are so far removed from the experience of those being called upon to make the valuation that doubt must exist on the reliability of the conclusions (Howe, 1991). The debate rages. And here I would like to close with one simple suggestion for discussion.

The least non-credible part of the valuation exercise is to ask what in fact individuals or families *have spent* on particular goods and services over a period, recorded in a diary. They might then be asked the question: what *would you* have been willing to give up in respect of these historical purchases in assessing the value to yourself of option, bequest or existence values? They are then trading off actual opportunities they have enjoyed. The answers could be given more credibility than the hypothetical.

REFERENCES

Barde, J. P. and Pearce, D. W. (1991) *Valuing the Environment: Six Case Studies.* London: Earthscan Publications.

Department of Trade and Industry (1985) *Burdens on Business: Report of a scrutiny of administrative and legislative requirements.* London: HMSO.

Howe, C. (1991) Frontiers in the Valuation of Non-market Amenities: Progress and Remaining Problems. Proceedings of International Conference in honour of Carlo Forte: Assessment Studies and Environmental Economics: New Frontiers in Evaluation. University of Naples.

Lichfield, N. (1960) Cost benefit analysis in city planning. *Journal of the American Institute of Planners*, Vol. 26, No. 4, pp. 273–279.

Lichfield, N. (1964), Cost benefit analysis in plan evaluation. *Town Planning Review*, Vol. 35, No. 2, pp. 160–169.

Lichfield, N. (1988*a*), Cost benefit approach in plan evaluation, in Barbanente, A. (ed.) *Metodi di Valuazione nella Pianificazioni urbana e territoriale: Teno e cosi di Studio.* Bari: Instituto per la residenzia e le infrastutture Sociali.

Lichfield, N. (1988*b*) *Economics in Urban Conservation.* Cambridge: Cambridge University Press, Part IV.

Lichfield, N. (1990) Plan evaluation methodology: comprehending the conclusion, in Shefer, D. and Voogd, H. (eds.) *Evaluation Methods for Urban and Regional Plans*. London: Pion.

Nijkamp, P. (1987) Culture and Region: A Multidimensional Evaluation of Monuments. Proceedings of the 27th European Conference of the Regional Science Association.

Nijkamp, P., Rietveld, P. and Voogd, H. (1990) *Multiple Criteria Analysis in Physical Planning*. Amsterdam: North Holland.

Pearce, D. W., Markandya, A. and Barbier, E. B. (1989) *Blueprint for a Green Economy*. London: Earthscan Publications.

Quinet, E. (1990) *The Social Cost of Land Transport*. Paris: OECD.

15

Environmental Quality and Value for Money in British Roads Policy

DEREK WOOD

Behind the building or improvement of a trunk road in Britain there lies a lengthy and procedurally complex process of decision-making. All the main decisions are made by politicians – government ministers – rather than administrators or transport specialists. At crucial stages in the process the issues which have to be decided are subjected to wide consultation and, in most cases, a formal Public Inquiry. At the end, the decision which is made is an act of political judgement; all relevant factors have to be weighed up and a balance struck between competing priorities.

The factors taken into account comprise, in particular, two broad groups which, under current practice, are loosely called 'economic' and 'environmental' and are often seen in opposition to each other. Thus, some schemes are promoted for the 'economic' benefits which they will confer upon the community, measured in terms of greater transport efficiency, perhaps at the cost of 'environmental' damage; others are promoted for local 'environmental' gains. A good example of the latter is a village by-pass which may, in some cases, have a minus 'economic' value. Formal procedures exist for the appraisal of these different types of effect, and for their presentation to the public and those who have to make decisions about them.

In September 1989 the Standing Advisory Committee on Trunk Road Assessment (SACTRA) was asked by the government to review the methods which it currently employs for assessing the environmental costs and benefits which flow from the building of trunk roads; and to re-examine the interrelationship of the so-called economic and environmental groups of effects which plays such a dominant role in the decision-making process. The results of that review were presented to the Secretary of State in November 1991, and our Report, and the government's Response, were published in March 1992 (Department of Transport, 1992). This chapter is an attempt to summarize our main findings and the government's reactions to them. The SACTRA Report ranges over a wide field. We looked at the existing practice which leads to a decision to build a road; the manner in which economic and environmental factors are currently evaluated, as part of the process; made detailed observations on that practice; and explored in some detail the question whether the link between cost effectiveness and environmental quality can be strengthened.

The subject was an unruly one in at least two respects. First, the environmental impacts of transport planning, road building and the use of motor vehicles are multi-faceted. They are difficult to capture and quantify, and cannot be reduced into one simple system of measurement. They range from global and national concerns about the warming of the atmosphere, the exhaustion of non-renewable resources such as fossil fuels or building materials, and the long-term effects of land take, through to local concerns such as noise levels, and community severance. Somewhere along that spectrum are effects upon landscape, heritage, water quality and animal and plant species. Some effects are perceived by individuals or the community; others are inexorable but invisible. Some are short term; others operate over a large timescale. Moreover, however carefully one classifies different effects, their importance can alter from case to case.

Secondly, the processes by which road proposals emerge and are brought to fruition are lengthy, and the imposition of a uniform method of appraisal at every stage in the process is likely to result in very important environmental considerations being overlooked.

How Roads Get Built

It is convenient to start by describing briefly how, in Britain, trunk road schemes become incorporated into the national roads programme, are evaluated, subjected to public consultation and inquiry and approved by Ministers. The detail is set out in Part II and Annex 3 of the Report. There is no single source from which road proposals emanate. They may be inspired by national transportation policy, but are at least as likely to result from local initiatives – Members of Parliament, local interest groups the local authority, or the regional offices of the Departments of the Environment and Transport responding to local needs and problems. In the latter type of case traffic congestion, the effect of heavy lorries on residential areas, road safety and various forms of pollution play leading parts.

When a need or problem is formally recognized by the Departments' regional office, it will be subjected to initial appraisal at that level. If the proposal involves a major route or corridor, a Route Identification Study will be carried out. This study will take broad environmental considerations into account, particularly questions of the effect of the line of the road on landscape and its effect upon national environmental policies, such as the undertaking given by the government to avoid so far as possible the construction or upgrading of a trunk road in a National Park. At this early stage a landscape architect, who may be an official or an independent consultant, is likely to be consulted. Once a route has been identified it will be split up into individual schemes for further study.

Scheme Investigation Studies result either from a Route Identification Study or from less extensive proposals limited to the solution of local problems. Those too are carried out regionally. Such a study will analyse the problems which have been identified and describe the options available for solving them, including the possibility that the existing network should remain substantially unaltered (the 'do-nothing' or 'do-minimum' option). Scheme Identification Studies will contain an initial economic assessment and some environmental assessment on matters such as the effects of the proposal upon landscape, heritage sites and its likely visual impact. The relationship of the scheme to local planning policies will also be explored. A Scheme Identification Study is more likely to identify areas for further study than produce any detailed data of its own.

When the regional office is satisfied that a case for the new route or scheme has been made out in principle it is submitted to the headquarters of the Department of Transport for consideration by Ministers for entry into the Roads Programme. For the purpose of decision-making at this stage only broad-brush economic and environmental assessments are available, and if the proposal is entered into the Roads Programme, further studies must be carried out before a firm intention to build can be made. Announcements of schemes which have reached this level of approval are made about every two years.

Schemes in the Roads Programme are given their place in an order of priorities. They are then in their due sequence more fully examined. Detailed analysis and modelling is carried out, including traffic surveys and economic and environmental assessment; and a report is obtained from the Landscape Advisory Committee, an independent body whose function is to advise on the visual effects upon the landscape of different options. When sufficient data have been assembled on the various options, including 'do-nothing' and 'do-minimum', they will be exposed to local public consultation by means of exhibitions and other forms of presentation. In the light of the results of the consultation, and the other data by now available, the Secretary of State for Transport selects the preferred route or scheme and in virtually every case it is submitted to a Public Inquiry. The Inquiry is conducted by an Inspector, appointed jointly by the Secretaries of State for the Environment and Transport from a panel drawn up by the Lord Chancellor. The proceedings at the Inquiry are quasi-judicial and follow the adversarial form of legal proceedings. The

Inspector submits a Report to the two Secretaries of State, together with his recommendations, for their decision. They may accept the preferred scheme, with or without modification, or reject it in its entirety. The final decision is subject to some legal controls. It can be overturned by the courts if there has been unfairness or procedural irregularity in the process, or if the decision-maker has ignored relevant factors or been influenced by extraneous ones.

Traffic Forecasting

All effects of schemes are evaluated against traffic forecasts, carried out in accordance with the technical guidelines contained in the Department of Transport's Traffic Appraisal Manual (TAM). The traffic using the existing network is analysed according to its quantity and type, and the origins and destinations of all trips. Forecasts are then made of the growth in that traffic, based upon the National Road Traffic Forecast. Forecasts are made on the basis of high growth (high economic growth and low fuel prices) and low growth (low economic growth and high fuel prices). A picture is thus obtained of the volume and type of traffic which might be found in the future on the existing network (that is, if the 'do-nothing' or 'do-minimum' option were followed). That same traffic is then, for the purposes of comparison, assigned to the proposed new network, on the bases, once again, of high and low growth. As is well known, some controversy surrounds this stage in the process, because the re-assignment model operates on a fixed-trip matrix. No assumptions are made either (1) that the number of trips made between existing origins and destinations will be increased or (2) that new trips will be generated between origins and destinations previously regarded by drivers as impractical. As a matter of common sense this approach is surprising because most new networks make driving more attractive and destinations more accessible from many other places. Actual experience of the use of some trunk roads, after construction, has demonstrated how difficult it is, if one bases forecasting upon a fixed-trip matrix, to present a reliable picture of the future effects of a proposed scheme. The cure is not, however, easy to find; and SACTRA is currently looking into the possibility of amending forecasting methods so that the prospect of induced or generated traffic can be properly taken into account in the appraisal of future schemes.

Cost-Benefit Analysis

From the 1960s onwards schemes have been subjected to a form of cost-benefit analysis, now embodied in a computer program known as COBA. The edition currently in use is COBA 9. Its aim is to quantify the economic costs and benefits of different scheme options, and compare them with the economic costs and benefits of the 'do-nothing' or 'do-minimum' options, using quantities based on high and low growth traffic forecasts. The variables which are taken into account are the following:

(a) TRAVELLING TIME

Calculations are made of journey times between links and of delays at certain junctions for all options. Figures are then derived for the time required for travelling between the same origins and destinations on the different networks. Monetary values are given both to time spent on travel in the course of work ('working time') and time spent on all other travel, including commuting to and from work ('non-working time'). The data for the proportion of trips which are 'working' and 'non-working', and the number of occupants in each vehicle for each type of trip are based on traffic surveys. The results are summed, taking both the high growth and low growth traffic forecasts, and a monetary comparison is drawn between the costs of travel on any proposed new road and those incurred on the existing network. The values for *working time* are based upon average wage rates and earnings surveys. In effect, therefore, these monetary differences are the extra costs incurred or the savings made by employers as between one road system and another. The values attributed to *non-working time* are based upon views and preferences stated by people in surveys and interviews, and currently stand at about one quarter of those for working time.

(b) VALUATION OF ACCIDENTS

The likely incidence of road casualties, both fatal and non-fatal, is calculated for all scheme options, and the results given a monetary value. The value given to *fatal accidents* is again based upon the amount people in interviews have stated they would be willing to pay to reduce the risk of a fatal accident. To that amount are added other resource costs, such as medical costs and damage to vehicles. *Non-fatal accidents* are valued by reference to the contribution which the victim would have made to the economy but for the injury, and an allowance for pain, grief and suffering. The unit of comparison is that of personal injury accidents per million vehicle kilometres, account being taken of the type of road, its length and the daily average traffic flow, the number and types of junctions and the number of links.

(*c*) VEHICLE OPERATING COSTS

The cost of fuel, oil, tyres, vehicle maintenance and vehicle depreciation are calculated for the different schemes. In broad terms, those costs are a function of distance and speed of travel.

(*d*) CAPITAL EXPENDITURE

The costs described in (*a*), (*b*) and (*c*) above are mostly costs incurred by users – travellers (including accident victims), their employers, vehicle owners. In addition, public expenditure is incurred in (*i*) building a new trunk road or improving an existing one; (*ii*) carrying out associated works on other utilities, such as the railway system, or drainage or other services; (*iii*) acquiring the necessary land and paying statutory compensation to other persons affected by the scheme who are entitled to it; (*iv*) promoting the scheme. All these costs are measured in the prices of a given year, the 'Present Value Year'.

(*e*) COST OF MAINTENANCE

Finally, future expenditure on repairing, maintaining, resurfacing and lighting the various schemes which are being compared is estimated.

Items *(a)*, *(b)*, *(c)* and *(e)* above are all recurrent costs. The annual cost of these items is calculated over a thirty-year period and discounted to the Present Value Year. Currently, the rate of discount is '8 per cent real'. These costs are then expressed in the end as a single, capital sum both for all options under review and for 'do-nothing' and 'do-minimum'. Any savings in the recurrent costs (capitalized) of a proposed scheme, compared with do-nothing or 'do-minimum', are then set off against the actual capital cost described in paragraph *(d)* above. The difference is called the scheme's Net Present Value (NPV), which may be positive or negative.

Environmental Assessment

The approach to environmental assessment is strikingly different. It was first subjected to critical scrutiny by SACTRA's predecessor, the Advisory Committee on Trunk Roads Assessment (ACTRA), under the chairmanship of Sir George Leitch (Department of Transport, 1977). When ACTRA embarked on its work, cost-benefit analysis was well-established, but the Department of Transport had come under heavy criticism for the lack of any corresponding procedure for evaluating and bringing into its assessment process all those other effects of a road scheme – particularly environmental effects – which were not to be found in COBA. ACTRA, in the result, broke some important new ground. It endorsed the criticism, and identified a large number of specific environmental effects which it considered should be formally evaluated. It also concluded that the quantification and description of these effects was a matter of professional judgement, and that they were not capable of reduction into monetary or economic units. They could not therefore be brought into the COBA program. In order, therefore, to ensure that all factors were given equal prominence in the decision-making process, ACTRA recommended that all the predicted effects – both those produced by COBA and the many others which were not – should be presented together in a special tabular form, called the Framework, which would enable Ministers and the public to ascertain the nature of the balance which would have to be struck between competing options.

It was a further recommendation of ACTRA that a Standing Advisory Committee should be established, and SACTRA was born. SACTRA's first task was to work with the Department on the development of the Framework, which has now become the standard medium for the presentation of all the economic and environmental effects of a road scheme which are currently measured.

In order to implement the recommendations of ACTRA it was also necessary for central guidance to be given on the technical assessment of environmental factors, and, again as a result of collaborative work between SACTRA and the Department, the latter has produced its *Manual of Environmental Appraisal* (MEA) (Department of Transport, 1983), first published in 1983. MEA serves two main functions. First, it gives detailed advice on how to draw up the Framework, and to the extent that the Framework embraces the non-environmental effects which are the output of COBA, MEA may be said to exceed the scope of its title. Secondly, it gives advice on the assessment of a number of specific environmental effects:

- traffic noise;
- visual impact;
- air pollution;
- community severance;
- effects on agriculture;
- effects on heritage and conservation areas;
- ecological impact;
- disruption due to construction;
- effects on pedestrians and cyclists;
- view from the road;
- driver stress.

Within the Framework all effects, those which are monetized and those which are not, are measured against six assessment groups:

Group 1   the effects on travellers
Group 2   the effects on occupiers of property
Group 3   the effects on users of facilities
Group 4   the effects on policies for conserving and enhancing the area
Group 5   the effects on policies for development and transport
Group 6   financial effects

It can be seen at a glance that there is no systematic correlation between COBA, the MEA list of environmental effects, and the six groups.

Use of the Framework

In the process of decision-making which has been described above, the Framework is formally introduced at two particular stages of great importance. First, when a series of options is presented for public consultation, and secondly when the Secretary of State publishes his preferred scheme, and it proceeds to Public Inquiry. Less rigorous appraisal is carried out at earlier stages in the process, which occur well before these two stages are reached; but that appraisal is heavily influenced by the form and content of the material which ultimately has to be produced. In a later report *(Urban Road Appraisal* [Department of Transport, 1986]) SACTRA expressed doubt as to whether the Framework, as a method of presentation, had fully lived up to expectations, and recommended its replacement with a more flexible form of document – an assessment summary report. It did not, however, seek to challenge the fundamental theoretical assumption upon which the Framework is based, namely that there is a set of effects, mainly of an environmental character, which cannot be expressed in monetary or economic terms and which must therefore be traded off against the outputs of cost-benefit analysis on the basis of discretion and political judgement.

EC Directive 85/337

The final component within existing appraisal procedures is the legal requirement to comply with the provisions of EC Directive 85/337. *The Assessment of the Effects of Certain Public and Private Projects on the Environment* which was adopted by the Council of the European Community on 27 June 1985, and came into force on 21 July 1988. The Directive requires an environmental assessment of certain types of major development to be carried out, and exposed to public consultation, before development consent is granted.

The Directive applies to virtually all important road schemes. It was given effect in England and Wales, in respect of such roads, by amendments introduced into the Highways Act 1980 under Statutory Instrument 1988 No. 1241. The legal requirements can be shortly summarized as follows. For any proposed scheme the Secretary of State for Transport must publish a statement containing information, so far as it is relevant to the project, and is reasonably capable of being obtained, on the direct and indirect effects of the project on the following:

- human beings, flora and fauna;
- soil, water, air, climate and the landscape;
- the interaction of the above two groups of factors; and
- material assets and the cultural heritage.

Such a statement must include at least (a) a description of the project including its site, design and size; (b) a description of the measures envisaged in order to avoid, reduce and, if possible, remedy significant adverse effects; (c) the data required to identify and assess the main effects which the project is likely to have on the environment; and (d) a non-technical summary.

The statement in question is called an 'environmental statement'. It is published with the Secretary of State's preferred scheme, in the period leading up to the last stage of the process – the Public Inquiry – and is considered at this Inquiry. It is closely linked to the Framework which, as has been seen, is produced both at the earlier public consultation stage as well as at the Inquiry, in that the Framework has been determined, under Departmental practice, to be the medium through which the information listed in (c) above – data for identifying and assessing main environmental effects – is presented. The Framework therefore appears as the very core of the text of the environmental statement.

The Future Development of Environmental Assessment

Out of this corpus of policy, practice and procedure a number of important questions arise and are addressed at some length in our Report. I will concentrate on three of them.

1. Do our current appraisal methods do justice to all the environmental effects of road building and road use?
2. Are we carrying our relevant environmental appraisals at the appropriate stage in the planning and decision-making process?
3. Do we strike the right balance between cost-benefit analysis and appraisal based on judgement?

Each of these questions has implications for academic research. There is a fourth question on which there remains disagreement between SACTRA and the government, and that is over the best way of presenting the results of environmental assessment for public and Ministerial consumption.

Is Appraisal Comprehensive?

This first question relates back to remarks made at the beginning of this chapter about the multi-faceted impacts of transport planning, road building and the use of motor vehicles. We have developed procedures which are good, at the level of individual schemes, at picking up most of the differences between various options, in terms of their local environment impact. If we build a by-pass around a village, or convert a dual-two-lane carriageway into a dual-three-lane carriageway, most of the local effects, and the differences between options, can be identified and measured. It may be argued that the list of impacts in MEA should be lengthened, and that is likely to happen in the light of experience.

In recommendations 16.32 to 16.34 of the Report we indicate the direction in which a new Manual should travel. We recommend that it should be greatly enlarged; that specific additions to the existing checklist should include the following: the effects of land take; loss of open space; water pollution; vibration; and a general heading for health and stress (as opposed to the more specific headings driver stress and effects on pedestrians and cyclists). We follow the recommendations contained in the SACTRA 1986 Report, and wish to see night-time noise and the social and environmental effects of blight and development potential included, and emphasize the importance of view from the road for inter-urban schemes.

But the more serious problem at present, as it seemed to the Committee, lies in our inability to connect decisions on specific schemes with the much larger environmental concerns with which we have now become preoccupied: global warming, the depletion of non-renewable resources, sustainability. It has become customary to say that these issues are too large to be comprehended within the type of decision which I have been discussing in this chapter. When an Inspector at a Public Inquiry is invited to make a recommendation in favour of, say, Route A (which by-passes the village to the south) against Route B (which by-passes it to the north) and 'do-minimum' (which involves some traffic management measures to the existing route passing through the village), the distinctions between those three options may in global terms be so fine that matters such as the comparative quantities of noxious gases emitted by traffic passing along each of the three networks are impossible to measure.

In the present state of scientific knowledge that proposition may be right in the case which I have mentioned. It may even hold true in the case of a more substantial proposal to build a new major route or corridor, such as the Trans-Pennine Route now under consideration, or the crossing of Twyford Down. If however it is right, it indicates that we must develop other appraisal procedures which will ensure that these large questions are resolved at some earlier stage in the process, when they can be properly reflected and translated into policy.

In its White Paper *This Common Inheritance* (Department of Environment, 1990) the government declared (see in particular para. 18.6) an intention to ensure that the environmental dimensions of policy-making at high level will be more rigorously examined. A good deal of work has already been carried out to implement that intention. In particular, the Department of the Environment's Paper 'Policy Appraisal and the Environment' (Department of Environment, 1991) contains valuable guidance on the development of strategic environmental planning, and has some interesting things to say about monetary assessment.

So far as roads are concerned, however, the connection between strategic environmental issues and strategic transport planning is poorly developed, and needs to be buttressed with much more detailed scientific and transport engineering study before it can be properly understood by decision-makers. A greater number of our more localized decisions about transport could then be better integrated into national environmental policy.

In the light of these considerations SACTRA has made a series of recommendations which advocate a more strategic approach towards the planning of the road network. They include the following.

16.05 An effective system of measurement must be capable of capturing all effects, and give them coherence with policies and decisions made at all levels in the planning of our transportation system.

16.07 Scheme assessments should in every respect be guided by explicitly stated policy objectives, which will provide a series of reference points against which competing options can be judged.

16.08 Environmental assessment on a scheme by scheme basis alone will not take account of all affects. There is a need for a strategic level of assessment.

. . . . .

16.11 An appraisal structure must be devised which will be adequate in geographical extent and timescale, and in its consideration of the combined and cumulative impacts of several schemes and policies.

. . . . .

16.15 Implementation of this new approach starts at the highest level with a setting of objectives or targets in relation to major impacts, and establishing procedures for monitoring and reporting progress towards their achievement.

16.16 The procedures for the initiation, design and approval of trunk roads should relate in both timing and content to those for land-use and transportation planning. If due consideration of these important matters is not given at the outset, they are likely to be lost altogether when the somewhat narrower choices between different schemes at a more local level have to be made. This implies some formal assessment of environmental impact at the regional level . . .

. . . . .

16.19 Similarly, where regional and more local environmental objectives have been adopted by local planning authorities which are relevant to roads, routes and schemes should be tested against these objectives also, at the Identification Stage. The results of this early appraisal should be available at the Public Consultation and Public Inquiry stages, so that the public may be satisfied that these matters have been fully taken into account, and to allow the results to be subjected to public scrutiny.

16.20 After a scheme has entered the Roads Programme, room should prudentially be left within the appraisal process to ensure that the differences between schemes which significantly effect national objectives are properly picked up. Strategic effects may be of importance in choosing between options.

The Time for Appraisal

The second question is closely bound up with the first. In our Report we have attempted to present two main ideas: that there is a spectrum of environmental effects varying in scope and importance from the general to the local, and that there is a continuum of decision-making, from the formulation of policy at the highest levels in government to the smaller scale and closer-grained process which produces a Decision Letter from the Secretaries of State after a Public Inquiry into a particular scheme. At every point along that continuum environmental questions are raised, differing in their content, which are important to people.

The task for the Department is to sort out and classify in a more systematic way than has hitherto been achieved the different types of environmental effects with which transport policy-makers are concerned, so that they can be more effectively matched with the sequencing of policy decisions themselves. It is likely that many effects will call for consideration many times over. It would be wrong to create the impression that these effects can be compartmentalized in a neat and tidy fashion. The intractable problem of the effects of transport planning upon changes in land use may be given as one example. But it is the very density of the problem which calls for a careful review.

Our Recommendations in relation to the timing of assessment are therefore as follows.

16.21 The statutory Environmental Statement required by EC Directive 85/

337 and the Highways Act 1980 should be preceded by two formal non-statutory Environmental Assessment Reports prepared (i) before a scheme enters the Road Programme and (ii) before options are presented for Public Consultation.

16.22 These Reports will successively deal with wider national and environmental issues, corridor and regional effects, and the local, detailed considerations arising out of scheme-options. The assessment reports should become increasingly detailed in coverage, such that the environmental assessment of a route-option should be readily developable into an Environmental Statement if that option finally goes forward to Public Inquiry.

16.23 The 'Environmental Assessment Report – Roads Programme Entry' must be available to those who subsequently undertake the principal work of environmental assessment and a summary of its main contents will be reported in the 'Environmental Assessment Report – Route Options'. This latter report will be a document which is available to the public for the purposes of public information and consultation and will be available for discussion at the Public Inquiry . . .

Cost-Benefit and Environmental Quality

The question whether the disciplines of cost-benefit analysis can be introduced further into environmental assessment has been fully debated in academic and technical literature and we have reached the point at which hard decisions have to be made by the government.

The SACTRA Report does not contain any original research into the subject which we have carried out ourselves, or have commissioned. However, concurrently with our work the Department had commissioned a detailed review of the problem from a consortium of consultants (Rendel Planning and the University of East Anglia, 1992) and we have had access to their material, which is published, in summary form, in the Transport and Road Research Laboratory's Contractors' Reports Series. Our role was to exercise independent judgement over the work which has been carried out by others, in order to identify any areas in which the greater use of monetary and valuation techniques could be applied to environmental effects in a manner which would make practical sense to decision-makers and command general public acceptance.

This is discussed in Part IV of our Report. In Chapter 13 we address the question as to whether it is acceptable in principle that any environmental benefits or costs should be evaluated in money terms. In so doing we were re-opening a question which ACTRA and SACTRA in the earlier Reports had firmly answered in the negative. It was their clearly expressed view that assessment should lie exclusively in the realm of professional judgement, and that monetary values had no part to play. In Chapter 14 we review the various valuation techniques which academic research and professional consultants have identified as particularly appropriate to the subject-matter. In Chapter 15, having persuaded ourselves that we should move cautiously away from the stand taken by our predecessors, we set out the areas in which monetary valuation techniques, should, in our view, be first attempted. Our main conclusions under this head are as follows.

16.40 We concur with the earlier Reports of ACTRA and SACTRA that a formal method of appraisal is required to furnish decision-makers with all relevant information in a form which will enable them to give due weight to all the disparate effects of competing proposals. Such a method is a tool in decision-making and not a substitute for it.

16.41 The use of a common unit of measure impacts of a different character will simplify the balancing exercise which has to be carried out.

16.42 Cost-benefit analysis and the use of money-values has advantages over other comparative methods; but there are limitations and weaknesses which must be acknowledged.

16.43 There are some environmental effects which cannot sensibly be valued; but there is no legitimate objection to valuing those effects which can be.

. . . . .

16.45 Effects which cannot sensibly be monetized include those which may cause social catastrophe or the loss of unique or sacrosanct assets; and cumulative or irreversible effects which fall on future generations.

16.46 Where actual costs are incurred by any agency or person, for example in mitigating, off-setting or cleaning-up the effects of damage or pollution, they should be included in the cost-benefit analysis where they can reasonably be calculated.

. . . . .

16.48 The costs of mitigation, clean-up and protection will always be relevant to decision making, even if they are not expected to be incurred in fact.

16.49 Values revealed by behaviour, for example increases or decreases in the price of houses following road construction, may be a valid measure of the effect of certain local and clearly perceived effects.

. . . . .

16.51 The 'travel cost' method is another type of analysis based on actual behaviour but we doubt whether the results obtained by this technique, in its present state of development, could be converted into economic value with any degree of confidence.

. . . . .

16.54 For strategic impacts which are not currently perceived by individuals and need to be dealt with at a social level, there are techniques of actual taxation or 'shadow pricing' for translating policy targets and constraints into money values.

. . . . .

16.58 Pilot studies should be carried out, in relation to a representative cross-section of schemes and policies, to judge the reliability of revealed values, contingent valuations and stated preference techniques in the specific area of transport-planning.

16.59 The results of these studies should be amalgamated into the actual assessment being carried out into the schemes in question, to test their effect on the balance of assessment overall.

REFERENCES

Department of the Environment (1990) *This Common Inheritance: Britain's Environmental Strategy*, Cmnd 1200. London: HMSO.

Department of the Environment (1991) Policy Appraisal and the Environment. London: HMSO.

Department of Transport (1977) *Report of the Advisory Committee on Trunk Road Appraisal* (Chairman Sir George Leitch). London: HMSO.

Department of Transport (1983) *Manual of Environmental Appraisal*. London: HMSO.

Department of Transport (1986) *Urban Road Appraisal: Report of the Standing Committee on Trunk Road Appraisal* (Chairman Professor Tom Williams). London: HMSO.

Department of Transport (1992) *Assessing the Environmental Impact of Road Schemes*, *Report of the Standing Committee on Trunk Road Appraisal* (Chairman Derek Wood QC). London: HMSO.

EC Council Directive (1985) On the assessment of the effects of certain public and private projects on the environment. *Official Journal of the European Communities*, L175, pp. 40–48.

Rendel Planning and the Environmental Appraisal Group, University of East Anglia (1992) Environmental Appraisal: A Review of Monetary Evaluation and other Techniques, TRRL Contractors Report 290.

16

Unresolved Questions of Environmental Valuation

KENNETH BUTTON

Derek Wood's chapter spells out very clearly the rationale underlying the way that environmental factors are currently included in transport infrastructure decision-making in the UK and provides an interesting history of how the assessment procedure has evolved over time. The process is certainly not single layered nor static as it has sometimes been portrayed by critics and, in particular, the historical perspective set out in the chapter shows the high degree of pragmatism, coupled with a certain amount of theoretical sophistication, which lay behind the current approach. The author also makes it clear that there are often no immediate and easy answers to resolving some of the admitted defects in the current methodology when it comes to embracing adequately environmental factors into the assessment process.

Nevertheless, and not withstanding the prospects of some changes in procedure following the current review exercise undertaken by the Standing Advisory Committee on Trunk Road Assessment (SACTRA), the existing approach does have serious limitations in the way it incorporates environmental considerations and it is not altogether clear that we can be optimistic about them being resolved in the near future.

In particular, while there has been considerable attention in the past few years on whether to incorporate more environmental factors into the COBA process or to improve the existing manual of Environmental Appraisal. This rather misses an important point. Any extensions to the COBA coverage of the environment or improvements to the 'Framework' are of little use if traffic forecasts continue to be as unreliable as they have been in the past. To be fair, this is a point briefly touched upon by Derek Wood but needs some further elaboration.

Firstly, many environmental effects of transport are directly related to traffic levels. This is because traffic flow influences traffic speeds and also often the 'smoothness' of the traffic flow. Some general indications of the

TABLE 1. Composition of exhaust gases at different stages in the motoring cycle.

| Pollutants | Composition of exhaust gases (parts per million) | | | |
	Idling	Accelerating	Cruising	Decelerating
Gasoline engines				
Carbon monoxide	69 000	29 000	27 000	39 000
Hydrocarbons	5 300	1 600	1 000	10 000
Nitrogen oxides	30	1 020	650	20
Aldehydes	30	20	10	290
Diesel engines				
Carbon monoxide	trace	1 000	trace	trace
Hydrocarbons	400	200	100	300
Nitrogen oxides	60	350	240	30
Aldehydes	10	20	10	30

TABLE 2. Emissions related to speed

| Miles per hour | Emissions (grams per mile) | | |
	Carbon monoxide	Hydrocarbons	Nitrogen oxides
25	55.47	8.75	5.13
40	37.24	7.07	5.85
55	31.66	6.30	6.85

implications of these two parameters on atmospheric pollution are seen in the, albeit now rather dated but still generally representative, data set out in tables 1 and 2. Since traffic characteristics also influence fuel consumption, there are also important links between congestion and emissions of global warming gases such as CO_2 which are highly correlated with fuel efficiency. They also influence the level of noise nuisance traffic creates.

Additionally, the monitoring which has been taking place of the existing trunk road planning process in the United Kingdom, and reported to the House of Commons Committee of Public Accounts (1989), reveals that traffic forecasts can be extremely inaccurate. For instance, after examining forty-one road projects, and comparing predicted and actual traffic flows on their opening, it was found that twenty-two had forecast flows which were within 20 per cent of actual flows while the other nineteen schemes had variations in the predicted level of between 50 per cent below and 105 per cent above the flows which materialized. Prior to any extensive further research on more specific environmental issues, it would be useful to gain better understanding of the outcomes of previous road assessments and to use that knowledge to produce more reliable traffic forecasts in the future. Would, for example, the same priorities have materialized in the road programme and, at the micro level, would the same design standards have been favoured?

Linked with this in some ways is the question of the limitations of the current appraisal system, which essentially involves assessing projects rather than strategies. The direct link with traffic forecasts is, as the author points out, the fact that there are no traffic generation effects allowed for in the existing COBA appraisal. Traffic effects are purely seen in terms of traffic distribution. Intuitively, to an economist at least, it seems rather rigid to assume that the aggregate demand curve for road travel is perfectly vertical and that traffic growth only occurs due to vertical shifts in the curve as the consequence of rising income, etc. Because, in relative terms, any particular scheme is small, traffic generation effects are certainly difficult to capture for an individual project, but this may not be the case either for a set of closely linked projects being carried out over a number of years in, say, a corridor (for example, a series of by-passes). Alternatively, it may be possible to capture some element of traffic generation factors by looking retrospectively at the actual aggregate traffic volumes associated with previous years' road programmes to gain some idea of the likely overall traffic effect of investing in the road currently in the road programme.

Secondly, in economic theory it is well established that, because of its relative nature, the application of cost-benefit procedures such as COBA to a series of projects can generate a positive social return for each. Yet, when these projects are all completed, society is actually worse off than at the outset (for example, Gorman, 1955). There are arguments that this type of effect exists on some corridors where individually by-passes meet the economic criteria laid down but, as a result of their construction, travellers switch from other modes (especially rail) which, because of their cost structures, are eventually forced to withdraw services. Again, looking back at situations where this may have occurred could provide some indications of the possibilities that even good project appraisal of schemes may be inadequate in the absence of good strategic assessment methods.

Thirdly, a considerable amount of work has already been done on evaluating many local effects of traffic (for example noise), and that the decision whether or not to include as standard practice some of this research in the appraisal methodology should be taken after its implications have been thoroughly explored for a number of actual case studies. One must agree that field trials are important in assessing the real limitations and strengths of putting money values on environmental costs and benefits. This would help to isolate the key practical problems rather more clearly than desk-top studies. Where I might disagree is that these studies should focus on cases, 'which raised difficult environmental issues which could not be evaded by decision-makers or the public'. Certainly these are interesting but equally, from the point of view of looking at what are likely to be more regular trade-off issues, there is a case to be made for including studies which are perhaps less dramatic in terms of environmental concerns.

What is also perhaps played down by the author is the fact that ongoing fundamental research conducted in parallel with these case studies should also yield substantial dividends. Looking back at the history of COBA, for instance, it is clear that independent work on elements of the package, relating especially to travel time values and to accidents, has considerably improved the current appraisal methodology – the same may well hold for local environmental effects.

Fourthly, with regard to the global and transborder environmental effects of transport, these are not embraced under the current umbrella of environmental effects considered in road investment appraisal and Derek Wood says little about them. This may obviously disappoint many environmentalists but equally there may be very good reasons why these effects should not be embraced within, say, an extended COBA or as part of a modified framework. First, it seems unlikely that it would ever prove possible to put a credible value on something like 'global warming effects'. Indeed, if one examines the current economic literature on the subject (which, perhaps some would say naively, assumes scientific bodies such as the United Nations' Intergovernmental Panel on Climate Change are producing reliable climatic forecasts) then there is not even a consensus about whether global warming should enter a cost-benefit analysis as a positive or negative item. Some economists such as Nordhaus (1989) suggest that it may have, overall, a neutral effect.

Of more importance, these types of large-scale environmental effect are probably more effectively treated at source rather than via indirect means such as adjustments to road investment appraisal procedures. The gases concerned can be handled via regulation (for example, at the simplest level the fitting of catalytic converters to reduce NOx) or via quasi-market techniques such as tradeable permit schemes. (The latter involving the government limiting, say, total CO_2 emissions and allocating the right to emit CO_2 by a permit system under which the permits, once issued, could be bought and sold so that they would be used most efficiently – for an account of similar schemes for other pollutants in the USA see Tietenberg (1989).) The requirement of the appraisal process then becomes one of allowing for the impact of such direct measures on future traffic levels – in other words it comes back to a traffic forecasting problem.

Finally, one topic which Derek Wood rather surprisingly did not raise was that of the discount rate to be employed if we are to introduce more environmental factors into COBA. One of the problems of environmental degradation is that, even if it is reversible, it has very long-term implications. The current rate of discount used in COBA is relatively high compared with those generally adopted in environmental analysis. Even if one treats global warming and similar issues independently, there may well be a case for re-examining the nature of the appropriate discount rate if more local environmental effects were to brought within a COBA framework. Attitudes towards the longer-term implications of increased noise and health damage associated with local pollutants may indicate the need for a lowering of the discount rate adopted.

REFERENCES

Gorman, W. M. (1955) The intransitivity of certain 'criteria' used in welfare economics. *Oxford Economic Papers (New Series)*, Vol. 7, pp. 25–35.

House of Commons Committee of Public Accounts (1989) *Fifteenth Report – Road Planning*, HC 101. London: HMSO.

Nordhaus, W. D. (1989) Slow the Greenhouse express: economic policy in the face of global warming, in *Brookings Report on Economic Activity*. Washington DC: Brookings Institution.

Tietenberg, T. H. (1989) Marketable permits in the US: a decade of experience, in Roskamp, K. W. (ed.) *Public Finance and the Performance of Enterprises*. Detroit: Wayne State University Press.

17

Transport Policy and Management

TONY MAY

This chapter considers the impact of transport on the environment. Its brief is wide; it covers the potential of transport policy, of infrastructure design and traffic control and management to contribute towards the development of environmentally friendly cities. In doing so it adopts a logical sequence, considering issues ranging from the broad to the specific. It analyses in turn:

- the overall trends in demand for travel;
- the potential of alternatives to travel;
- the encouragement of less intrusive patterns of travel;
- means of reducing the environmental impact of vehicles;
- means of achieving environmentally enhanced design of infrastructure.

It focuses primarily on person travel, but considers briefly in each section aspects of freight movement for which the environmental arguments are different. It primarily addresses issues in urban areas; it should be noted that the problems, and solutions, for inter-urban travel will differ. It does not consider issues of environmental evaluation, since these, although critical to the development of transport policy, are covered by Quinet and Wood (this volume). Each section identifies policy issues and potential research topics which arise from the discussion. These are summarized in a concluding section.

Overall Trends in Demand for Travel

In forecasting the growth of transport demand, the past is often taken as a guide to the future. An illustration of potential future traffic growth is given by the National Road Traffic Forecasts (NRTF) issued by the UK Department of Transport (Department of Transport, 1989). Prepared in 1989, they envisage traffic growth of between 24 and 47 per cent between 1988 and 2000, reflecting alternative assumptions about national economic growth. By 2025, these growth figures increase to between 83 and 142 per

TABLE 1. Predicted growth rates (per cent per annum) for motorized travel in selected conurbations and nationally.

	Trips	*Trip-km*	*Car trips*	*Car-km*
London 1986–2001	0.4	0.4	1.3	1.4
Birmingham 1985–2010	1.0	1.2	1.2	1.4
Edinburgh 1990–2010	0.6	1.1	1.1	1.4
Nationally* 1987–2025	N/A	N/A	N/A	1.8 to 3.3

* all traffic.

cent. The extended roads programme announced early in 1990 would add about 2 per cent to England's road capacity in the foreseeable future, mostly on the inter-urban network. The implications of such forecasts for increased congestion and for the environment, especially the emission of oxides of carbon and nitrogen, are potentially very serious.

The scale of these problems will depend on the rate of growth of travel demand and on the facilities provided to meet that demand. These two are interrelated, in that the supply of transport facilities, and the cost of using them, will influence the demand for their use; while increasing demand will, if past policies are continued, encourage an increase in supply. It is therefore difficult to specify a level of latent demand for future travel. The approach that has been adopted in recent studies is to predict changes in the factors influencing demand, such as the distribution of population, employment, income levels and car ownership, and to assume a 'do-minimum' transport policy in which only those policy changes already committed are implemented. This enables the problems which would arise if no new policy were adopted to be identified.

Table 1 summarizes the predictions of rates of growth in travel from three recent UK studies in London, Birmingham and Edinburgh, and compares them with the NRTF predictions of growth in car use.

It can be seen that there is considerable uniformity in the estimates for car travel growth, with predicted increases in car-km of 1.4 per cent per annum, representing a 32 per cent increase over twenty years. These estimates are lower than those for national traffic, reflecting the lower levels which have traditionally been experienced in urban areas. Results over the last decade suggest that traffic growth rates have typically been around 1 to 2 per cent per annum on the approaches to urban areas, 3 to 5 per cent on interurban roads, and 5 to 7 per cent on motorways.

However, it is worth noting that some urban areas are already experiencing substantially higher growth rates. The low growth prediction for Cambridge, for example, is 2.9 per cent per annum.

These estimates are inevitably dependent on the assumptions made for economic development and incomes. In Edinburgh a range of scenarios was produced which suggested a range of 0.6 per cent to 1.3 per cent in trip-km and 0.8 per cent to 1.6 per cent in car-km (May, Roberts and Holmes, 1991).

Generally these predictions suggest that trip-kilometres will rise more rapidly than trips; in other words average journey length will continue to increase. This is a trend which has been apparent for several years in the UK. Comparison of the 1965 and 1985 National Travel Surveys indicates that, over that twenty-year period, total passenger travel, in person-km, increased by 61 per cent (a rate of 2.4 per cent per annum). Further analysis indicates that the 61 per cent was explained as follows:

- increased population   4 per cent;
- more journeys   22 per cent;
- longer journeys   35 per cent.

Thus the largest single cause of traffic growth has not been people making more journeys (the usually understood result of increased motorization) but people travelling further to carry out the same activities. This is particularly marked with journeys to work, whose average length increased by 58 per cent over the same period. Increased journey lengths inevitably mean less reliance on those modes which are more suitable for short journeys: walking, cycling and, to some extent, the bus.

These results are for the nation as a whole, but similar results can be found from comparison of the 1975 and 1985 data for London. NTS shows an 11 per cent growth in person-km by London residents, at a time when population fell by 5 per cent. In this case, the growth is made up roughly as follows:

- lost population   −5 per cent;
- more journeys   4 per cent;
- longer journeys   12 per cent.

This analysis suggests that one of the major causes of traffic growth has been the encouragement of longer journeys.

The predictions in table 1 also suggest that car use will rise substantially more rapidly than overall travel. Again this is a trend which is apparent from past data; the National Travel Survey indicated a 101 per cent growth in car user-kilometres, or 3.6 per cent per annum, over the period in which total travel grew by 61 per cent. One other indication from the Edinburgh study had been that demand for growth is likely to be greater

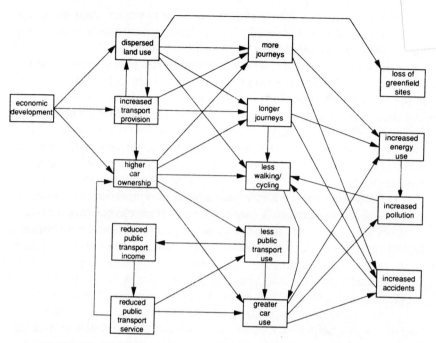

FIGURE 1. Interactions contributing to unsustainability in urban travel.

in the peaks than at other times, with a predicted 1.2 per cent per annum growth in trip-km in the peaks and 0.9 per cent per annum off peak.

Thus the past trends and future predictions indicate as average values for urban areas:

(i)   an increase of around 0.6 per cent per annum in journeys;
(ii) an increase of around 0.4 per cent per annum in trip length, giving an increase of around 1.1 per cent per annum in trip-kilometres;
(iii) an increase of around 0.2 per cent per annum in the proportion of journeys made by car, giving an increase of around 1.4 per cent per annum in car-user kilometres;
(iv) an increase of around 0.2 per cent per annum in the proportion of journeys made in the peaks, giving an increase of around 1.2 per cent per annum in peak travel.

These trends are encouraged by a number of factors, including the trend to lower density development, the construction of larger, more remote, schools, shopping centres and hospitals, provision of transport at less than the marginal cost, and discouragement of shorter journeys, as a result of worsened conditions for walking and cycling, and reduced levels of bus service. As figure 1 indicates, these factors are to a considerable extent interrelated.

In the freight sector, too, overall travel, in both tonnes lifted and tonne-km, has been increasing average journey lengths particularly in the 1970s. Since 1969, tonnes lifted have increased by 11 per cent, while tonne-km have risen by 67 per cent. The factors underlying these trends are less well understood, but it appears that they have been induced by a decline in the share which transport represents in the overall distribution process, and the greater emphasis on 'just in time' delivery. The first has made it more attractive to concentrate stock holdings in fewer developments, thus increasing the area covered from each; the latter has made it more important to provide additional freight movements to meet customers' requirements.

A key challenge for the future will be to attempt to reverse the processes which have led to increases in journey length. If people can be encouraged to carry out the same activities close to home, it should be possible significantly to reduce overall travel, and hence its impact on the environment, without diminishing the richness of the opportunities available to the individual. The processes underlying decision-making for freight movement are more rigid, and their reversal may therefore prove more difficult.

In both passenger and freight travel, the most pressing need is for research which helps explain more fully the causal processes which underlie the growth in journey length and thus helps improve our capability to predict future trends. For passenger travel, this needs to be investigated for different journey purposes, and also by considering individuals' overall travel diaries. It will be necessary also to consider separately the changes arising from life cycle changes, from changes in the location of home and workplace, and from changes which arise while these other factors remain constant. Where changes are induced by the decisions of others, such as employers and developers, these, too, need to be investigated. For freight movement, an analysis is required by commodity type, and in terms of changes induced by the customer, the shipper and by developers. It will require a more thorough understanding of the dynamics of each industrial sector than is apparent in current freight forecasts.

In advance of such research, it is possible to envisage changes in journey length being induced by changes in land-use planning, in the information available to those making locational and travel decisions, and in the costs of travel. The second and third of these are considered in the next two sections. Research in the first of these areas, commissioned by the Department of the Environment, is already underway. It is designed to assess the extent to which planning controls and planning guidance can help to achieve a reduction in the carbon dioxide emissions generated by transport. It is uncertain as yet how comprehensive that research will be, but it is almost certain that it will identify the need for further work. Related research, funded by the EC, is already beginning to produce interesting comparisons between the UK and other European countries (Roberts and Rawcliffe, 1991).

At a fundamental level, there is a case for research which helps identify patterns of land use which are less demanding of transport, and more consistent with a transport system in which users respond to the true marginal costs of their journeys. While such an analysis could focus on the link between transport and land use, it could also consider urban and regional forms which are more energy-efficient overall. It is by no means clear what the implications of optimizing the energy requirements of both buildings and transport are for either built form or transport.

At an applied level, it is clear that more research is needed into the likely effects of trip planning ordinances which are being used increasingly in the US to attempt to ensure that new developments make fewer demands on travel. It is clear from assessments to date that little is yet known about their impact on locational decisions, on actual investment in transport systems, or on overall levels of travel (Wachs, 1990).

If such planning controls are to be envisaged in the UK, it will be important to ensure that the responses of developers, and of those who use the resulting developments are well understood.

SUMMARY OF RECOMMENDED RESEARCH AREAS

1. Investigate the causal processes which have led to increases in the length of passenger journeys, by purpose, and as induced by life cycle changes and location changes; and use these to predict future trends.
2. Investigate the causal processes which have led to increases in the length of freight journeys, by commodity type, and as induced by customers' and shippers' decisions and underlying industrial dynamics; and use these to predict future trends.
3. Investigate the factors affecting developers' decisions in choosing development sites, and their resulting contributions to (1) and (2) above.
4. Identify land-use patterns which are less demanding of transport and more consistent with higher cost transport facilities.
5. Study the impact of trip planning ordinances on development decisions and the provision and use of transport facilities.

Alternatives to Travel

To an extent it may be possible to remove the need to travel altogether for certain journeys. Telematics have for some time offered the potential for remote working, remote shopping and remote personal business activities. Their impact on travel has, however, been somewhat uncertain (Salomon, 1985). It appears that the journeys foregone in favour of telecommunications may well be more than offset by the new journeys promoted by enhanced information on the potential for travel. A move towards a higher cost travel market could, however, change the situation markedly. If travellers had to pay the full marginal costs of their journeys, they could be expected to find telecommunication more attractive, while at the same time being less attracted to the new travel opportunities on which information was provided. The recent Dutch national transport policy review estimated that telematics had the potential to replace 8 per cent of personal travel. If that personal travel were to become more expensive, this may well be a substantial underestimate.

There probably is a case for further investigation of the extent to which person travel, for different purposes, could be replaced by a range of telematics facilities, in contexts within which the costs of travel are increased substantially. It will be necessary to distinguish these responses from others, such as reductions in the frequency or length of travel, which could arise without replacement by telematics.

All of these responses could be induced by a further development in telematics, the development of trip planning systems. These represent a means of providing information to existing and intending travellers, including the most appropriate location in which to satisfy an activity need, the optimum departure time and mode and, in real time, the best route, service and parking facility. As such, they subsume current developments in real time route guidance and passenger informations systems, and can provide information not only during the journey, but before it starts and even, on a longer time scale, before locational decisions are taken (Hopkinson and May, 1990).

As with other forms of telecommunications, it is uncertain whether such systems will induce more efficient travel patterns, or encourage increased travel by making users more aware of the opportunities available. Much depends on the extent to which current travel patterns are suboptimal as a result of inadequate information.

A recent paper identified the following research needs in the field of trip planning systems (Hopkinson and May, 1990):

(i)   the optimality of existing travel decisions;
(ii)   factors affecting the supply of trip planning information;
(iii) the actual and perceived information needs of users;
(iv) design features which would encourage information retrieval;
(v)   user response to pre-trip and in-trip information;
(vi) systems response to information provision.

Of these topics (i), (v) and (vi) will be particularly important in understanding their contributions to environmental impact. Some work in these areas has recently been started (May, Preston and Roberts, 1991).

SUMMARY OF RECOMMENDED RESEARCH AREAS

6. Assess the potential for telematics systems such as home working, teleshopping and teleconferencing to replace travel in conditions in which travellers incur their full marginal costs.
7. Investigate the extent to which existing travel decisions are suboptimal, and could be enhanced by improved information.
8. Determine the user response to pre-trip and in-trip information from trip planning systems and their derivatives.

The Encouragement of Less Intrusive Means of Travel

Once the overall demand for travel has been determined, it can be accommodated in a range of ways, which have differing environmental impacts. The most important determinant is the choice of mode of travel; broadly the impact of passenger travel is least for walking and cycling, followed by rail and bus, followed by shared cars. Per passenger-km, single occupant cars and, in a different way, motorcycles, will have the greatest impact. For freight, the mode choice argument is more complex. Rail and waterborne freight offer little alternative in urban areas, and will usually require road delivery to the customer. There is a choice of size of vehicle, with trans-shipment being an option in large urban centres. Here the environmental impact is determined both by the resulting number of vehicle movements and their physical scale. Some further applied research may be justified into the environmental case for influencing choice of freight vehicle size in urban areas. Although modal choice is the dominant issue, choice of time of travel and route may be important if they help reduce congestion, and avoid environmentally sensitive times of day and locations.

Our understanding of the ways in which passenger modal choice can be influenced in urban areas has increased substantially in recent years. Table 2, taken from a recent study in Edinburgh (May, Roberts and Holmes, 1991), indicates that it is possible to develop strategies which achieve lower levels of fuel consumption and casualties, and higher environmental quality, despite an anticipated 23 per cent increase in person-km over the study period. The most effective strategies are likely to be ones which integrate a number of related approaches and include public transport investment, traffic and environmental traffic management, limitations on fares increases and the introduction of road pricing. Such strategies may also help to influence the overall level and distribution of travel. However,

TABLE 2. Performance of selected strategies in Edinburgh, compared to 1990.

Strategy	Do Minimum	C1[6]	C2	C3	C4	C5	C6
Access by car	− − − − −	+++	−	++	− −	++	− −
Access by bus/rail	− − − −	+++	+++	+++	−	+++	−
Environmental quality	− − − − −	+	− −	+	− − −	+	− − −
Local economic activity	− − − −	++++	−	++++	− −	+++	− − −
Fuel consumption	+16%	−2%	+7%	0	+10%	+1%	+12%
Casualties	+ 7%	−8%	−1%	−7%	+ 2%	−7%	+ 3%
Benefits (£m NPV)	N/A	+410	+300	+330	+180	+310	+110
Finance (£m PVF)	N/A	−260	−270	−100	−160	+ 10	0
Capital costs (£m 1990)	N/A	530	520	530	340	530	340

Key:	<	Worse				Better	>
	− − − − −	− − − −	− − −	− −	−	0	+	++	+++	++++	+++++

NPV: Net Present Value (a measure of economic efficiency) relative to Do Minimum.

THE SIX COMBINED STRATEGIES

Strategy	C1	C2	C3	C4	C5	C6
Finance[1]	High	High	Medium	Medium	Low	Low
Infrastructure[2]	NS EW WR	NS EW WR	NS EW WR	NS WR	NS EW WR	NS WR
Capacity reduction (%)[3]	10%	10%	25%	10%	25%	10%
Fares level (%)[4]	−50%	0	−25%	0	−10%	+25%
Road pricing[5]	Yes	No	Yes	No	Yes	No

Notes:
1. High: £200m–£300m PVF;
   Medium: £100m–£200m PVF;
   Low: Zero financial outlay
2. NS: North-South Light Rapid Transit;
   EW: East-West Light Rapid Transit;
   WR: Western Radial
3. Percentage reduction in city centre road capacity.
4. Percentage change from level anticipated in 2010.
5. Inclusion or otherwise of a charge of £1.50 to enter or leave the city centre throughout the day.
6. C1 to C6 relate to different strategies being evaluated in Edinburgh.

these impacts appear likely to be of second order by comparison with changes in mode and time of travel. Indeed some strategy elements such as public transport investment and fares reductions may actually encourage increased travel which may later be susceptible to transfer to car. While such approaches are now well documented, they are still largely based on predictive models. As these strategies are implemented, it will be important to ensure that their effects are carefully monitored.

Unfortunately, studies in lower density areas, where public transport is already a minority mode, indicate that the growth of car use is a more intractable problem. More generally, the most appropriate transport policy measures for increasing walking and cycling are less clear. Research could therefore usefully focus on means of using transport policy to reduce car use in lower density areas, and to increase walking and cycling overall. It may be, however, that land-use planning offers a more effective way of achieving these results.

While the policy approaches to be adopted are generally well understood, at least in the larger urban areas, there are still considerable barriers to progress. The most serious concern imbalances in the way in which financial support for transport infrastructure and operations is justified and in the methods for investment appraisal of road and public transport projects. More specifically the reluctance to consider road pricing as a solution is also an impediment. These issues are, of course, ones of policy rather than underlying understanding. They are, however still ones to which research can contribute. The government has already announced its intention to embark on a programme of research into urban congestion and it would be appropriate for research council funded research to complement this. Particular areas could include that of environmental evaluation in both financial and investment appraisal (see Wood this volume) and the design impact and appraisal of road pricing systems. Some research on the latter is already in hand (Chartered Institute of Transport, 1991).

SUMMARY OF RECOMMENDED RESEARCH AREAS

9. Assess the overall environmental impact of alternative sizes of freight vehicle, including trans-shipment, in urban areas.
10. Monitor the effectiveness of integrated transport strategies as they are implemented.
11. Identify appropriate transport policies for reducing car use in lower density areas, and assess their contribution relative to, and in conjunction with, that of land-use planning policies.
12. Explore ways of encouraging a transfer of travel to walking and

cycling, and assess their contribution to environmental conditions as part of an overall transport/land-use strategy.

13. Contribute to the Department of Transport's intended research programme into urban congestion.

14. Enhance the procedures for environmental evaluation as a contribution to the development of a common financial and investment appraisal method for urban transport projects.

15. Develop and assess the impact of alternative road pricing structures and systems.

Means of Reducing the Environmental Impact of Vehicles

Once the overall pattern of mode choice, time of travel and routeing has been determined, the environmental impact is determined largely by the vehicles themselves and the way that they are used. The environmental impact of vehicles is likely to be reduced by a range of developments, including increases in fuel efficiency, conversion to alternative motive fuels, control of atmospheric pollutants and noise emissions, increases in vehicle safety and, to a limited extent, reductions in visual impact. While between them these measures are likely to reduce the specific environmental impact of individual vehicles, it is clear that they are to some extent in conflict with one another in their effects; more seriously their impact is likely to be eroded by the underlying growth in vehicle use (Department of Energy, 1990). The technology of improved vehicle design is outside the scope of this book. However, it will be important to be clear as to the predicted impact of such design improvements when assessing the need for other means of environmental enhancement, and their resulting impact.

The main parameters of patterns of vehicle use which affect the environment are flow, composition and speed. Flow and composition are largely determined by measures considered in previous sections, although local environmental traffic management measures can influence the use of specific roads. The effect of speed is more complex. Higher speeds create higher noise levels, increased emissions of oxides of nitrogen and higher fuel consumption, which in turn increases carbon dioxide emissions. Accident rates may also be increased as will sense of danger. Lower speeds are usually associated with more variable traffic conditions, in which greater energy consumption arises from successive acceleration, deceleration and idling. As a result noise levels and carbon monoxide emissions are increased, accident rates may increase, and the resulting queues cause visual intrusion and inefficient use of space. One approach increasingly being encouraged in urban areas is the use of traffic calming to limit vehicle speeds but at the same time avoid unnecessary queuing and variability in traffic conditions. While it is generally accepted that such changes will be environmentally more acceptable, there is little information on the impact either on emissions or attitudes and perceptions. This is an area in which further research is needed, and can usefully be coordinated with the traffic calming schemes now being introduced. More generally, research is needed into the environmental consequences of alternative operating speeds, as part of the input into policy decisions on speed limits.

One interesting argument advanced with traffic calming schemes is the suggestion that they might induce a reduction in car use. In practice, the main aim has been to reduce the environmental impact of a given flow of traffic, but early schemes such as Oxford Street have been quoted as evidence that traffic flows can be reduced by imposing controls in the way in which roads are used. It appears that such effects can arise in city centres, where the opportunity to park, and to drive around searching for parking space, is reduced. If they can be achieved in other parts of urban areas where through traffic predominates, this will be of considerable significance in the treatment of environmental impact, and in encouraging increased walking and cycling. It will be important to conduct empirical research to assess the scale of such impacts from experimental traffic calming schemes. This is a specific example of the more general need to monitor the effectiveness of new transport policy initiatives.

One other aspect of the use of vehicles is the impact of parking on the environment. Much of the concern here is with the visual impact of parked vehicles and with their requirements for space. The alternatives, including modal transfer, off-street parking and park and ride, are well understood, but their assessment could be enhanced by improving our ability to evaluate the visual and land consumption impacts of parked vehicles. Past experience indicates the difficulty of evaluating such aspects of visual quality.

SUMMARY OF RECOMMENDED RESEARCH AREAS

16. Assess the impact of traffic calming, and resulting lower and more uniform speeds, on emissions and on public perception of traffic impact.
17. Investigate more generally the environmental costs of alternative traffic speeds.
18. Assess the impact of traffic calming measures on levels of vehicular traffic and on the encouragement of walking and cycling.
19. Develop means of evaluating the visual and land consumption impacts of parking.

Environmentally Enhanced Design of Infrastructure

One of the responses to transport problems continues to be investment in new infrastructure. The work on integrated transport strategies has demonstrated that new roads can be beneficial if they enable traffic to be diverted from environmentally less suitable roads, and that new public transport infrastructure can contribute by attracting a transfer from car use. However, any new infrastructure will have environmental impacts in terms of its land requirements, visual impact and severing effects on the area through which it runs, as well as those impacts which result from the traffic which it generates. Design can assist to reduce these impacts in two broad ways. The first and more conventional, is to add to the design, and the resulting financial and space requirements, by landscaping and provision of barriers and crossings. These approaches are generally well understood, although there may be a case for further research into the relative environmental benefits and costs of alternative right of way cross-sections. The extreme of this conventional approach is the building of new roads (as well as rail lines and busways) in tunnels. Oslo has already adopted this approach to considerable effect, and both Paris and, to a lesser extent, London are considering limited access tolled tunnel road networks. Some research is needed into the operations of such networks, their integration with conventional networks and parking facilities, and their impact on mode choice and on congestion on the remaining, free, road network.

The second, and less conventional, approach is to reduce the design standards of new infrastructure to enable it to be integrated more acceptably into the existing built form. This is already being done with some of the recent developments in light rail systems, but road design is still tied to rigid design standards. It may well be that lower standard, and hence lower speed, roads will be perfectly adequate in urban areas where overall traffic levels are being regulated by other means. Research is needed into the environmental and other benefits and disbenefits of a wider range of design standards for urban roads.

There is increasing interest currently in the redesign of existing infrastructure. Some aspects of traffic calming schemes, and the more substantial projects to redesign urban road layouts pioneered by the Dutch, change the allocations of road space and the materials used in surface treatment, and in some cases use these devices to influence the way in which drivers use the road space. One of the stimuli to redesign of road space in UK towns and cities has been the realization that many continental towns have dramatically improved the appearance of town centres, residential areas and main roads, and hence changed the nature of the activities on them. At the same time, there is uncertainty, in advance of experimentation, on the types of design which are likely to be considered acceptable, and those which will positively influence driver behaviour. Both of these are issues which can be assisted by visualization in two, or preferably three dimensions. Integration of three dimensional visualization of such designs into driving simulators will further help in identifying the potential impact on the behaviour of drivers and other road users.

SUMMARY OF RECOMMENDED RESEARCH AREAS

20. Assess the environmental benefits and costs of alternative cross-sections and frontage treatments of road and rail infrastructure, including landscaping and barriers.
21. Investigate the design, operation and impact of limited access tolled road tunnel networks.
22. Evaluate the environmental and other costs and benefits of a wider range of urban road design standards.
23. Two and three-dimensional modelling of the visual impact of alternative designs of urban road space, and the simulation of their impact on road user behaviour.

Research Recommendations

The preceding review has identified twenty-three possible research topics, which are listed in table 3 for completeness. This list includes a wide range of types of topic. Some are of greater importance and potential impact than others. Those with the highest priority are likely to be topics 1, 2, 4, 7, 11, 14, 16, 22.

TABLE 3. Possible research topics.

---

1. Investigate the causal processes which have led to increases in the length of passenger journeys, by purpose, and as induced by life cycle changes and location changes; and use these to predict future trends.
2. Investigate the causal processes which have led to increases in the length of freight journeys, by commodity type, and as induced by customers' and shippers' decisions and underlying industrial dynamics; and use these to predict future trends.
3. Investigate the factors affecting developers' decisions in choosing development sites, and their resulting contributions to (1) and (2) above.
4. Identify land-use patterns which are less demanding of transport and more consistent with higher cost transport facilities.
5. Study the impact of trip planning ordinances on development decisions and the provision and use of transport facilities.
6. Assess the potential for telematics systems such as home working,

teleshopping and teleconferencing to replace travel in conditions in which travellers incur their full marginal costs.

7. Investigate the extent to which existing travel decisions are suboptimal, and could be enhanced by improved information.

8. Determine the user response to pre-trip and in-trip information from trip planning systems and their derivatives.

9. Assess the overall environmental impact of alternative sizes of freight vehicle, including trans-shipment, in urban areas.

10. Monitor the effectiveness of integrated transport strategies as they are implemented.

11. Identify appropriate transport policies for reducing car use in lower density areas, and assess their contribution relative to, and in conjunction with, that of land use planning policies.

12. Explore ways of encouraging a transfer of travel to walking and cycling, and assess their contribution to environmental conditions as part of an overall transport/land-use strategy.

13. Contribute to the Department of Transport's intended research programme into urban congestion.

14. Enhance the procedures for environmental evaluation as a contribution to the development of a common financial and investment appraisal method for urban transport projects.

15. Develop and assess the impact of alternative road pricing structures and systems.

16. Assess the impact of traffic calming, and resulting lower and more uniform speeds, on emissions and on public perception of traffic impact.

17. Investigate more generally the environmental costs of alternative traffic speeds.

18. Assess the impact of traffic calming measures on levels of vehicular traffic and on the encouragement of walking and cycling.

19. Develop means of evaluating the visual and land consumption impacts of parking.

20. Assess the environmental benefits and costs of alternative cross-sections and frontage treatments of road and rail infrastructure, including landscaping and barriers.

21. Investigate the design, operation and impact of limited access tolled road tunnel networks.

22. Evaluate the environmental and other costs and benefits of a wider range of urban road design standards.

23. Two and three dimensional visualization of alternative designs of urban road space, and simulation of their impact on road user behaviour.

Some are more fundamental in nature (topics 1, 2, 3, 4, 7). Some are more applied (topics 6, 8, 9, 11, 12, 13, 14, 15, 17, 19, 20, 21, 22, 23) while some need to be associated empirically with the implementation of experimental projects (topics 5, 10, 16, 18).

Some are more appropriate for economic and social research in transport funding (topics 1, 2, 3, 4, 5, 7, 14, 19) while others are more appropriate for science and engineering research in transport (topics 9, 17, 20, 21, 22, 23). Some are appropriate for both (topics 6, 8, 10, 11, 12, 13, 15, 16,

18). Some are particularly suited to industrial sponsorship (topics 3, 6, 9, 15, 20, 21, 22, 23), It will be important, however, not to compartmentalize this suggested programme too rigidly between the different funding sources for academic transport research in the UK (traditionally the ESRC and SERC) as most topics have economic, social and technological attributes which interact strongly. It will be important to reflect this in the research conducted and in its funding.

REFERENCES

Chartered Institute of Transport (1991) *Paying for Progress*. Supplementary Report.

Department of Energy (1990) *Energy Use and Energy Efficiency in UK up to the Year 2010*, Energy Efficiency Paper 10. London: HMSO.

Department of Transport (1989) *National Road Traffic Forecasts (Great Britain)*. London: HMSO.

Hopkinson, P. G. and May, A. D. (1990) Travel Demand Growth: Research on Longer Term Issues. The Potential Contribution of Trip Planning Systems. WP 308, Institute for Transport Studies.

May, A. D., Preston, J. and Roberts, S. (1991) ITE The Specification of Trip Planning Systems. Proposal to SERC Transportation Subcommittee, May.

May, A. D., Roberts, M. and Holmes, A. (1991) The Development of Integrated Strategies for Edinburgh, in *Proceedings of PTRC Summer Annual Meeting*, PTRC: London.

Roberts, J. and Rawcliffe, P. (1991). Fission or fusion? in *Proceedings of PTRC Summer Annual Meeting*, London: PTRC.

Salomon, I. (1985) Telecommunication and travel – substitution or modified mobility? *Journal of Transport Economics*, vol. 19, no. 3, pp. 219–235.

Wachs, M. (1990) Regulating traffic by controlling land use. The Southern California experience. *Transportation*, vol. 16, no. 3, pp. 241–256.

ACKNOWLEDGEMENT

The author is grateful to his colleagues, and particularly to Professor Chris Nash and Dr Peter Hopkinson, for their contributions to the ideas outlined in this paper. He takes full responsibility, however, for the conclusions drawn and the resulting recommendations.

18

Do Transport Policies Meet Needs?

JOHN ROBERTS

Some say that the map of the world would be incomplete without Utopia. Others believe Utopia has no place there, for the concept implies a finite, unchanging state which would not further human interest and development, nor be capable of sustaining integration of the whole living world. Whichever track we travel on, we need at least intermediate and enviable goals toward which we can progress.

What is needed and what is available are two different things. Only by renting a 'Mount Palomar telescope' would it be possible to see a set of palpable transport goals in Britain, yet the present transport problems are legion.

Tony May's chapter suggests a wide range of deficiencies within our current life systems, which refer in one way or another to the way we move ourselves and goods around – deficiencies which are widely recognized, thanks to intensive media attention and a remorseless output of questioning reports to sustain them.

We see a lot of familiar faces in the May paper: an apparently inexorable rise in journey lengths, in themselves increasingly made by car; decreasing public transport patronage (and who would be surprised when one sees what deregulation has often done to the quality and price of bus services – for example, the Sheffield Household Survey 1990 found a 34.2 per cent shift from bus to car for work journeys from 1986, the time of bus deregulation and the end of cheap fares (Sheffield City Council, 1991)); environment as a free good, happily exploited by the car user; an – unchanged – downmarket view of those on feet or bicycles; policies to reduce personal injury accidents that certainly achieve some welcome reductions in death and maiming, but at the cost of a reduction in non-vehicle users' accessibility; and a whole range of placebos offered by politicians in lieu of real investment in the right places.

All of these issues demand change, not least of the politicians who caused them. It may be a deniable truth, but political adherence to *laissez faire* policies appears difficult to reconcile with the kind of changes that are necessary. So, unless the political ideology changes, achievement of new and widely supported objectives must come from without. Where might that be? Some examples would be accelerated resource depletion, or a popular revolt against untenable environmental conditions, or the sea rising faster and higher than anticipated, or the sun increasingly becoming either invisible or more visible, or a different and less sectarian view filtering down from the European Communities.

Before losing our hair at the rate many trees are losing their leaves (64 per cent of UK trees are damaged in some way by acid rain, and Britain is the second worst performer of all, East and West, European nations) we should first examine the potential of a new, or refurbished, political ideology. It is perhaps too much to hope that we shall see a third force, somewhere between the extremes of capitalism and communism, but we might achieve a government one of whose useful characteristics was a willingness to intervene in and regulate the affairs of the private state.

This new administration would re-establish reasonable powers once held by town planners to determine the spatial distribution, and interrelation of homes, work and all the other human activities that flow from wealth achieved in that way – the continuum of acquisition, consumption and waste creation, health care, learning, recreation, defence. This could be part of a 'mediocosm' (a system neither tiny nor vast), a close-knit unity where many facilities were within walking distance of the home and of each other, while most of the remainder were a bike/bus/tram/train ride away. It is too idealistic to imagine the airlines would cease operations, but their air pollution and spatial demands might be reduced somewhat.

As May frequently notes, the land use/travel relationship is crucial. If it could be reorganized, rapidly in terms of new building, slowly in terms of the existing fabric, then I imagine we would not have to introduce measures to phase out the private car; it would phase itself out when it no longer had much of a function, and its continuing users faced derision: a situation not too dissimilar from cigarette smoking – who would have believed even ten years ago that the entire London Underground system would by now be smoke-free, as would one or two enlightened airlines? Once a critical mass is reached, change can take place quite rapidly.

While May is aware of the importance of land-use/travel relationships, he may not be aware of the extent of work being done. Yes, the Department of the Environment (in association with the Department of Transport) commissioned a study aimed at carbon dioxide emission reductions, but TEST started a study with more fundamental aims two years before that. The Rees Jeffreys Road Fund supported first a literature review of land use and trip generation, and then what became a large pilot study comparing car dependence in the new cities of Milton Keynes and Almere in the Netherlands. The two cities were designated about the same time, have similar target populations, and cover a similar surface area: but there the similarities cease. Almere's buses, cyclists and pedestrians are all separated from the cars, the latter having very modest roads, and the residential area ones are scarcely wide enough for two cars to pass – when they have coped with frequent humps. To take one example of what this means, figure 1 compares parental attitudes toward child play and travel (see also Roberts and Rawcliffe, 1991)

The third stage of the TEST study is now underway and is intended to be undertaken among the developed nations. The case studies themselves, however, are at the 'medio-scale' noted above, with interviews (and travel diaries, as desired by May) with about 1000 persons in small areas – no more than 1-km radius – experiencing some land-use and/or transport innovation. There will also be control studies where nothing much is happening to subvert the *status quo*. 'Innovation' might be an attempt to increase residential densities (as in suburban Toronto). It might introduce new day-to-day facilities, or improve a transport interchange, or construct light rail, or insert area-wide traffic calming or pedestrianization. In this

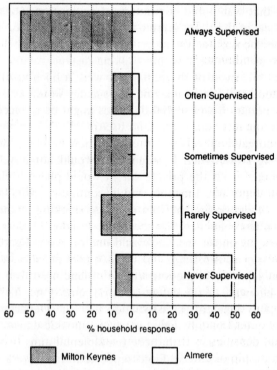

FIGURE 1. Level of supervision of children's local travel and play in Milton Keynes and Almere (data derived from all households interviewed with children under 12 years).

way it would be possible to learn what effects these might have on modal choice when related to residential density and land use configurations.

The 'trip degeneration' study is important because it seems to matter, and seems to echo many of May's concerns. And, it is worth noting that OECD have their own study on land use and transport, with case studies in a number of member nation cities. Ironically, Britain which had a planning system admired worldwide, started dismantling this at just the time when Germany was tightening its powers against out-of-town shopping, and some time after France had done the same. Germany and France had both experimented with relaxation of control only to regret the adverse consequences for their existing town centres (TEST, 1989). So, it would appear that Britain's 'more remote shopping' is a governmental encouragement to longer trip distance and higher levels of car ownership. And this is reflected across all types of activities which now seem to be more spatially dispersed.

But to return to the pursuit of my never-to-be-completed Utopia. What does my enlightened government do about its continuing soak-up of suppressed demand, a blotting paper that soon becomes super-saturated? Well, they certainly do not widen it. They might consider that motorways are rapidly becoming the poor person's railway, though nowhere near as efficient – railways generally do keep moving. The media often show motorways as continuous lines of vehicles any one of whose movement, when it happens, is controlled by those before and after in what is effectively a wagon-load train. So, the natural corollary is to expand rail and reduce its fares, thus overturning the income differential aspect, and thereby capturing large numbers of motorway users. A recent comparison of the environmental impacts of road and rail (TEST, 1991) confirms once and for all the extraordinary lead that rail has over road in its impact on global warming.

There is an important comment on p. 237 of May's chapter where it is said 'A key challenge for the future will be to attempt to reverse the processes which have led to increases in journey length'. Such action would have some bearing on car use, so there is modest scope for enthusiasm, as there is in table 1's lowest trip and trip-km growth rates for London (p. 233). Certainly parts of London have, through historical accident, got something right, and this is the propinquity of services to where people live: this happens throughout the inner city and in town centre and subcentre pockets of outer London. Table 1 suggests immediate action in tightening residential densities in Birmingham and Edinburgh. It is unfortunate that the relationship of undefined 'trips' to 'car trips' cannot be perceived. One other point on the table's commentary: is it assumed that the predictions precede the policies, or do the two meld in some way? If the latter, then the sentence 'These estimates are inevitably dependent on the

assumptions made for development and incomes' should probably become
'. . . development, incomes and transport policy at local and national
levels'. Traffic growth in Cambridge is high: is it in any way related to
the attempt to squeeze bikes out of the city centre? Traffic growth in
Birmingham is high – is that in any way related to Black Country Development Corporation, City of Birmingham, and government promises of new
roads in and around Birmingham?

One other comment is necessary on May's section 'Overall Trends in
Demand for Travel', before moving on to later sections. This concerns
his figure 1. It is unclear whether this is meant to suggest a global model
or simply one for Britain, for there would appear to be differences even
within other European nations. Economic development can produce quite
different results. One might be dispersed land use. Another can be
explained by the fact that people often locate their home by house price.
They may *desire* central or inner-city living, but this is not affordable. If
their income increases (through economic development) their first action
may be to move closer to the city centre. For many people in this fix the
journey to work distance may be proportional to house cost + rail season
cost.

Those who do opt for dispersed living are likely to incur substantial
impacts upon environment and transport. This is abetted in at least two
ways: first, where long-distance commuting is encouraged because, for
distances up to about 60 miles from London, rail season cost appears to
be inversely proportional to distance travelled. The scattergram in Figure
2 shows seventeen BR stations at varying distances from London, and the
1991 cost of a monthly season ticket interpreted per mile distant from
London. The details are tabulated in the Appendix, but what stands out is
that, in environmental and transport infrastructure terms, the relationship
ought to be the other way round – the further you travel, the more it
costs per mile. Second, for those hooked on suburban living next to the
countryside (which probably will successively move away from them
during a twenty-year stay in such a house, as others have the same idea,
and rings of residential development are added) *their* high incomes will
mean they have a prestigious company car plus expenses, this again
encouraging long-distance travel.

The box below 'increased transport provision' in May's figure 1 should
discriminate between infrastructure and services, both having significant
but quite different transport – and environmental – consequences. And
the box below that, 'higher car ownership', is likely to be subject to the
same questions raised on the 'dispersed land use' one.

On the right of May's figure one very important box is missing. This
would be labelled 'urban destruction to accommodate the car'. There
might be another connected with the glib eradication of SSSIs, NNRs,

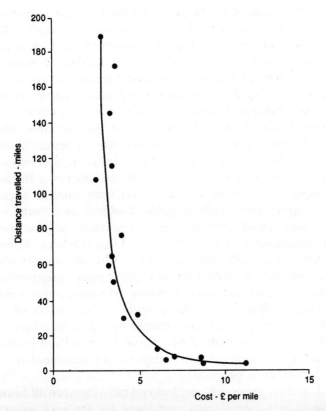

FIGURE 2. Relationship between distance and monthly fare cost for BR stations directly accessible from London.

parts of AONB and, similar heritage areas simply to 'satisfy the demand for personal transport', a phrase which has unfortunately crept back into officialese when the Minister of Transport announced his Department's proposals for enlarging the M25 in September 1991.

Moving on to May's section on Alternatives to Travel, it is interesting to see that he raises the issue of telematics, and their influence on home- or near home-working. Excellent ways of reducing travel demand, but how much take-up would there be? He quotes a Dutch estimate of 8 per cent of personal travel being potentially replaceable by telematics, but it may be significant that in the Netherlands distances between places are generally shorter than in Britain. It is worth remembering that there are many social reasons for travel – to get away from home, to mix with a range of work colleagues, to widen the range of mid-day facilities at your disposal, to behave illicitly, and so on.

May's section 'The Encouragement of Less Intensive Means of Travel' is provocative. Its very first line says 'Once the overall demand for travel

has been determined, it can be accommodated in a range of ways. . . . '
Although May may have intended to say 'reduced demand resulting from
the satisfaction of various energy and environmental objectives', this
should have been clearly stated. Many readers are going to ask whether
we should go on unquestioningly satisfying the demand for travel by *any*
mode, and permitting development which creates transport demand? Or
should we be more discriminatory, and subject to fierce cross-examination
only increased vehicular transport movements? Or only those which have
an environmental impact rating of *x*/person-km or, better, *x*/trip? These
issues seem to me to be a long way from resolution. In many cases the
questions have not even been asked – well certainly not in Britain.

May seems to be looking sideways at Germany when he suggests that
'some strategy elements such as public transport investment and fares
reductions may actually encourage increased travel . . .' Germany is the
apogee of integrated transport demand satisfaction. It has built motorways
within 5 km of practically everyone living in what was the west, but it has
simultaneously used a car fuel tax to improve public transport radically.
The upshot is vastly enhanced mobility. What we must work for is
enhanced accessibility, remote from which is the concept of satisfying
every whim to travel anywhere, mainly by environmentally offensive
modes like the car or aircraft. And, of course it is not just whim-satisfac-
tion – in many cases land-use dispositions and low densities have enforced
a new requirement to 'get moving'.

Table 2, p. 240, shows that car, bus and rail access can all be improved
for the same high capital costs, and these are the only options where
environmental quality is even modestly improved. Local economic activity
also improves greatly in each of these three options. However, it appears,
as if the variables are unconnected – should we expect increased access
by car to have an adverse environmental impact, or to be part of an all
round increase in access which leads, in each option, to environmental
improvement? It may simply be that portrayal of complex variables within
such a table is too difficult to do convincingly, without much more expla-
nation.

In conclusion it is suggested that transport policy was out of sync with
real need, and people's perceptions. Simply to build more roads because
there are more cars because there are more roads because . . . is no
solution, and most people recognize this – as is made clear in the results
from ten surveys undertaken in the last three years. Improving/subsidizing
bus and rail attracted between 48 per cent and 88 per cent agreement in
five national surveys, and over 65 per cent in three London surveys.
Building new roads/motorways/car parks only had two out of seven
national surveys with greater than 50 per cent agreement, and none in
London. Taking national and London surveys together, only three out of

nine had less than 50 per cent agreement for banning/restricting cars in central areas. Each of these surveys provides more evidence of public disenchantment with excessive vehicular traffic.

These comments started by asking whether any sensible changes *could* take place within a free market, unregulated, non-interventionist climate, and saw many difficulties. Is it the rulers or their advisers? This is a research topic in its own right, to add to May's list, but these comments might end by offering one solution to this problem. Looking around in London one has the feeling that we are living in a world largely determined by accountants and. financial advisers. So, the Canary Wharf tower is accountant's architecture, while the ticketing system of London Underground, or British Rail's taking off of trains to meet government profit targets, is accountant's transport. Imagine my satisfaction to come across a paper by Gray (1991). You will have to look at the references to see its significance.

REFERENCES

Gray, R. H. (1991) The Accountancy Profession and the Environmental Crisis (Or can accountancy save the world?) Inaugural Professorial Lecture, Dundee University.

Roberts, J. and Rawcliffe, P. (1991) Fission or Fusion? in *Proceedings of PTRC Annual Summer Meeting*. London: PTRC.

Sheffield City Council (1991) Integrated Transport: South Sheffield Demonstration Corridor. Committee Report, 24 January.

TEST (1989) *Trouble in Store? Retail Locational Policy in Britain and Germany*, A report for the Anglo-German Foundation. London: TEST.

TEST (1991) *Wrong Side of the Tracks? Impacts of Road and Rail Transport on the Environment: A Basis for Discussion*. London: TEST.

Appendix

BR provided 1991 information on monthly season tickets for seventeen stations directly accessible from London. The cost was then divided by the distance from London, giving a monthly cost/mile. Figure 2 (p. 253) plots distance against cost/mile, while the table below gives the base data, ranked by distance, and by cost/mile covered by the season ticket: (see table on p. 256)

There are some anomalies within the table. Apart from a broad inverse relationship between unit cost and distance travelled, there is evident pricing up of the most congested lines. Otherwise, what explains the great difference between Exeter and York? Why is Peterborough's unit cost so much higher than York's when they are on the same electrified line? Why, for that matter, do Harlesden and Willesden Junction have such different rates for virtually the same distance on the same line? Oxford and Cam-

bridge appear to have special privileges. Could the pricing system be
somewhat arbitrary in its operation?

Station	Distance from London, nearest mile	Monthly season £	Monthly cost/ mile £	Rank low=1
York	189	564.5	2.995	2
Exeter	174	644.4	3.703	8
Cardiff	145	500.0	3.44	5
Birmingham	115	399.4	3.465	6
Bournemouth	108	271.2	2.5	1
Peterborough	76	304.6	3.995	9
Oxford	64	213.6	3.364	4
Cambridge	58	189.4	3.266	3
Brighton	51	178.6	3.502	7
East Grinstead	30	148.7	4.916	11
Sevenoaks	29	128.3	4.582	10
Surbiton	12	76.5	6.375	12
Wimbledon	7	51.1	7.048	14
Harlesden	6	51.1	8.52	16
Willesden Junction	6	36.5	6.64	13
Alexandra Palace	5	40.4	8.08	15
Finsbury Park	3	28.8	11.52	17

19

Efficiency and the Environment: Possibilities of a Green-Gold Coalition

PHIL GOODWIN

There is a view that the development of environmentally friendly transport policies will be inherently difficult – and perhaps ultimately unsuccessful – because the economic advantages of policies which are *unfriendly* to the environment are so powerful.

This view has been expressed in a number of different forms, and it can take on a variety of different political positions. One version perceives green opposition to road building, for example, as an essentially destructive and negative interference with necessary improvements to the infrastructure. An Anonymous (1990) leader entitled 'How can Transport afford the Environment?'in *Transport* (the Journal of the Chartered Institute of Transport) argued:

> Concessions to environmental pressures have resulted in straitjackets from which extrication is going to be expensive and painful . . . Butterflies obstruct the route of one new road project, the traditional path of frogs (or was it toads?) another, new rail lines (the Heathrow/Paddington as well as the high speed Channel Tunnel links) are priced out of the private contractor's purse and prospect of an economic return by the requirement for environmental protection. . . . Can we, as a Nation, accept a continuation of these obstructions of 'Better Transport for Great Britain'? If we wish at the minimum to hold our place in any league of national prosperity, then the answer must be NO . . . We must respectively suggest to the Secretary of State for Transport, 'our' Secretary of State, that in future public pronouncements, instead of stating his determination to improve the environment while developing a better transport infrastructure he reverses the order of those priorities.

Such an implied hostility between environmental and economic interests is also contained, for example, in arguments which lead to totally opposite conclusions. Nader (1965) pointed out:

> In fact, the gigantic costs of the highway carnage in this country support a

service industry . . . Traffic accidents create economic demands for these
services running into millions of dollars . . . A great problem of contemporary
life is how to control the power of economic interests which ignore the
harmful effects of their applied science and technology.

More recently, Ullrich (1990), also highlights the substantial commercial
interests built around the car market:

In industrialised countries, however, the car is not a normal consumer article
with a typical market economy cycle from manufacture, sale, usage, to waste
management. Today, very extensive and powerful service and user infrastructures are associated with the car. This 'system of motorisation' embraces the
car industry; an unknown number of suppliers from the chemical and metal
industries; the oil industry; roads suitable for cars; the road construction
economy; the filling station network; repair operations; accident hospitals;
traffic police; traffic courts; insurance; car lobby associations; car scrap
dealers; car graveyards and so on . . . The characteristics of MIT (motorised
individual transport), such as confidence in progress, economic freedom,
product decay and its role as a technically coagulating symbol of the industrial
dynamic, produce an extremely convenient dream-child for the industrial and
capitalist economy and consumer society . . . In the technological system of
motorisation there is a whole range of detrimental effects which are not
capable of compromise and therefore cannot be erased by any positive effects.
Constitutional status must be conceded to such natural sources of relief as
the right to undisturbed sleep, clean water and pure air.

Both Nader and Ullrich propose (though I hasten to add that this is not
their whole argument) that economic agencies should be restricted by
legal or constitutional means from the damaging activities that their own
self-interest leads them to, and might therefore find the 'straitjacket' meta-
phor more appropriate than was intended. However, if it is true that
societies as a whole have to choose between environmental and economic
advantage (for the sake of convenience labelled as 'green' and 'gold') then
certain implications will certainly be argued.

First, green policies will involve some *overall* reductions in production
of wealth, and therefore material standards of living as currently defined.
Of course, there is a separate argument that the quality of life in other
senses might improve, but still there will be less money and fewer things
to buy.

Secondly, either such reductions will be reasonably evenly spread among
the population, or some groups will be cushioned from falls in their
standard of living (either by reason of their power in one scenario, or
their need in another). If evenly spread, then there will be a very wide
constituency of economic opposition to the changes. If unevenly spread,
then there can be some self-interested support, but by the same token the
losers will be more seriously affected, and will therefore have a more
vigorous and determined opposition.

Thirdly, the choice between green and gold policies, therefore, presupposes intense political conflict, the upsetting of powerful vested interests, active involvement from the representative institutions of those interests, and in the normal way for such battles, exaggeration, propaganda, demagoguery, lies, vacillation, compromise and instability. The argument would be presented by one side as Enlightenment against Mammon, and by the other as Progress against Luddism.

Fourthly, the outcome of such a battle does not seem to be certain. Prevailing political ideologies are perhaps more aware of the power of commercial markets and the profit motive than has always been the case, and current global historical movements seem to reinforce that power. This makes some green campaigners pessimistic about the chances of success. On the other hand, there is an apocalyptic version of the green analysis that sees any economic advantage being so overwhelmed by the exploding pressure on resources from developing countries that the appearance of power, based on vested interest, will be swept away.

I cannot say whether the basic contention from which such prospects arise – the proposition that environmental improvement depends on accepting lower economic standards – is true or not for the *generality* of overall policies. In the fields of space heating, agriculture, industrial production, building, leisure activities, housing, animal husbandry, diet, education, service provision and administration it may be that such choices have to be made, in whole or in part. If so, then as citizens we shall all have to confront these issues and determine our individual positions and preferred political solutions.

But in the transport sector I would argue that by and large the entire structure of the argument is invalid.

In seeking to decouple 'environmentally friendly' from 'economically inefficient' I advance three propositions and one axiom. The propositions are:

1. Environmental costs are real economic costs.
2. Environmental benefits have a real economic value.
3. There is being constructed an environmentally friendly transport policy that is economically more efficient than those which have been predominant.

The first two reflect fundamental questions of what we mean by the word 'efficiency'. They are well established theoretically and reasonably easy to demonstrate. However, they would not cut much ice if it were not for proposition 3, which arises not from any fundamental questions of theory or definition, but from an assessment of the specific characteristics, within the transport sector now, of the implications of traffic growth.

The axiom is that if there are net benefits to be had from a policy which is economically and environmentally advantageous, but politically unpopular because of its negative effects on some groups, it must be possible to devise *some* method of implementing it which can be politically popular.

Proposition 1: Environmental Costs are Real Economic Costs

A notion has grown – paradoxically encouraged by the very use of social cost-benefit analysis that was designed as its antithesis – that there are two different sorts of economic costs, with unequal status.

Taking the case of the roads programme, for example, first there are the 'real' costs, which represent the actual payments of money, for labour, raw materials, land purchase, compensation and maintenance. These costs are identified in the budgets of a national or local government department, can be controlled, overspent or underspent, cut or reallocated. They are added into recognizable totals, set against the public expenditure targets, and (it seems) directly comparable with the flows of real money which condition the activities of any private company, household or individual. They are measured in units of money, because they *are* in units of money. The basic test of their reality, perhaps, is that they can be audited.

Secondly, there are the 'social' costs, which in some cases even those who estimate and count them do not fully believe to be real in quite the same sense. The 'cost' of wasted time to commuters, or of the unpleasantness of traffic accidents are surely agreed to be important policy considerations, but the calculations seem notional. It is very difficult to track down exactly where the real sums of money are which correspond with these entries to a cost-benefit calculation, and the idea that an accountant could be invited to follow the audit trail to ensure that these sums are all properly receipted and banked is, unfortunately, absurd.

It may well be necessary to add the two classes of cost together the fulfil Treasury requirements for approval for a road scheme, but at the end of the day there remains a very widespread feeling (from which the author is not totally immune) that the costs which can be audited on a balance sheet have some more concrete existence than those which derive from assumptions, axioms, mathematical formulae and surveys. This feeling persists even through the admittedly shaky reality of some accounting conventions on depreciation and the like.

But this will not do. There is another, perhaps more important dimension of environmental accounting, which cuts completely across this distinction between real money costs and notional social costs. Even if we confine our attention solely to the auditable impacts, the point about environmental processes is that the consequences of an action can fall on different agencies from those who initiate them.

A good example to consider is the effects of road salting. Here (and quite apart from calculations about the balance between the money cost of the salt and the social cost of any accidents due to ice) there are definite money costs imposed; the cost to private and company vehicle owners of maintenance and repairs to counteract the corrosion, and the cost to downstream water users (for example, factories) of any desalination that may be necessary. All these costs are unchallengeably real; the point is not that they do not enter into a balance sheet, but that they *do not enter the balance sheet of the agency responsible for salting.*

Similarly, some of the air pollutants emitted by vehicles used by individuals and companies cause definite health problems – irritation of respiratory, eye and other systems, carcinogenic effects, impacts on the central nervous system and other damage – which involve treatment by doctors and hospitals, loss of productive capacity, and support from public social service agencies or private insurance arrangements. Unlike the case of those traffic accidents where fault can be clearly identified, there is rarely if ever the opportunity for those who meet these costs, from their household, company or taxpaying budgets, to identify the source of the costs and recover them by way of compensation. But these costs, also, are unchallengeably real; the point is not that they are not incurred, but that they are not incurred in a way which associates them with their cause.

Consider the case where an environmental effect like this is understood with a reasonably acceptable level of scientific confidence, and its financial costs can be estimated with a reasonably acceptable degree of economic accuracy. In that case the 'Polluter Pays' principle would say that some system should be designed for visiting these costs on those who cause them, rather than collecting them in a haphazard fashion either from those who suffer from them (the desalination case) or from taxpayers in general (the health service case).

It is clear that such a principle is, in general, going to be 'green' in its effects. This is because the individuals and agencies causing the pollution now have an incentive not to do so – they save money by causing less – and indeed the amount they save, being related to the costs of cleaning up the damage, is an approximate guide to how much less pollution it is, on balance, worthwhile to cause. So there will be less pollution.

The question to be addressed though, is – would the operation of such a principle be 'gold'? The instinctive reaction of both companies and individuals, is to assume not. The imposition of such procedures is resisted because it would 'put additional costs on businesses at a time of economic difficulty' or 'increase the tax burden'. But that interpretation is fundamentally one-sided; it omits the basic fact – without which one would not have suggested such a solution in the first place – that those costs are already being met by companies and individuals. They are already paying for the extra costs to their productive processes, and in general taxation. The 'polluter pays' approach only differs from the starting point in two respects:

(a)   If there were no net change resulting in the amount of pollution caused and the cost of remedying it, the total outlay would stay the same, but be met by different people. This is a question of equity, not efficiency; it will surely be the general case (though admittedly not universal) that it is more equitable to visit the costs of pollution on those who cause it than on everybody else.

(b)   Since there ought, if the scheme is well judged, to be a reduction in the total amount of cost-inducing pollution, then there will be a reduction in the total costs induced. Therefore the economy as a whole is relieved of a burden, not troubled with a new one.

There is a net financial benefit from this approach. The individuals and companies who benefit most are those who cause little pollution, but meet the costs of the pollution caused by others. Their bill will go down. The individuals and companies who do not benefit in their own accounts are those who at present are causing pollution but picking up less than their share of the cost of remedying it. Their bill will go up. This seems fair. But overall, the financial benefits to the first group will be greater than the financial losses to the second group. This is efficient.

If this argument is valid, individuals and companies should be campaigning for green cost recovery, since they have more to gain than lose. The reasons why this is not happening on a large scale need to be understood – they are obviously crucial for political acceptability – and one might suggest that it is in part connected with a degree of cynicism about increases in some costs being offset by reductions in others, and in part to simple ignorance on the part of the potential payers about how much they are already paying in disguised form.

The argument, at root, implies that there is money to be made from the imposition of 'polluter pays'. There must, therefore, be some form of implementing it in which the financial advantage can be coupled to the environmental advantage.

Proposition 2: Environmental Benefits Have a Real Economic Value

It is convenient here to address not those financial benefits which are the simple converse of the costs discussed above (to which of course the same argument may be applied), but the environmental benefits whose cash value is less obvious. Like leisure time savings, or reductions in accidents, there are disagreements about how sensible it is to accord a money value to benefits which are not traded in a market, which do not enter on anybody's income and expenditure account, and for which the economist's enthusiasm for attributing values is not always matched by everybody else's.

This chapter will not rehearse the case for and against incorporating money values for environmental impacts in social cost-benefit analyses since, although that would provide useful information for a green-gold collaboration, it is not a necessary or sufficient condition for it. The question is, would the outcome of such analyses demonstrate that the interests of those whose incomes depend on efficiency harmonize with the interests of those seeking to improve the quality of the environment.

Four cases may be discussed where this should apply.

First – for completeness, though perhaps it should not need saying – is the recognition that economic efficiency is no less threatened than any other sector by those global environmental threats that now have to be considered as possibilities, if not certainties. If global warming, the ozone layer and acid rain are to be taken seriously as potential dangers to human survival or social stability, then it is perfectly apparent that business profits and national incomes would not be immune.

There is no *inherent* reason why those concerned with business or the national economy should come to a different assessment of the scientific evidence or immediacy of these processes. Global environmental effects, from this point of view, might be compared to the use of poison gas for war, which was outlawed while other equally unpleasant weapons were not; it is extremely difficult for its users to insulate themselves, or friendly parties, from its effects. Similarly the grandchildren of shareholders, politicians, captains of industry, pop stars and chartered accountants will have to breathe the same air as the grandchildren of the poor, powerless and dispossessed. The issue here is only the balance of the scientific evidence.

The second case is more homely. It is useful to remind ourselves that economists exist to provide satisfaction to human appetites for food, warmth, shelter, recreation, culture and such happiness as can be gained from the material goods and non-material services that are produced and exchanged. There js a somewhat arbitrary and changeable line (based mainly on a recorded act of sale) separating those goods and services which enter into conventional national income accounts and those that do not, but in terms of the physical and spiritual welfare provided, we must surely include meals cooked at home as well as those in a restaurant, care provided by relatives as well as by strangers, and free concerts as well as charged ones. The looseness of the dividing line is seen on those occasions when it is bridged; for example, in a court award for loss of the services of a wife, or compensation for loss of light.

I am not here saying 'the best things in life are free' or 'money cannot buy happiness' or 'spiritual values are as important as material ones', but rather that there is a whole class of goods and services that are completely economic in character but do not enter fully into markets for reasons that are social or historical or technical. Some minor change in technology or fashion or legislation can tip them from one side to the other.

To give an example; consider the minor but annoying nuisance of noise such as personal stereo sound leakage or portable telephones on trains, or the more substantial impacts of industrial or traffic noise. At present these are considered as environmental nuisances, constrained by politeness or legislation. The only economic impact is when regulation might demand some costly sound reduction to be inserted into a machine – a financial cost with no corresponding financial benefit to offset it – or when compensation is payable. But there exists a device (at present, I think, cumbersome, costly and not entirely efficient) which matches the pattern of sound waves emitted by a noise source and itself emits an 'anti-noise' designed to leave the air undisturbed, hence quiet. If such a device could be produced at a cost comparable to the cost of noise-producing machines, like a little portable radio, it is possible to envisage that it would have a very substantial market. The invention of the device would itself transform our perception of whether 'quiet' was a marketable commodity or a non-economic environmental attribute. (It could also raise very profound questions of rights; if you are allowed to let your noise reach my ears, am I allowed to let my quiet reach yours – i.e. neutralize your cell-phone? And in the industrial case, who should pay for the device, the sufferer or the noise-maker?)

Such a device is not on sale. However, the fact that it could be demonstrates that people can consider quiet as something with a value to them.

More practically, another example of ways in which an improved quality of environment can have a clear economic advantage is seen in the transformation of thinking about shopping centres which has already swept much of central and northern Europe, and is starting to influence Britain – the realization that pedestrianization and reduction in car traffic can increase trade by making the town centre more attractive, rather than reduce it by making it less accessible.

The third class of real economic benefits achievable through environmentally friendly policies relates to the as yet unexploited advantages of genetic diversity. To some extent this remains an act of faith, but there are sufficient examples of the discovery of new medicines in the tropical rain forest, and new food sources from combinations of the genetic bank of old species, to give cause for suspecting that there is much still to be discovered.

Fourthly, there are profits to be made from the environmental protection industry itself.

Proposition 3: There are Environmentally Friendly, Economically Efficient, Transport Policies

All the above argument would avail little if it really were the case that those transport policies which made the greatest contribution to economic well-being were also those that caused the greatest damage to the environment. Received wisdom suggested that this was true for many years. That is no longer an accurate description of the argument about transport policy.

This may be seen by considering the convergence of two lines of argument, in which new directions for transport policy are derived either from environmental considerations (both global and local) or from economic considerations (primarily the impact of congestion and traffic delays on personal and business efficiency).

Concerning the environment, a key statement is that made by a meeting of the Ministers of Transport of nineteen European countries (and with general support from other countries present including Australia, Canada, Japan and the United States) in November 1989 (European Conference of Ministers of Transport, 1990). The meeting adopted unanimously a resolution which went considerably further than any previous multinational statement of its form, and which indicated a number of emphases that had not previously been very apparent in British government thinking, including

. . . Governments should review the use of taxes and/or regulations for motor vehicles to ensure their consistency with the goal of reducing fuel consumption and emissions . . .

A full range of possible measures that can be taken to reduce transport's contribution to the 'greenhouse effect' be set out together with the costs and practical problems of implementing them. . . .

That traffic management be used to further environmental objectives in transport policy, both in relation to demand management and in relation to changing modal split . . .

It is necessary, in accordance with the Polluter Pays principle, to introduce systems of supplementary charging for environmental damage caused . . .

That effective and acceptable means of reducing the use of private car in urban areas need to be applied . . .

That assessments of infrastructure investment proposals should include traffic and environmental evaluations of the alternatives, including . . . extending railway or other public transport infrastructure and that of not building the infrastructure.

Concerning arguments of economic efficiency, we have noted elsewhere (Goodwin et al, 1991) the development of a sea-change especially in the way that urban transport policies are now discussed.

But the initiatives designed to provide enough capacity to keep pace with increasing car use never actually provided enough road space to do so, let alone provide enough additional capacity for other road users, including freight, which many thought should have an economic priority. As a result, traffic continually expanded much faster than the capacity of the network, 'spilling over' into previously less congested places and times of day. This gave an extra boost to the fear – continually repeated over several decades, but difficult to prove or disprove – that extra roads themselves induced the extra traffic to fill them up . . .

In April 1989 the Department of Transport issued some revised traffic forecasts (the earlier forecasts having underestimated traffic growth). These forecasts suggested that economic growth and existing trends would result in traffic levels by the year 2025 that would be between 83% and 142% higher than in 1988 – i.e. broadly double the current levels . . . a traumatic effect on the thinking of people involved in the planning and provision of transport services – it seemed neither possible to fit such traffic increases into any realistic road network, whether improved or not, nor a very good idea to try to do so even if it were possible . . .

The single most important conclusion of the resulting discussion was the proposition that there is no possibility of increasing road supply at a level which matches the growth rates in demand. It follows logically that (a) whatever road construction policy is followed, the amount of traffic per unit of road will increase, not reduce, i.e. congestion will get more severe or more widespread, and (b) demand management would therefore become the centre of transport policy; if supply cannot be matched to demand, demand has to be matched to supply . . .

A key feature of the new approach is the understanding that all the different parts of transport policy have to be in harmony with each other – it is no use planning the amount of road space, and public transport capacity, the parking provision and the patterns of land use with different and competing objectives. And it is also realised that to achieve that will require a wide range of different levers, prices, markets, laws, enforcement resources and institutions.

The specific mix of these will vary from place to place, but there are certain common themes. These are:

-   A very substantial improvement in the quality and scale of public transport provision, in some cases by new light rail or other high capacity reserved track systems, in others by extensive bus priority measures. This is almost completely agreed in principle, though there is not yet agreement on how to achieve it.

-   Traffic calming, both as a set of detailed engineering techniques to reduce traffic speed in residential and central areas (by speed humps, chicanes, restricted road width, etc) and also as a general strategy to tilt the balance of advantage in favour of pedestrians, and sometimes cyclists. These measures, together with pedestrianisation of a scale so far more familiar in European than British cities, are designed to improve the quality of life rather than mobility as such, and are a necessary component in compensating for the loss of some expectations of car access.

– Advanced traffic management systems, including automatic driver guidance and integrated signal control, to get the most efficient use out of the existing network – no longer defined as the maximum throughput of vehicles, but allowing for a safety margin between traffic levels and capacity, and also making provision for priority for the most efficient classes of vehicles or other local priorities (often mentioned are buses, delivery lorries, emergency services and disabled travellers).

– There is an increasing interest in the contribution that road pricing could play in knitting together the other policies (e.g. by providing some margin of unused road space with which to deliver the environmental improvements and public transport priorities) and, unlike all physical methods of restraining car use, producing a large revenue which could be used to fund the other improvements. Road pricing is politically controversial, and is likely only to be acceptable if it is carried out as part of a total programme of improvements, with safeguards to ensure that the revenue is used for this programme and that groups who lose out are more than compensated with other advantages. It has another advantage; by ensuring that the prices that are charged for transport services are approximately in line with their costs, the market can work more efficiently as between the different methods of transport, and the resulting traffic levels will be those that are economically merited.

– In this logic, the need for new road construction is seen to follow from a consideration of how much traffic it is desirable to provide for, which will be influenced by the combined effects of the policies described. There will still be occasions when new road construction is clearly justified – for example, in connecting a new industrial or residential development to the network – but construction 'to meet demand' is no longer the core of a transport strategy.

One of the great difficulties that has been experienced in the past in experimenting with one or other component of this list of policies, has been the political resistance from individuals or interest groups who feel their freedom to pursue their private and company interests is under threat from planners or bureaucrats motivated by dogma, rather than legitimate social objectives. Perhaps there has been an element of truth in this, on occasion. But now the situation is different; it is traffic growth, and inappropriate responses to it, which constitutes the threat to economic efficiency and a decent quality of living.

Conclusion

The proposition here is that capacity cannot grow at the same rate as the traffic forecasts, and it is therefore necessary to give priority to essential passenger and freight movement (by traffic management and road pricing) and encourage a greater use of public transport. These policies are derived entirely from arguments of economic efficiency – but turn out to be precisely those policies which contribute most to the protection of the environment. Similarly, the environmental preference for non-mechanized methods of travel, primarily walking and often cycling, are found to be those that enable town centres to become attractive and viable with consequent improvements in trade.

This is not to say that vested interests in other outcomes are non-existent, or that full agreement yet exists on the way such policies ought to be implemented, or how to meet their costs, or how far the same logic applies to inter-urban or rural travel. But for the large bulk of urban movement there does seem to be a case for expecting those with a commercial and economic motivation in the attractiveness and competitiveness of an area to find common cause with those driven by aspirations for environmental improvement.

This common cause does not need to derive from or depend on a common ideology or philosophy. It arises because there are potential net benefits to be shared. Hence the importance of the axiom – if these benefits exist, there must be *some* sharing of them which can produce a lobby powerful enough to secure implementation, by outvoting or compensating those who would lose. In one application, it is suggested ('The Rule of Three') that the road space and financial benefits of road pricing are divided between increased traffic speeds, added public transport priority and environmental enhancement. In another, the Freight Transport Association has recently accommodated to the recognition of limited road capacity by suggesting that buses and lorries share in an expanded programme of priority lanes.

I propose, therefore, that not only is transport able to make a significant contribution to environment policy, but that it may be able to make the pivotal contribution. Far from change involving, 'such draconian measures that they themselves would be politically unacceptable', we should be able to chart a path where, step by step, people are given opportunities to benefit themselves, their communities and their economies by recognizing the reality of environmental costs and reducing their impact.

REFERENCES

Anonymous (1990) How can transport afford the environment? *Transport*, January/February.

European Conference of Ministers of Transport (1990) *Transport Policy and the Environment*. Paris: ECMT/OECD.

Goodwin, P., Hallett, S., Kenny, F. and Stokes, G. (1991) Transport: the New Realism, Transport Studies Unit, University of Oxford, March.

Nader, R. (1965) *Unsafe At Any Speed*. New York: Grossman.

Ullrich, O. (1990) The pedestrian town as an environmentally tolerable alternative to motorised travel, in Tolley, R. (ed.) *The Greening of Urban Transport*. London: Belhaven Press.

Index